MEDIA OF COMMUNICATION
Radio, TV and Video

MEDIA OF COMMUNICATION
Radio, TV and Video

Suraj Singh

CENTRUM PRESS
NEW DELHI-110002 (INDIA)

CENTRUM PRESS
H.O.: 4360/4, Ansari Road, Daryaganj,
New Delhi-110002 (India)
Tel: 23278000, 23261597, 23255577, 23286875
B.O.: No. 1015, Ist Main Road, BSK IIIrd Stage,
IIIrd Phase, IIIrd Block, Bangalore-560085 (INDIA)
Tel: 080-41723429
Email: centrumpress@gmail.com
Visit us at: www.centrumpress.com

Media of Communication: Radio, TV and Video

First Edition, 2010

ISBN 978-93-80836-13-3

PRINTED IN INDIA

Printed at Mehra Offset Press, Delhi

Contents

Contents

Preface

In communication, media (singular medium) are the storage and transmission channels or tools used to store and deliver information or data. It is often referred to as synonymous with mass media or news media, but may refer to a single medium used to communicate any data for any purpose. Media technology has made communicating increasingly easier as time has passed throughout history.

Today, children are encouraged to use media tools in school and are expected to have a general understanding of the various technologies available. The internet is arguably one of the most effective tools in media for communication. Tools such as e-mail, MSN, Facebook etc, have brought people closer together and created new online communities. However, some may argue that certain types of media can hinder face-to-face communication and therefore can result in complications like identity fraud.

In a large consumer-driven society, electronic media (such as television) and print media (such as newspapers) are important for distributing advertisement media. More technologically advanced societies have access to goods and services through newer media than less technologically advanced societies.

In the era of social media, our networks are much larger than they have ever been, and we have more ways to communicate with those in them. Today, thanks in large part to social media, we have many different levels of communication, each with a specific purpose and etiquette. When we do not understand the role of these levels, they can become huge time wasters. When we do understand them however, they can help us more effectively engage and navigate these new waters. The public reply provides an open and transparent channel for people to interact with public figures, brands, and each other, without the pressure of response that comes with e-mail. Public interactions are a great starting point for engagement that never existed before social media, and if done correctly, can often lead to more fruitful direct communication.

Chapter 1

Paying for the Video Revolution

In 1978, the new video technologies of cable TV and home video were relatively uncommon, with fewer than 20 percent of U.S. households receiving cable and just over 1 percent owning videocassette recorders. Just ten years later, both technologies were represented in a majority of households, with 51 percent receiving cable and 58 percent owning videocassette recorders. The social implications and policy consequences of this "video revolution" are the subject of continuing research.

This chapter focuses on the changes in spending patterns that made possible the swift diffusion of new video technologies. Using methods originated by McCombs and extended by Wood, we examine consumer spending on the mass media during the decade when cable television and video recording and playback became majority technologies.

Consumer spending has been thought to be a constant fraction of consumer income. This "constancy principle" would imply that new mass media technologies could be supported only by spending taken away from the income share of established media technologies. As a result, new technologies could threaten the survival of existing technologies.

However, if the constancy principle failed to hold, even for a few years, consumers might devote an increased share of their mass media expenditures to adopting new technologies. Later, when long-term constancy reasserted itself, the new technologies would have become established without having displaced the older mass media.

McCombs originally identified mass media spending as a broad aggregate of six categories of consumer spending kept by the U.S. Department of Commerce. Those categories are newspapers, magazines, and sheet music; books and maps; radio and television receivers, records, and musical instruments; radio and television repairs; motion picture admissions; and other paid admissions.

The "mass media" aggregate was expanded by Wood to include the then-emerging videodisc and cassette technologies as well as expenditures on cable television services. The previous studies examined yearly national data on mass media spending and income from 1929 through 1981, before the new video technologies had become firmly established.

The constancy principle can be formally described as the invariance of the proportion of consumer income spent on the mass media aggregate, regardless of changes in levels of income, changes in mass media technologies, or the passage of time. Function A goes through the origin of the graph and remains in place over time. Along that function, consumers adjust their media spending with the passage of time and changes in income, but they always spend the same fraction on media.

In this hypothesis, new technologies can gain a share of income only at the expense of existing technologies. For example, first-run movie theaters might lose income share to home video, or book publishers might lose out to cable television. In the absence of sufficient growth of income, the actual number of dollars spent on the older media would decline, possibly endangering those media's survival.

Constancy could fail to hold in a variety of ways. For example, a function like A could rotate upward or shift upward in parallel fashion. In either case, the fraction of income spent on mass media would change. Because of the multiple ways in which constancy might fail, no one test can indicate decisively whether constancy is present.

Although other interpretations of constancy are possible, we focus here on the more conventional income-share and time-trend tests, which use correlation studies or the statistically equivalent regression approach. The regression approach has the advantage of facilitating corrections for serially correlated error terms, which commonly occur in annual time-series data.

If the fitted function intercepts the vertical axis below zero (function B), then mass media spending as a fraction of income increases if income goes up. The test for constancy is therefore a test of whether the intercept of the fitted function is statistically different from zero. The time-trend constancy test uses multiple regression to estimate the relationship between mass media spending, disposable income, and a time-trend variable.

Including a time-trend variable means that the interpretation of the intercept term is no longer a straightforward indication of the constancy of spending on the mass media. If the regression coefficient of the time-trend variable is not significantly different from zero, the relationship between income and mass media spending is considered constant over time. A coefficient statistically different from zero would cast doubt on the constancy hypothesis.

To test for the presence of constancy, we must examine both the incomeshare and time-trend interpretations. It is possible that time-trend constancy would hold while income-share constancy is violated. This would indicate that over long periods of time people spend a constant fraction of their income on the mass media but spend greater proportions of income for shorter intervals. These short-term violations of constancy could be sufficient for new technologies to become established, before mass media spending returned to long-term constancy.

To test the constancy hypothesis during the time of rapid change in video technologies, we extended the data series of earlier studies through 1988. In addition, we amended some of the pre-1981 data because of revisions made by the U.S. Department of Commerce.

For this study, new video technologies were videodisc, videocassette recorders, and cable television services.

Videodisc spending first showed up in the government figures for 1981. Videocassette recorders were significant enough to report for the first time in 1975. Cable television had been reported as early as 1955, but it remained a minority technology, with less than 20 percent penetration of households as recently as 1980.

Tests confirmed that serial correlation was present in the time-series sample, with t-statistics for 1929-1988 significant at p d".01. Our regression tests corrected for this serial correlation of error terms and incorporated corrections for taxation of personal income and length of sample period.

Period, when new video technologies became majority technologies, was characterized by an increased share of income being spent on the mass media. The fitted function has an intercept statistically different from zero. Consumers also had spent an increasing share of income on the mass media in 1959-1968 and a decreasing share in 1949-1958 and 1969-1978. The overall constancy for 1929-1988 thus masked significant decade-long departures from constancy.

Departures from constancy could imply dramatic financial gains for new technologies, in times of increasing income share for the mass media, or large losses of revenue for all technologies, in times of decreasing income share for the mass media. The income share spent on mass media is plotted against time and broken down into print, audiovisual, and new video components. The figure reflects increasing income shares for the mass media in 1959-1968 and in 1979-1988, the period of special interest here.

This confirms the long-term constancy of the relationship between mass media spending and consumer income. The time-trend variable is not statistically different from zero; consumer income retains a high degree of explanatory power. The result confirms the absence of persistent increases or decreases in mass media spending over time. The data show that consumers' willingness to spend an increased share of income on the mass media in 1979-1988 prevented major losses by print and conventional audiovisual media. In 1979, mass media spending commanded a 2.57 percent share of income. If that share had remained constant over the decade, consumers would have spent only $89.4 billion on the mass media in 1988 instead of the $113.8 billion that they actually spent. Had consumer spending obeyed the constancy principle for 1979-1988 while new video technologies were adopted, there would have been a dramatic loss of revenue by older technologies.

Although the income share of print media appears to be declining, higher overall levels of income allowed for actual increases in spending on print media. As the totals indicate, real consumer expenditure was higher at the end of the decade than the beginning, despite some year-to-year reductions. Consumer expenditure is, of course, only one variable influencing the survival of specific media; rising costs of production could doom an older media technology if consumers did not increase their spending to keep pace.

The data for 1979-1988 show that new technologies entered the mass media market, attracted significant consumer spending, and did not displace or endanger older technologies. It is possible that the dramatic upturn in consumer spending on the mass media that began in 1979 marks the beginning of a longterm departure from constancy.

The introduction of new video technologies may have structurally changed consumer spending, making consumers willing to spend a greater proportion of income on the mass media at the expense of nonmedia goods and services. Such a structural change could leave room in household budgets for older and newer technologies alike. Since the video revolution is a relatively recent occurrence, however, statistical confirmation of this change may be years in coming.

Chapter 2

News Media Coverage of Popular-culture Culpability

Throughout the twentieth century, certain segments of society have blamed the products of popular culture for lowering moral standards and inciting "had" behaviour. After World War I, for example, many blamed movies for bringing the "loose morals" of Europe to America, resulting in women taking up smoking and wearing dresses that exposed their calves.

In the 1950s, parents worried that doo-wop and rock and roll would provoke sexual promiscuity in their teenage sons and daughters. And in the 1980s, a group of concerned parents known as the PMRC labeled the music of Madonna, Michael Jackson, Motley Crue, and others as a "contributing factor" in teen pregnancy and suicide.

In the 1990s, popular media products (including movies, recorded music, television talk shows, the Internet, tabloid newspapers, and video games) were blamed, at least in part, for a number of high-profile tragedies. Among these were the car crash that killed Princess Diana, the murder associated with the "Jenny Jones" show, and the shootings at several high schools in the United States, including the massacre at Columbine High School in Littleton, Colorado.

In news coverage of these tragedies, the mainstream news media seemed to lead the charge against their popular brethren by unabashedly reporting on, if not initiating, the finger-pointing. This study explores how and why the news media came to assign blame to products of popular culture in coverage of the three recent high-profile tragedies mentioned above. We chose these three events because we see them as variations on a theme: well-publicized, wide-reaching events in which a tragedy occurred that involved popular media in some way and in which a large component of the news discourse that followed involved the blaming of popular media for the tragedies.

We argue that the ways in which the "elite" news media covered these events were not isolated or unique but rather exemplified widely held assumptions, common practices, and consistent perspectives regarding news, popular media, and audiences. We see the analysis of three cases, rather than only one, as compelling evidence of the universality of the themes we raise.

Through case studies based on qualitative content analysis of English-language newspaper coverage of these three events, we will answer the following questions:

- *RQ1:* How did the reporting of each story-Princess Diana's death, the "Jenny Jones" talk show murder, and the Columbine High School shootings-evolve over time?
- *RQ2:* At what point in news coverage of each story did popular-culture culpability arise, and from what source(s) did the blame originate?
- *RQ3:* In news coverage of each story, how were products of popular culture such as video games, the Internet, the paparazzi, and talk shows blamed for each tragedy?
- *RQ4:* How might we explain the news media placing the blame on popular culture?

After presenting the case studies, we employ several theoretical frameworks to discuss why popular-culture products, and occasionally their producers, were blamed for these tragic events.

Our goal is not to exonerate popular-culture products or their producers but to understand how and why they were implicated in news coverage of the tragedies. This research topic has the potential to reveal a great deal about the practices-and perhaps even the motivations-of those involved in the creation and control of the news. Yet little research has been done on the relationship between the "elite" news media and the various forms of "popular" media, those which serve to entertain more than to inform.

Analyses of news media blaming popular media products for causing or contributing to high-profile tragedies are rare. Thus, we briefly review the few studies that look specifically at the coverage of these three tragedies by the news media to provide context for the rather novel study at hand. We also provide a brief overview of the history of blame being assigned to popular media by entities other than the news media.

Finally, we turn toward more broad theoretical foundations that can be applied to the particular occurrence of assignment of blame by news media to popular media. News coverage of the three tragedies studied here implicated many typos of entertainment media and popular culture, all of which have been the subject of similar criticism as well as of more formalized research scrutiny in the past. One popular media form that was blamed, in part, for the Columbine tragedy was recorded music.

In social scientific research, exposure to violence in recorded music has been associated with antisocial and destructive behaviour, as well as sex-role stereotyping and negative attitudes toward women.

Yet a direct causal relationship has been elusive because of both the difficulty in extracting the influence of song lyrics in complex decision-making processes and the finding that up to 30% of those adolescents listening do not know the lyrics.

The evidence on the topic is sufficient, however, for the American Academy of Pediatrics to make recommendations to parents about "reducing the potential negative effects of music lyrics and videos". There also exists an extensive history of blaming violent films for encouraging antisocial behaviour, as was also the case in news coverage of the shootings at Columbine.

Among the more recent contributions to this literature are analyses finding increases in aggression levels after exposure to violent films, often greater for those aggressively inclined prior to exposure. Similarly, a growing body of research links video-game use-raised as a causal factor for the Columbine shootings-with increased aggressive behaviour and desensitization toward violence.

Other research has found elevations in aggressive play rather than aggressive behaviour directed toward others following violent video-game use. Two other aspects of popular culture widely blamed in the three cases examined here, particularly in the Columbine case, include television violence and extensive news coverage of violent events (because such coverage may lead to copycat behaviour). Both have received attention in studios too numerous to identify here, yet Berkowitz, Surette, Comstock and Scharrer, and Potter provide informative overviews of each.

Analyses of the amount or treatment of violence in newspaper content are surprisingly scant. One exception is Clark and Blankenberg's study of violence across different types of media that found about 18% of newspaper front pages featured violence. There is also a growing amount of research on the topic of news coverage of violent events involving youths, an issue relevant to the Columbine tragedy.

For example, an analysis of local television news in California found that over half of the nearly 1,800 stories analysed that contained violence featured youths, similar to the 48% of violent stories that involved children found in an earlier study. A similar study in California the following year found 68% of all violent stories involved youths.

To our knowledge, no scholarly research has linked daytime television talk shows or tabloid publications-the two remaining objects of blame in these cases, particularly in the "Jenny Jones"-related murder and the death of Princess Diana-to adverse media effects, though they have certainly been criticized in the news media. One exception is a study by Tavener, who argues that daytime talk shows elicit moral panics among middle-class cultural critics and mainstream journalists but that, in fact, shows such as "Jerry Springer" and "Jenny Jones" serve to reinforce middle-class values and mores.

However, a few studies conducted over the last decade have examined the often controversial content of talk shows. Brinson and Winn report one reason for the format's popularity has been an increased emphasis on interpersonal conflict. Critics of the "Jerry Springer Show" suggest the show's premise is to spark controversy and conflict in the hopes of elevating the conflict to a physically violent level.

As the trend of revealing "secrets" or disclosing private information in front of a national audience became more popular, a few researchers began to explore the role of these programs in society and the nature of talk-show guests themselves. Anderson and Oliver suggest that talk shows are "modern, mass mediated freak shows", and critics, ranging from journalists to political figures to a talk-show host have charged talk shows with emphasizing sexual themes, sexual practices, and sexual deviance.

Abt and Seesholtz found in their analysis of talk-show content that talk shows are dominated by sexuality, themes of deviance and psychopathology, and self-disclosure of private facts.

Greenberg and colleagues found in their analysis of 110 talk-show episodes that sexual activity was a major issue of discussion in 36% of the shows and discussion of criminal acts was a major-issue in 24% of the shows. Brinson and Winn analysed representations of interpersonal conflict in 40 randomly selected talk shows and found aggressive behaviour in approximately 25% of the shows.

In another area of talk-show research, Priest and Dominick examined the relationship between talk-show participants, their exposure to television, and their reasons for choosing to disclose sensitive and private information in a public forum.

They found that participants on the "Donahue" show reported a "pragmatic attitude toward talk shows as a forum to reach a number of audiences".

Though some talk-show guests were aware that they might face ridicule or embarrassment on the programme, they were willing to do so in order to "evangelize" their issue or position. In another investigation of self-disclosure on talk shows, Peck found that talk-show participants viewed the talk-show stage as an extension of therapy, thereby enabling talk-show participants to perceive their participation on the show as a step in the healing process.

A few studies have looked specifically at news-media coverage of one of the three tragedies analysed in this chapter, Princess Diana's death. Real (2000) used print and broadcast news coverage of Diana's death and funeral to explicate a theory that the media serve a religious function in modern society. Real did not focus on the "elite" media blaming popular culture for the tragedy, but he suggested that "the intense controversy over the possible role of media paparazzi in her death functioned largely as a displacement attempting to find blame to explain away the unexplainable finality of death".

Eichholz studied the extent to which German and American newspapers (both "elite" and tabloid) criticized tabloid photographers and the tabloid press for their purported role in Diana's death. He found that "on average, elite newspapers devoted 25% of their coverage to the role the media played, compared with only 5% that the tabloids devoted to the media's role". Eichholz also found "the elite media were more willing to voice media criticism because they aimed most of their critique at the tabloids and the paparazzi, while at the same time differentiating themselves from these groups".

Bishop, whose study is most similar to the study at hand, focused primarily on how the news media (both print and broadcast) actively differentiated themselves from tabloid publications in their coverage of Diana's death. Through textual analysis, Bishop identified a pattern of coverage that served to distinguish "elite" journalists and "elite" media from tabloid-press photographers and tabloid publications.

Bishop found that journalists for the "elite" media

"struggled to keep their readers and viewers aware that the paparazzi, and British and American tabloids, did not practice journalism with the same level of professionalism".

MEDIA DISCOURSE AND "SERIOUS" vs. TABLOID JOURNALISM

In addition to the particular studies cited above, the works of Bird, Jensen, Pauly, and Eason contribute to our theoretical framework for interpreting the mainstream news media's handling of the three high-profile events studied here. This framework views communication as a symbolic social practice and media content as the negotiated outcome of the social practices of its producers and the public.

Bird writes about supermarket tabloids as cultural phenomena, existing "alongside and because of other cultural phenomena" rather than merely as disconnected parts. She stresses the importance of considering intertextuality, or the relationship of one media product to other media and oral traditions, when studying the role of a media product (in her case, tabloids) in people's lives.

Bird argues that the writer, the reader, and the content itself contribute to "the cultural phenomenon of the tabloid", and she counters criticism of tabloid journalism by "serious" journalists with evidence of the close connection between "serious" and tabloid journalism, both past and present. The connections to be made with our study are several. First, we must consider the cultural phenomenon we are examining, the assignment of blame in newspaper journalism to elements of popular media, in context with other cultural phenomena.

If popular media are being portrayed in a negative light in print news media and the reader is a fan of popular media, a complex intertextual scenario may transpire. How audience members read news coverage that places responsibility for social ills on popular media may certainly be mitigated by audience members' own relationships with popular media.

Also relevant to our study is the relationship between "serious" journalism and tabloid journalism. In our study, we expect tabloid journalism will be directly implicated in both the "Jenny Jones" and the Princess Diana cases. In the Columbine case, we expect that the popular, entertainment-based media (video/computer games, movies, television shows, recorded music) will be implicated in press coverage.

Central to our discussion of the treatment of these entities by journalists employed at major newspapers is the apparent division between the popular and the "elite" being drawn by the "serious" journalists in non-tabloid publications. We argue that in order to point the finger of blame at media in general but deflect blame from one's own media outlet, this delineation is drawn. Yet, as Bird suggests, the distinction between "serious" and popular media is not one of opposite sides of a polemic but rather of blurry points on a continuum.

Jensen analyses decades of discourse about ill effects associated with media, although she examines scholarly arguments made by media critics whereas we examine news articles appearing in major newspapers. Jensen argues that when critics rail against the powers and persuasions of media, the underlying assumptions and beliefs they are advancing are fundamentally complaints about modernity or what modern times have wrought.

She does not attempt to determine whether there are unfavorable influences of the media on society or on individuals but rather she analyses the discussion or discourse surrounding that topic. We adopt the same stance in our study in that we do not attempt to determine whether the popular media discussed in newspaper coverage of these three events are to blame for the three tragedies. Rather, we examine the process by which they were blamed, in discourse located in newspaper coverage of the events.

Jensen's argument about modernity can be applied to our study. It is possible that though media criticism is easier to articulate as a cause for these tragic events, perhaps truer culprits are modern issues and circumstances. Among these are an emphasis on commercial interests (e.g., ratings for Jenny Jones, money for the photos of Princess Diana, sales or ratings for the movies, music and video games mentioned in coverage of the Columbine shootings) or the alienation and disconnection experienced by many in contemporary life (e.g., the ostracism of the Columbine perpetrators, the claims of humiliation for the Jenny Jones assailant, the identification with and adoration of Princess Diana).

Jensen presents the key media criticism arguments advanced by Macdonald, that media and mass culture jeopardize the presence of high art; Boorstin, that "pseudo events" created by the media and presented to audiences as fact obscure the truth; Ewen, that consumer culture promotes an ideology of consumption that functions as an agent of social control; and Postman, that television has led to the transformation of serious and important aspects of public affairs into entertainment, thereby robbing audiences of information they need to conduct themselves as citizens.

Jensen identifies a common element in these criticisms: each suggests media change us, as audience members, by offering something more appealing or easier to make sense of compared to those things that would be better for us. Implicit in this criticism are the beliefs that there is consensus regarding what is good for society and that ordinary citizens themselves cannot be trusted to know what that may be. However, in media criticism the blame is often not directly placed on the audience for choosing lazy or flashy options; instead blame is placed on the media for duping the audience into doing so by presenting no better options.

These notions about audience preference and this sense of protectionism are central to our study. The angles chosen, words used, and sources employed in reporting about these events (as part of the social process of news gathering) may reveal a similar "elite" protectionism and unflattering belief about the nature of audience preferences and desires. The news coverage may imply that members of the news media know what is best in order to protect the masses and to sustain social order.

By assigning responsibility to popular media for these three tragedies, "serious" journalists can adopt a prescriptive stance toward improving social conditions by leading audiences away from the ostensibly harmful and salacious content in the popular media to which they are presumably drawn. Jensen discusses the moral element in the comparison of tabloid journalism with "serious" journalism, with the distinction drawn between the two indicating "a moral tension between self-indulgence and self-denial".

The loyalty of tabloid journalists to audience interests and therefore profit making is contrasted in media criticism to the loyalty of "serious" journalists to "higher" processes of rationality and the virtues of high culture.

The distinction is made more obvious in the aspect of media-influence discourse that refers to the "lowest common denominator" presumably appealed to by certain types of media content such as tabloid journalism or popular media. A particular view of audiences as being ill equipped for reason and inevitably drawn to more "shallow symbolic forms" underlies this commonly used phrase.

This is central to our discussion in that implicit in the criticism of popular media by elite news media is a sense of shamefulness associated with "pandering" to "base" human instincts toward violence (Columbine, Jenny Jones), intrusiveness (Jenny Jones, Princess Diana), and sex (Jenny Jones).

An essay by Pauly about media mogul Rupert Murdoch in Carey's Media, Myths, and Narratives also informs this discussion of "elite" and "non-elite" media. Murdoch was criticized for his use of "promotional journalism" and accused of devaluing journalistic ideals by not "honoring the stylistic conventions that journalists used to defend the social importance of their occupation".

Pauly discusses the defensive strategy of distinguishing between information and entertainment as a primary means of defining "elite" and "non-elite" media. Yet, he argues that this is an artificial construction since news content is increasingly presented in a manner and in a context that seeks to entertain:

Because mass-circulation dailies comprise vast and varied symbolic materials, different groups can argue that the 'essential' part is the one that they most enjoy or that sustains their sense of identification. Thus the professional journalist emphasizes the investigative role of the newspaper out of proportion to the actual number of stories undertaken.

In other words, the investigative, purely informational, "factual" content in a daily newspaper is a small portion of the whole, but is magnified in importance by those with a vested interest in arguing the difference between "serious" and tabloid journalism. This argument is at the centre of our study, which suggests that in order to blame some aspects of media and popular culture, newspaper journalists must imply that this content is fundamentally different (and comparatively "worse") than what they transmit to audiences.

The alleged dichotomy between "what audience members want" and "what audience members need" is also raised in Eason's essay in Carey's Media, Myths, and Narratives, in which Eason discusses the controversy surrounding the fabricated elements in Janet Cooke's award-winning news story, "Jimmy's World." Eason argues that journalism has experienced an evolution away from the repertorial function of transmitting facts and more toward the creation of "reality " with the words and elements of a story chosen by journalists.

We argue similarly that the journalists in the news stories we reviewed about these three high-profile tragedies create a reality in which popular media and popular-culture products bear responsibility for the tragedies. Although the journalists whose stories we review presumably did not fabricate any information they conveyed, they did choose to highlight certain "facts" that appear to have made their stories more marketable to a large audience while downplaying other "facts" that may have been deemed of less interest to readers.

FACTORS AFFECTING MEDIA COVERAGE

A somewhat different though complementary view of the phenomenon of popular-culture culpability is seen from the perspective of Shoemaker and Reese. Their approach examines how media content is influenced by factors in the context in which it is created.

Though one could view their theoretical perspective as examining media content as shaped by external social processes in a unidirectional (external forces lead to media content) manner, we argue that their theory can be expanded to examine the interrelated, multidirectional, dynamic relations between all elements-content, producers, public. In Mediating the Message, Shoemaker and Reese identify five major spheres of influence on media content, from the most microscopic to the most macroscopic.

We use these labels to identify sources of influence on the producers of news content as well as on the content itself. Though the labels are presented individually, we argue for their overlapping, multidirectional relationship with content as journalists go about the social practice of determining how to cover "the news." We introduce the levels of influence here briefly and will then apply them to each of the three events examined in this chapter.

The most microscopic level of influence on media content is the individual level, that is, the influence exerted by the individual reporter or columnist, the copy editor, and the editor-each person who has a hand in creating the news content. This can include deciding what constitutes news, selecting the angle of the story, writing the story, and editing it. Some of the factors that influence content decisions at the individual level are personal feelings, tastes and preferences, values, opinions, and the professional backgrounds and training of those directly involved in content decisions.

The media routines level focuses on the routines, or standard procedures, for gathering and disseminating news. Among the influences found at this level are news values-those characteristics that make an event newsworthy, such as deviance from the norm, sensationalism, prominence, proximity, timeliness, conflict or controversy, human interest, and impact on audience members or society as a whole.

Other media routines include objectivity, the five "Ws" (answering who, what, when, where, and why in every report), pack journalism, competition, reliance on other media for information or for whole stories, localism (getting the local angle on a story that takes place far away), simplicity (offering pat "answers" because complex situations are hard to explain and hard for readers to understand quickly), and over-reliance on a handful of sources.

The next level of influence, moving toward a more macroscopic perspective, is the organizational level. Analysis at the organizational level focuses on the impact of policies, managers, and owners of the organization in which the media content is produced. It is difficult to discuss influences at this level, as we do not know what went on in each newsroom during coverage of these three events. However, the opinions of upper management or concerns of those in the circulation or advertising-sales departments can influence coverage, as can organizational policies such as the degree of autonomy allowed to each reporter.

The extramedia level has to do with elements and factors outside of the media organizations themselves, such as news sources, advertisers, government, interest groups, and the audience. This level includes actual, direct influences as well as the influence that news media personnel's perceptions of what these entities might do or how they might feel that also shape content.

While influence of advertisers might weigh against extensive blaming of popular culture in news coverage, for example, pressure from some interest groups and activists, as well as governmental concern, could weigh toward the pursuit of this angle. In terms of perceptions of audience preferences, some journalists may believe that audiences want to see and read about violence, sensationalism, scandal, and the lives of celebrities.

This perception could have a profound impact, because giving the audiences "what they want" will presumably sell newspapers and space to advertisers. Thus, angles that have popular appeal may be advanced while more esoteric or abstract angles, such as the notion that society in general is responsible or that a complex nexus of forces are at fault, may take a back seat.

The notion of audience preference is also a cultural one.

de Mooij argues the one such preference that is culturally bound is America's adherence to a cause-and-effect paradigm. She argues that it is a cultural norm in the United States to expect to have a logical explanation for any given event and that any event has concrete and measurable answers to the question of what caused it.

Journalists, if following this cultural norm or if presuming audiences follow it, may provide a concrete explanation rather than leave the tragedies unexplained. Subscribing to this cause-and-effect paradigm can be viewed as an individual influence on the part of reporters and editors, an extramedia influence that takes the shape of conceptions about audience preferences, or an ideological influence that entails broad-based cultural and societal beliefs.

The ideological level includes the influences that broad systems of beliefs and values have on the news-gathering process. Among the factors at play here are notions of "elite" and "popular" media, representations that define "mainstream" and "deviant" content, and the concept of hegemony. The latter suggests that entities enjoying political and economic power in existing societal structure will act in the interest of thwarting social change in order to protect their dominant status.

We predict that these three case studies will show the use of defensive strategies when other media are, indeed, blamed. Through the use of labels such as "tabloid," "paparazzi," and "trash TV" to draw theoretically distinct lines, journalists may construct readings of their own stories as the dominant discourse and those of "tabloid" media and "trash TV" as deviant.

A subtext exists in this type of criticism that suggests a need to save people from their own tastes in media and popular culture. This is similar to the points raised by Bird and Jensen above, and is the central theoretical element of the study at hand. de Mooij's suggestion that as part of American culture, we-as members of society-need someone or something to blame whenever there is a tragedy, also has implications for hegemony and social order.

In order for members of society to feel secure about the world around them, there has to be a rational cause, with a clearly identifiable source of blame, for each event. Thus, it is much more satisfying to place blame on a specific, tangible targetin this case, the non-elite media-rather than advancing the more unsettling notion that something is amiss in society at large.

PRINCESS DIANA

The first case study involves the death of Princess Diana of Wales and the automobile accident that took her life and the lives of Dodi al Fayed and Henri Paul on August 31, 1997. The accident occurred shortly after midnight in Paris when the Mercedes Benz in which the princess and her friend were travelling crashed in a tunnel near the Seine River. Dodi al Fayed and Henri Paul, the driver, were found dead at the scene. The princess died a few hours later of injuries she sustained in the crash.

The event was reported in newspapers around the world. The larger U.S. and U.K. newspapers gave extensive coverage to the event in the days following the crash. For example, on the first day of coverage The London Observer ran 28 articles, The New York Daily News ran 10 articles, and The Atlanta Journal and Constitution ran four articles.

This case study is based on analysis of those articles and others that were published in English-language newspapers from the day of the crash, August 31, 1997, through the day of Diana's funeral, September 6, 1997, when the focus of coverage shifted from the accident to the funeral. The articles were retrieved from the General News archive of LEXIS-NEXIS Academic Universe. In all, 507 stories were reviewed for relevant content, and those with relevant content were studied more closely.

Often, the first news reports of a tragic and unexpected event will present only the basic facts of the story, answering the fundamental journalistic questions of who was involved, what happened, when it happened, and where it happened, without speculation as to the causes of the event. It usually takes another day or more for the "how" and "why" questions to be answered.

However, this was not the case in the early reporting on Princess Diana's death. Answers to the "how" and "why" questions were included in the initial reports of the event because tabloid-press photographers were said to have been chasing the princess's car at the time of the accident. Approximately 11 photographers, sources said, some on motorcycles and others in a car, set out after Diana and Dodi's Mercedes when it left the Ritz hotel in Paris.

The photographers were apparently trying to get pictures that would confirm rumors of a romance between Diana and Dodi. Several sources in the earliest stories claimed that the photographers caused the accident. Among them were Paris police, unspecified police, French journalists (their sources unnamed), a photographer for a London paper, Agence-France Presse (the French news agency), and British reporters.

No eyewitnesses to the crash were quoted in the early coverage-in other words, no source knew for certain that the photographers had actually caused the accident (and some sources even claimed that the car had lost the photographers). In spite of this, the idea that the photographers caused the accident became a part of every story reporting the facts of the event.

The Boston Heraldbegan an article by Joseph Mallia with "Princess Diana and her companion Dodi Fayed were killed in a high-speed car crash early today in a tunnel near the Seine River in Paris, as their Mercedes was being pursued by photographers."

The Hindu of India began a story with "Britain's Princess Diana and her millionaire companion, Dodi El-Fayed, were killed in a car crash early on Sunday while being chased by photographers on motorcycles in a road tunnel in the French capital Paris."

The third paragraph of an Associated Press story that ran in The Buffalo News on August 31 read "The crash happened shortly after midnight in a tunnel along the Seine River at the Pont de l'Aima bridge. It came as paparazzi-the commercial photographers who constantly tailed Diana followed her car, police said."

POPULAR-CULTURE CULPABILITY

During the week after the fatal crash, when coverage of the event was at its most intense, nearly every article contained at least one source who blamed the producers of popular culture for Diana's death. Among these were family members and family representatives, dignitaries, ordinary citizens, and journalists themselves.

Other sources who blamed "the paparazzi," "the press," "the media," or "the tabloids" (sometimes including tabloid-style television shows) were an Arizona talk-radio host and many of his callers, Britons living in the United States (usually interviewed in pubs), un-named TV commentators, and David Perel, executive editor of the American tabloid The National Enquirer.

Perel was quoted in several newspapers as saying that reckless action by the paparazzi probably caused the accident. Some family members of the crash victims extended the blame to all photographers who pursue celebrities for photos to be printed in tabloid newspapers. Ellen Tumposky and Mike Claffey of The New York Daily News (Aug. 31) reported "The dead Egyptian playboy's father, Mohammed Al-Fayed, blamed the tragedy on the paparazzi, who were being held for questioning by Paris police.

There is no doubt in Mr. Al-Fayed's mind that this tragedy would not have occurred but for the press photographers who have dogged and pursued Mr. Fayed and the princess for weeks,' a spokesman for the Egyptian billionaire said."

The Houston Chronicle reported "(Michael Gibbons), a spokesman for Buckingham Palace, noting that the incident occurred while the couple were being chased by photographers, said it was 'an accident waiting to happen.' he repeated the palace's anger at the actions of photographers who pursue the royal family around the world."

Other family members blamed not only tabloid-press

photographers but also the editors and publishers of gossipy tabloid publications. The London Observer was one of the first to report a scathing statement from Diana's brother. "This is not a time for recriminations," said Earl Spencer, "but I would say that I always believed the press would kill her in the end.

But not even I could imagine that they would take such a direct hand in her death as seems to be the case. It would appear that every proprietor and editor of every publication that has paid for intrusive and exploitative photographs of her, encouraging greedy and ruthless individuals to risk everything in pursuit of Diana's image, have blood on their hands today."

None of the first-day stories reporting the reactions of world leaders and diplomats (such as President Clinton, the Singapore government, and the Pope) contained quotes that blamed popular culture. However, on the second day of coverage, several French government officials made statements blaming the paparazzi, as reported in The Hindu.

The president of the French Parliament, the former prime minister, Mr. Laurent Fabius said that death precipitated by paparazzi proves that "photos, words and attitudes can also, in a certain sense, kill. These people must now face their responsibility." The government's spokeswoman, Ms. Catherine Trautmann, who is also France's Culture Minister, was more vehement in her denunciation of the paparazzi.

Princess Diana was the victim of the stubbornness of the press, she declared. "The singlemindedness of the press had increased dramatically these past weeks The circumstances of her death have thrown up questions about the functioning of this profession and above all of our society," Ms. Trautmann added.

Among the stories that reported the reactions of ordinary citizens, most contained at least one source who blamed either the paparazzi who pursued the Mercedes or the press in general. Most of these "average-citizen" sources did not distinguish between the popular press and the elite press or their producers, nor did the reporters attempt to make any distinction for the sources. The blame laid by these sources was among the most vitriolic. The New York Daily News reported:

Britons in New York mixed their grief at Princess Diana's death with criticism of the press for its relentless pursuit of her Beverly Dorking, 25, of Leeds in northern England, said, "she's been dogged and hounded by the media. They've been in her face since she was 19, and now they've taken away the world's most popular woman." Nicola Shigley, 24, of northern England, predicted a backlash against the media. She accused the media of spending "the last 10 years trying to put the woman to an end."

The San Diego Union-Tribune reported '"The press has a lot to answer for,' said Mary Simpson, also of Liverpool. 'They hounded her to death. Literally, now.'" The Seattle Times reported "Mitch Lease, 23, reflected bitterly on the circumstances of her death, a chase by photographers. I think the media should have given her a break a long time ago, and now they've killed her.'"

The London Observer reported "In one bitter outburst on BBC TV, a woman demanded that a reporter and his cameraman slop filmmg. 'You've done this Io her,' she screamed. 'You're to blame. The media, the papers, all of you.'" Some articles blamed popular culture by quoting other publications and thereby demonstrating what seemed to be a world-wide consensus as to who was to blame for the tragedy. A London Observer article read:

The French newspaper Liberation gave over its whole front page to a picture of (Diana) with the headline, "One photo too many. " Italy's La Stampa took up the same theme, stating tersely: "Dead for a photo" Hong Kong newspapers agonised over their own home-grown paparazzi, with the Oriental Daily News recalling that a local pop singer, Leslie Cheung, had crashed his Porsche while being pursued by photographers.

It branded paparazzi as "criminals of a thousand years." The Daily Star, a Bangladesh newspaper, said that "Western press and society will need to embark on a long search of their souls to come to terms with the sense of guilt Diana's death must generate."

Alongside the just-the-facts stories and reaction stories were articles focused primarily on the causes of the accident. Many of these stories found some aspect of popular culture (either the photographers who chased Diana's car that night, tabloid-press photographers in general, tabloid newspapers, the editors and publishers of tabloid newspapers, or any member of the press who had purchased paparazzi photos) to be at fault. The tone of these articles was often angry and disgusted.

Earl Spencer's statement was used in several of these stories as a starting point for further discussion of the role of the paparazzi in Diana's death. Dave Walker, writing for TAe Arizona Republic (Sept. 1), began such a story by asking "Do the media have blood on their hands for the death of Princess Diana? That's what her brother, Earl Spencer, suggested in the aftermath of the car wreck"

Walker went on to cite several sources who agreed with Spencer, including Dodi's father, Mohamed al Fayed, unnamed network television commentators, and Phoenix-area talk-radio host Charles Goyette, whom Walker quoted: '"The media are clearly to blame,' said Goyette, summing up the majority opinion among his callers. 'The consumers of this trash don't have the culpability, the media do.'"

An article in The Glasgow Herald quoted a source who followed Spencer's lead and blamed all the producers of tabloid newspapers: "the Prince of Wales's biographer Jonathan Dimbleby said: 'It isn't only the reporters and photographers, it's those who hired them.' He added: 'It's the editors and proprietors who too often, offer glossy excuses about the public interest who need now to examine their consciences.'"

Some of the stories that discussed causes were actually editorials expressing the views of the writer or writers. For example, The London Observer (no by-line, Aug. 31) expressed the following opinion: "Anyone in the British Press who has bought and used the pictures snatched by paparazzi on so many previous utterly private occasions helped ensure that the ravening pack would be on the trail on Saturday night." Some of these articles were written in a narrative stylo, retelling the facts of the story dramatically while characterizing the photographers as degenerates.

For example, Michael Daly of The New York Daily News (Aug. 31) wrote: No matter how fast her car sped through the Paris night, the paparazzi on the motorbikes were sure to stay right behind her, for she was with the man said to be her lover (T)he following Sunday, she was swarmed by those only interested in violating her private life.

They were still after the couple when she arrived in France. The hounds kept baying, right up to early this morning, when motorcycles sped after Diana's car along the Seine. Her pursuers were right out of the 1961 movie "La Dolce Vita," in which a photographer named Paparazzo chases his prey on a motorscooter (T)hey chased the biggest score ever right to her death.

The frenzy that began with "The Kiss" ended in two children being left without their mother. Similarly, Luke Harding, Owen Bowcott, John Hooper, Paul Webster, Alex Bellos, Stephen Bates, and Chris Mihill of The London Observer (Aug. 31) wrote: Even before Princess Diana and Dodi Fayed had strolled through the baroque central corridor of the Ritz hotel in Paris.

The paparazzi were lurking in wait (Diana and Dodi's) presence was common knowledge among the small, ruthless, multilingual band of photographers who pursue her, very lucratively, for a living Around 7 p.m. on Saturday Diana left the Ritz in a chauffeur-driven car to do some shopping in the Champs Elysee.

The press pack were, reportedly, in close pursuit Quite a few stories blamed "the press" in general or "the media" in general, not distinguishing the mainstream press from the tabloid press. Among these were stories reporting that Diana herself had condemned the practices of the British press in an interview published in a French newspaper the week before the accident.

J. Frank Lynch of The Atlanta Journal and Constitution (Aug. 31) reported "In Great Britain, 'the press is ferocious," Diana said in the article in the French daily Le Monde. 'It forgives nothing and is only hunting down mistakes. Each act is twisted; each gesture is criticized."'

SHANING THE BLAME

A number of stories about the causes of Diana's death divided the blame among several culprits. One of these culprits was Henri Paul, the driver of the Mercedes. On the first day of coverage, many articles noted that Paul had been driving at a speed well above the limit and that he lost control of the car, thus implying that the accident was at least partly his fault.

When the news of Paul's very high blood-alcohol level (which was more than three times the French legal limit) was released on day two, he became the target of finger-pointing in many more articles. However, none of the stories that blamed Paul let the producers of popular culture off the hook completely. An editorial in The Arizona Republic (no byline, Sept. 3) argued:

The swift and reckless rush to judgment, the desire to fix certain blame for the death of Diana, is also destructive and promises to leave victims. Misplaced blame might mask sorrow's pain, but it does not heal. Diana Spencer, queen of celebrity, died from the impaired judgment of millions. We'll name a few.

The paparazzi, a subset of photojournalists identified first and perhaps forever as the villains who ended the strange, fairy-tale existence of a lovely young woman, continue to receive disproportionate blame. Seven photographers face some type of charges related to the fatal crash. So what of the judgment of those editors and publishers who buy sleaze and resell it under some loose definition of news? Impaired? Morally warped? Yes. And, so whal of the judgment of millions of readers who purchase the product now blamed for the death of a princess? Impaired? Warped? Yes. However, in this tragedy, the person whose impaired judgment seems most responsible for the death of Princess Diana, is the man behind the wheel of the car carrying her and her boyfriend

One of the few articles to seriously consider the culpability of Henri Paul was published by The Boston Globe (Sept. 1). (This story also contained several sources who blamed the paparazzi at the scene and the press in general.) Author Peter S. Canellos wrote:

Ralph Whitehead, a journalism professor at the University of Massachusetts, said all the hand-wringing over the misdeeds of media is "a momentary hysteria."

Unless proof emerges that paparazzi on motorcycles actually interfered with the progress of Diana's car, responsibility for the accident should rest with the driver, he said. The Mercedes limousine was traveling faster than 60 miles per hour-perhaps much faster-in a tunnel where the speed limit is 30, police said. The princess and her companion, Dodi Fayed, did not appear to be wearing seatbelts.

"What would Diana and the rest of the people in the car have lost if they'd been overtaken by photographers?" Whitehead said. "If you're a celebrity, you have a right to regard the paparazzi as a pain in the neck. But it's not the right response to put your life in jeopardy by speeding away."

For a few days, there was a bit of a tug of war between those sources representing the photographers (primarily their lawyers) and those representing the driver (the Fayed family and Paul's co-workers). Some of the stories printed on days two through seven offered opinions as to which party deserved more blame, while others blamed Western society as a whole for its fascination with celebrities.

In an article called "Time Has Come to Point Finger in Right Direction," Steve Wilson of The Arizona Republic (Sept. 3) wrote "I would like to interrupt all the finger-pointing in Princess Diana's death-do the paparazzi or the drunken driver deserve the most blame?-for this important message: It's the culture, stupid. Or more precisely, it's the stupid, celebrity-obsessed culture."

Mickey H. Osterreicher of The Buffalo News (Sept. 4) wrote: As a photojournalism I am ashamed and embarrassed by the accusations that "paparazzi, " photographically pursuing the princess, were the cause of the accident. Given that factor, along with alcohol and excessive speed, the comparative negligence in this case would appear to be endless. In a larger sense, we are all somewhat responsible. This tragedy sadly illustrates the life and times in which we live.

POPULAR-CULTURE EXONERATION

In the other cases we examined, some journalists and sources came to the defence of the popular-culture products that were widely blamed for the tragedies. In the case of Diana's death, the paparazzi, the tabloids, and their producers were never fully exonerated. However, quite a few stories published in the days following the crash placed primary responsibility on the readers of tabloid newspapers-for encouraging the practices of the paparazzi.

An editorial in The Atlanta Journal and Constitution (Sept. 1) blamed the consumers of popular culture: "Princess Diana, perhaps the most recognizable woman in the world, was so beautiful and compassionate that people everywhere fell in love with her. And then they loved her to death. The insatiable demand for gossip and pictures involving Diana sot the stage for her tragic end.

" The editorial went on to blame the tabloid audience more explicitly: "The way to stop the stalking is to quit buying the trashy publications that pay for paparazzi pictures. This week, many of Diana's loyal fans will be weeping for their tragic heroine, but if they had not purchased the papers that exploited her in the first place, she might not be dead."

Others concurred. The Arizona Rcpublic's Dave Walker (Sept. 1) wrote "Some observers blame tabloid readers for creating the high-dollar market that would send photographers on a high-speed chase through Paris. " Walker cited "Mary-Lou Galician, an associate professor at the Walter Cronkite School of Journalism and Telecommunications at Arizona State University" as saying "that paparazzi command huge fees for celebrity photos because there's a market demanding them. 'The mathematics suggest that millions of people want these things,' she said. The public has to assume ultimate responsibility and not blame the messengers.'" Interestingly, several other factors could have served to exonerate the photographers and tabloids, at least partially, but these factors were largely ignored by the writers who sought to answer the "why" question.

Among these factors are the 15 minutes it took for an ambulance to reach the Mercedes, where Diana was rapidly losing blood; the fact that neither Diana nor Dodi was wearing a seat belt; the claim made by a few sources that the Mercedes had escaped the photographers before the crash; and, finally, the fact that no one really knew if the photographers actually caused the accident.

Instead of emphasizing or even just exploring these factors, the newspapers chose to focus most of their coverage (and most of the blame) on the paparazzi, the tabloids, their editors and publishers, and the readers of these popular publications.

CONNECTIONS WITH THEORY

Many of the theoretical arguments made by Pauly, Eason, and Bird were apparent in this case study of press coverage of Princess Diana's death. The fact that the photographers who were following Diana were employed at tabloid newspapers invited the discourse of "serious" versus "tabloid" journalism seen throughout the coverage.

The tone of condemnation and blame in coverage of Diana's death was typically directed squarely at the tabloids rather than at press coverage in general, just as in the pointed criticism of fabricated news stories and the reproach of the practices of Rupert Murdoch.

As Bird found in her analysis of tabloid newspapers in general, the tabloid photographers, in this particular situation (as well as editors, reporters, and owners) were implicated for their "base" profit-seeking and sensationalism which was implicitly contrasted with the elevating of the public service function of the "elite" press.

The theoretical contributions of Jensen also apply. In fact, the Princess Diana coverage stands out because the audience was also drawn into tho blame for its apparent attraction to sensationalism and intrusive fascination with the private lives of famous people. This element of the coverage reveals a view of the general public as drawn to "what is bad for them" that Jensen discusses as an underlying element in major strains of media criticism.

By implicitly making a distinction between the "popular" and "elite" news media, the newspapers we reviewed were able to deflect criticism from themselves and take an allegedly prosocial stance as watchdogs standing guard against the practices and content of other media institutions, thereby protecting the public.

Finally, we may also examine the press coverage of Diana's death via the levels of influences of news media content as advanced by Shoemaker and Roese. At the individual level, for instance, reporters may have empathized with Diana's plight of being followed and photographed all the time and thus been more inclined to blame the accident on those who hounded her.

Individual reporters (and their higher ups) may also have been motivated to try to make sense of and elevate the status of the death of Diana because her life was so extraordinary. In other words, death caused by a car crash-even one in which the driver was under the influence of alcohol-seems too mundane for a princess and a woman of such stature.

Thus, the pursuit ofthat car by paparazzi adds a glamorously tragic element befitting a princess as well as a moralistic element that may help channel the widespread anger and sadness caused by her death. This is exacerbated by the immediate removal of Henri Paul from ongoing blame due to his own demise. The tabloids provide an enduring, monolithic institution to blame rather than one unknown and unknowable individual.

Finally, the professional background of newspaper journalists might have made them prone to view the paparazzi as reckless or unruly because freelance photographers are not required to have journalism training or to adhere to a professional code of ethics, whereas most newspaper journalists are. Media routines were also apparent in the coverage. The selection of sources certainly shaped the stories that were written.

Many newspapers reported either the prepared statements of the victims' family members or the comments of celebrities, all of which sharply criticized the paparazzi. Localism produced some of the most vehement sources. The Britons interviewed in American pubs were quick to blame not only the photographers who chased Diana's car but all tabloid media.

This would also serve to separate the "elite" news media from the presumed culprits (though, in the case of Diana's death, a few writers did admit to guilt on the part of the "elite" media, especially after the wall-to-wall coverage of Diana's death in the "elite" media).

Extramedia influences on coverage were also apparent. Some sources called for government intervention in the practices of tabloid photographers after Diana's death. Notions of audience preference may well have facilitated the pursuit of the paparazzi angle through the view that many readers of the "elite" press would welcome the criticism of the tabloids and find this element of the event emotionally charged and fascinating.

Influences presumably occurred at the ideological level as well. The potential dissonance involved in newspapers reprimanding other types of print media was alleviated by the strategy of distinguishing between "them" and "us. " This is apparent in the many markers labeling tabloids as a separate entity in "elite" press coverage.

We can also see evidence of the cultural belief in the cause-and-effect paradigm in press coverage that is, in fact, magnified here clue to the fact that Diana was the subject of admiration and adulation in many parts of the world. Her revered status may well have heightened the typical North American tendency to try to find a cause for every event, a solution for every "problem."

The criticism of the paparazzi, as well as the alcohol level of the driver, surfaced as an attempt to explain what essentially a senseless death was and thereby to diminish readers' fears, discomfort, and, in some cases, grief. Finally, ideological beliefs about the nature of the masses were also apparent in the Diana case, as some newsppers placed part of the blame squarely at the feet of the public, whose taste for sensationalism, the papers claimed, is merely answered by tabloid publications.

THE "JENNY JONES" MURDER

In 1995, television talk-show host Jenny Jones arranged for Jonathan Schmitz, 34, to appear on her show as a part of her signature "secret admirer" segment. Schmitz was told in front of a national audience that his secret admirer was Scott Amedure, 32, a gay friend. Three days after the show was taped, Schmitz shot Amedure to death.

News coverage of the event quickly focused on the way Schmitz was brought in front of a national audience and "humiliated" as the subject of a gay fantasy. Subsequent news coverage was dominated by finger-point-ing-who should be blamed for the death of a talk-show guest?

Schmitz was convicted of murder in November 1996, and in May 1999, the Amedure family won $25 million in a negligence suit brought against the "Jenny Jones Show" and Warner Brothers, Jones' employer. Over the five years in which the story has been reported, the object of blame has fluctuated. News stories about the Jenny Jones talk-show murder centreed around four points in time: the initial shooting, a rash of follow-up stories blaming "trash TV" for the murder, Schmitz's first trial, and Schmitz's second trial.

The analysis below reflects quotes taken from newspapers across the country from the day after the murder through August 1999 when Jonathan Schmitz was convicted for a second time in the shooting death of Amedure. Articles were retrieved using the news category in ProQuest. In all, 326 articles with relevant content were reviewed.

This case study attempts to illustrate how the print news

media covered the Jenny Jones case, with an emphasis on analyzing the sources of blame. News stories on the first day after Scott Amedure's death reported the event as just another murder. Furthermore, news stories published that day implicated Jonathan Schmitz alone for Amedure's murder.

While the firstday stories mentioned the "Jenny Jones Show" because both men were guests on the show, neither the show and its producers were directly implicated for the murder until a few days later. Shauna Snow, writing for The Los Angeles Times, dealt with the facts alone in her story on March 10, 1995.

A gay man who took his penchant for talk shows to heart and appeared on the "Jenny Jones Show" to reveal his secret crush on a heterosexual man has been shot dead, and police said the object of his affection admitted the killing. All other stories examined that were published on the first day after the event contained a similar, just-the-facts approach.

POPULAR-CUTURE CULPABILITY

After initial news accounts reported who, what, where, when, and how, analysis and interpretation began to appear in stories about the murder. The "Jenny Jones Show" and the show's producers came under fire the day Jonathan Schmitz was arraigned on first-degree murder charges. In a Washington Post article (no byline) on the second day after the murder, March 11, 1995, the finger pointing at the "Jenny Jones Show" began.

Producers of the "Jenny Jones Show" have come under attack by Michigan prosecutors who allege the nationally syndicated talk show is partly responsible for the murder this week of a guest who professed to have a crush on another man Oakland County Prosecutor Richard Thompson said the talk show's "ambush" tactics-in which guests learn of shocking personal details on camera-may be partly to blame for the death.

A Tacoma News article published March 11, 1995, was one of many newspapers to describe the segment as "ambush television." Call it ambush television. It's the latest weapon in daytime talk-show wars, and now it's had deadly consequences. The formula is simple: Bring guests on the air, set off conflict and embarrass them before a national TV audience. Maybe even embarrass them to death.

The "Jenny Jones Show"' brought on John Schmitz, a 24-year-old man from Orion Township, Mich., and told him that a 32-year-old acquaintance, Scott Amedure, was his secret admirer. Today, Amedure is dead and Schmitz has been charged with murder.

The "Jenny Jones Show" was further implicated for Amedure's death later in that first week of news coverage after Prosecutor Thompson alleged the talk show was not only partially responsible for the murder of Amedure but also for the "poisoning of society." An article in The Detroit News quoted Thompson as saying Schmitz was "ambushed on national TV, the suggestion being that all Schmitz did was ambush back" at Amedure.

While the other two cases studied here were front-page stories from day one, the "Jenny Jones" talk-show murder only began to make the front page after the talk show's culpability became a part of the story. Most stories, such as this story from The State Journal Registerpublished on day two, contained harsh criticism directed toward the show and its producers and cited ratings as the rationale behind the segment.

A talk show focusing on "Secret Admirers" led to the killing of one guest, allegedly by another. Is 'The "Jenny Jones Show'" to blame? And was this a tragedy just waiting to happen? Yes to both questions, according to talk-show critics, who argue that anything goes to boost ratings.

As the story became more prominent, analysis of the event became the "new" news. The event was frequently the subject of newspaper editorials and columns, and these columns went beyond implicating the show and its producers for Amedure's murder-the authors accused the talk show of "trashing society."

By the time this Phoenix Gazette story ran on March 14, many of the "elite" newspapers had spent the previous three days analyzing the culpability of the talk show and its producers. "Our concern now is for the family and friends of the deceased and (for) maintaining the sanctity of the police investigation and the case," Jim Paratore, president of Telepictures Productions, which produces the "Jenny Jones Show," said.

His concern comes a couple of shotgun blasts too late. And his rejection of blame is cynical and without merit. Do Jones or the show's producers ever investigate the temperaments or personality traits of those they seek to embarrass? Did they know anything about Schmitz, or about submerged feelings he may have about homosexuality?

Obviously not. Nor did they care. Someone else pulled the trigger, but they were the ones who blindly spun the chamber. For that reason, they are all accessories. Howard Rosenberg of The Los Angeles Times on March 17, 1995, blamed the daytime talk shows for what he called rampant misbehaviour on the part of daytime television talk shows that play loosely with the lives of some of their guests by seeking to embarrass them with the cameras rolling.

Schmitz is surely a man driven by inner demons that "Jenny Jones" didn't know or care about when its staff plotted this high-risk farce, which, in the case of these two men, was based on the premise that a homosexual coming on to someone who is apparently straight equals titillation.

Elsewhere in the column, Rosenberg blamed the "Jenny Jones Show" for driving a mentally unstable Schmitz over the edge in the cause of ratings. "If Schmitz is guilty, he's the one who pulled the trigger. But if so, it was 'Jenny Jones' along with the laws allowing him to purchase a shotgun with apparent ease that provided the trigger."

It was at about this point (one week after the murder) that the theories of "who is at fault" seemed to coalesce among the different sources. Schmitz's attorney wholeheartedly defended his client's actions, suggesting the talk show "goaded a lunatic" to take desperate action.

Many of the news stories published at the same time took a similar tone. It was in these articles, published from two days to two weeks after the murder, that the popular-culture culpability angle became so evident. Newspaper headlines alone clearly directed responsibility to the talk show.

- "Critics Link Slaying to Contentious Talk Shows" (News Tribune, March 11, 1995)
- "Ambush-Style Talk Shows Are Playing with Fire" (Detroit News, March 11, 1995)
- "Critics Say Talk Show Partly to Blame in Talk-Show Slaying" (Sun-Sentinel, March 11, 1995)
- "TV's Gutter Talk-Sleaze Takes a Terrible Price" (New York Newsday, March 13, 1995)

Nationally known newspapers such as The Detroit News, The Washington Post, The Los Angeles Times and The Chicago Tribune covered the murder and arraignment from a seemingly objective standpoint; however, the sources used in each of the stories-Schmitz's attorney and Schmitz's family members-primarily represented just one side.

The tone in the newspaper stories was not overtly critical, but the inclusion of some points of view and not others suggested the "elite" media were condemning the actions of the daytime talk shows.

Not surprisingly, the Detroit newspapers dedicated a great deal of space to the story, and Ron French of The Detroit News wrote several articles and columns dealing with the issue of culpability.

His parents can't understand how a son who cried when he ran over a toad with the lawn mower could shoot a man. "It's darker on this side of the gun," Allyn Schmitz said. "This terror we had lived with came in a worse form. He didn't kill himself, but he killed himself in another way.

His life is taken away by prison and by Jenny Jones." Neal Gabler of The Houston Chronicle also faulted the show for putting the gun in Schmitz's hand. How the producers of the "Jenny Jones Show" must have grieved.

During a segment entitled "Secret Admirers," they had surprised a male guest expecting to meet a female admirer by springing a male acquaintance insteadNaturally, the producers made professions of regret, but one suspects what they really regretted was the killer's indecency of not having pulled out his rifle and committed the crime before their cameras. Now, there would have been a ratings coup.

The "Jenny Jones" talk-show murder all but disappeared from newspaper headlines within the first month after the murder. However, as the case moved closer to the trial stage, news stories blaming products of popular culture started to reappear. It was at this time in late 1995 when many politicians jumped on the bandwagon of condemning the daytime talk show for broadcasting "daytime TV smut.

"It was also during this time that parents and politicians alike decided daytime television needed regulation. Harry Levins' story in The St. Louis Post Dispatch, October 28, 1995, reported on a "band of influential Washingtonians" who led a campaign of taking the talk show to task, calling it "a matter of citizenship." The main critic of the daytime talk shows was former Education Secretary William Bennett, quoted in The Detroit News.

"There was a time," Bennett said Thursday, "when personal failure or marital failure, subliminal desire, and perverse tastes were accompanied by a sense of guilt or embarrassment. Today, these are a ticket to appear on the Sally Jesse Raphael show to be broadcast for children to watch," Bennett said. "This cultural rot is polluting America."

Many news organizations relied regularly on sources such as Prosecutors Thompson or Burdick or politicians such as Bennett, Joseph Lieberman, or Sam Nunn, who were very outspoken about the liability of the talk show. Thompson readily blamed the "Jenny Jones Show," Jenny Jones herself, and the talk show's producers for the murder. Friends and family members of Amedure rarely appeared as sources in news stories.

Yet family members and friends of Schmitz were frequently quoted, as were psychologists and analysts hired by the defence team. Furthermore, newspapers used Thompson and Burdick as sources more than anyone else. Therefore, the voices most critical to the talk show were the ones most frequently cited.

In addition to presenting relatively one-sided stories, news organiztions can be considered to have pandered to the audiences of the popular-culture products they were criticizing by giving the story so much news coverage. Joanne Jacobs of The Tulsa World, November 14, 1995, reported on what it was she thought the public wanted.

It's estimated that a million teen-agers and 650,000 pre-teens turn on daytime sleaze, and absorb its perverted values Trash-talk hosts claim their shows serve as morality plays, with the studio audience cast as judges. This lets viewers revel in the lurid confessions and confrontations. Then they get to condemn it. Small-town morality lives, only with hotter gossip and a better choice of sins.

EXONERATING POPULAR CULTURE /SHAKING THE BLAME

As the implication of a popular-culture product in the murder case became old news, new theories of blame started to circulate. During this time, a few weeks after the murder, two key suspects shared the blame for Amedure's murder with the "Jenny Jones Show"-Jonathan Schmitz himself and what was called the "homosexual panic defence." Paul E. Gainor, reporting for The Detroit News, March 26, 1995, was one of many who explored this theory.

Richard S. Sinacola, a Royal Oak therapist for 12 yearssays the case of Scott Amedure and John Schmitzmay have involved homosexual panic as a trigger point Sinacola theorizes that Schmitz "couldn't handle the fact that it involved homosexuality." For him, it touched on some deep-seated homophobia What he was killing was not so much the victim, but his own sense of homosexuality in the victim.

The "homosexual panic defence" theory quickly took centre stage in news articles after stories about Jenny Jones' irresponsible behaviour began to subside. The homosexual panic defence made headlines a few weeks after the murder and reappeared as a secondary object of blame when the media began covering Schmitz's first trial. From The Seattle Times, reporter not listed, on October 6, 1996:

Focusing on the "Jenny Jones Show" shifts blame away from the defendant to homophobia Society's problem is not that these TV shows are on. Society's problem is that we've created a world where a guy feels he can go out and kill a guy because he is gay.

As the "hate, not humiliation" theory became the new focus of news stories, a small contingent began to blame Schmitz again for the murder. Robert Strauss of The Los Angeles Times said that Schmitz would have to be pretty gullible to have no idea what he was in for on the "Jenny Jones Show." Strauss argued that even if the show's producers encouraged Amedure to be "flamboyant" toward Schmitz, Schmitz still purchased the gun, sought out Amodure, and killed him.

UNIQUE ELEMENTS

While Scott Amedure's death is undoubtedly a tragedy, his death did not reach the magnitude, in terms of press coverage or public outrage, of the Columbine High School shootings or Princess Diana's death.

The "Jenny Jones" talk-show case also differed from the other two cases in that it involved two trials and a negligence suit brought against the show. In the late fall of 1995, hearings on the "Jenny Jones" murder case began, and throughout late 1995 and 1996, the "Jenny Jones" talk-show murder began making news again.

While more than six months had passed between the murder and the first round of hearings, Jenny Jones, the show, and its producers still remained the objects of blame for Amedure's murder. As the trial neared, Schmitz's new defence attorney again tried to focus on the talk show's tactics.

While on the stand, Jenny Jones herself maintained that Schmitz knew his secret admirer could be a man or a woman. Ron French, for The Detroit News on February 21, 1996, wrote several stories about the trial stages of the case. Defence attorney James Burdick will try to deflect responsibility for the slaying from his client to the "Jenny Jones Show" and its ambush interview tactics.

Schmitz claims he was misled by producers who persuaded him to fly to Chicago to appear on a show about secret admirers. On November 12, 1996, Jonathan Schmitz was convicted of second-degree murder, yet jurors for the trial said the show deserved at least some of the blame. Ron French of The Detroit News, November 13, 1996, covered the case's outcome from the jury's point of view.

"We saw the show as a catalyst for this," said juror Joyce O'Brien. "They destroyed one person's life and his family, and another young man is dead and his family ruined. It is a terrible injustice all because of the show." As the trial came to a close, reporters from the "elite" media again began bashing the "Jenny Jones Show," the show's producers, and daytime TV for the "corruption of society".

An Associated Press story, written by Frazier Moore, discussed the details of the verdict in a November 29, 1996, column. Obviously Jonathan Schmitz wasn't prepared for what he got by Jones or any of the Jenny Jones staff. Quite the opposite. Evidence indicates that for the sake of lively talk TV, Schmitz was set up to believe he would be meeting the girl of his dreams. Instead, he met Jenny Jones.

After the much-publicized trial and verdict, the two years following the trial, 1997 and 1998, were fairly quiet. News of the murder and trial popped up sporadically, mostly in the form of editorials. Schmitz was convicted in 1996, but in 1998, his conviction was overturned on a technicality in an appeals court. In May of 1999, a jury awarded the Amedure family $25 million in a negligence suit against the "Jenny Jones Show." From a Los Angeles Times story (byline merely indicating it was from wire reports) on May 15, 1999:

A jury finds the "Jenny Jones Show" liable for the 1995 shooting death of Scott Amedure, a gay man who admitted during a never-aired show that he had a crush on Jonathan Schmitz. The jury awarded $25 million in damages to Amedure's family, saying the show tricked Schmitz and humiliated him into committing the murder.

In September 1999, Jonathan Schmitz was convicted for the second time in the death of Scott Amedure. Circuit Judge

Wendy Potts handed Schmitz a 25 to 50-year sentence-the same sentence he received in his first trial. The $25 million civil-suit award for the Amedure family represents a new turn in state and federal courts holding entertainment media liable for a tragedy.

Culpability in the "Jenny Jones" talk-show murder case was easier to prove than the culpability of the violent video games, music, and films linked to the Columbine High School shooting and of the paparazzi linked to the death of Princess Diana. The title of the segment, "Secret Admirers," the "ambush-style" tactics, and the notion that a talk-show guest was allegedly "goaded" to "act flamboyantly" have all been cited as evidence that the show and its producers incited the murder.

CONTEXT OF POPULAR-CULTURE BLAME

At the same time the entertainment industry was being held accountable for Scott Amedure's death, news of other tragedies, including the Columbine High School shootings, hit the airwaves and newsstands, and some producers of popular culture were again the target of blame.

From the time of the murder to the time of Jonathan Schmitz's first trial, the "Jenny Jones Show," the producers of the show, daytime talk shows in general, homophobia, and Schmitz had all been blamed for the death of Amedure. The news stories acknowledged Schmitz was responsible for pulling the trigger; however, many reporters seemed intent on finding an additional source of blame.

Through the selection of sources used in news stories to the focus of the news stories themselves, the "elite" media seemed to assign blame to the "less-than-legitimate" talk shows. Within a month after the murder, many of the "elite" media jumped on the bandwagon of accusing the popular media of polluting America. From The Washington Post, on October 31, 1995:

Still, there's no question many talk shows exploit and often humiliate people for entertainment-especially the ambush-style programs like the infamous Jenny Jones episode that was accused of sparking a murder. Some of the news stories even tried to draw distinctions between audiences of the "trashy" daytime talk shows and the audiences for other news-oriented programs. Sharon Waxman in The Washington Post described viewers of the daytime talk shows as "gullibleoften unemployedleeches" who had nothing better to do than to live vicariously through the lives of other "trailer park trash."

This cycle of blame became all the more evident as Jonathan Schmitz headed into his first trial and then his second trial. "Elite" newspapers such as The Washington Post, The Los Angeles Times, The Dallas Morning News, The Detroit News, and The Chicago Tribune appeared to draw a clear distinction between themselves and the popular media.

Furthermore, these news outlets criticized the talk shows for uncovering secrets, exposing wrongdoings, and "harping on the perversion in society." Yet many of these publications were doing the same thing by giving the story so much coverage. The difference is that the talk shows were reaching one audience, and the "elite" media used the same "trash" to reach another audience.

During the four-and-a-half-year-long evolution of the story, several theories of blame circulated. While the blame was shared, the daytime talk shows took the biggest hit for allegedly causing a larger social problem, "cultural pollution." Jonathan Schmitz's lawyer, James Burdick, said when Jenny Jones asked her television audience, "Is your life better than television?," culpability rested in her hands and in the hands of the show's producers. Burdick's contention is that in Jones' quest to focus on the drama of interpersonal conflict in a public forum, she theoretically put the gun in Schmitz's hands.

CONNECTIONS WITH THEORY

Pauly's (1992) discussion of the "elite" media's criticism of Rupert Murdoch parallels the "elite" media's criticism of the talk shows in the "Jenny Jones" case. Rupert Murdoch was accused by many in the "elite" press of devaluing journalistic ideals, and in a similar sense, journalists covering the "Jenny Jones" case accused the talk shows of not maintaining a high standard of practice.

This can be seen quite clearly as many newspaper reporters covering the story implicitly or explicitly distinguished themselves as "serious" journalists. Media mogul Rupert Murdoch was criticized for his style of promotional journalism, and the news organizations covering the "Jenny Jones" story capitalized on the promotional qualities of the pop-culture products they were criticizing by giving the story so much news coverage.

The news media would have a difficult time rationalizing the prominent play the story received, especially the length of time the story was in the news, because over the course of time, new details were not uncovered. More simply, the story was essentially old news with a high level of sensationalism and a presumed high level of public interest.

It seems fairly clear that as news editors made decisions regarding the newsworthiness of the story, promotional journalism was a driving factor in continued coverage. The examples from the "Jenny Jones" case parallel Bird's (1992) discussion of the way "serious" journalists speak out about "low taste."

The "elite" journalists and the sources they chose made overt references to the media producers they felt were responsible for Amedure's death. Adjectives such as "trashy" and "tabloid" clearly placed the talk shows in a very different category from the "elite" journalists; thus, by distinguishing the talk shows as a media product very different from what the journalists were producing, the journalists were able to keep the blame away from themselves.

The "elite" media's classification of the talk shows as "smut" entertainment is what Jensen would classify as an assumption of the masses as the "lowest common denominator." As the "elite" newspapers critiqued their popular media counterparts by using words such as "trash," "smut," or "tabloid," they elevated their own status by drawing a clear distinction between themselves and those ostensibly not like them.

One application of Jensen's theoretical framework to this study is an understanding of how the popular media were blamed for each of the tragedies. In the "Jenny Jones" case, the "elite" journalists accused the talk shows of pandering to the "sick" predilections of viewers-in a sense, doing anything for ratings.

The talk shows were blamed for giving audiences what they wanted rather than news and information they needed. In many news stories, the "elite" journalists directly condemned the talk shows, the talk show producers, the talk show guests and the talk show viewers of lowering the cultural standard of art in America.

This analysis can also be tied to McDonald's discussion of journalists speaking out against "low taste." In the "Jenny Jones" case, some newspaper quotes actually addressed this issue explicitly, arguing that part of the blame lies squarely at the feet of the public whose taste for sensationalism is merely answered by television talk shows.

Shoemaker and Reese's discussion of the five levels of influence on media content is central to explaining much of the coverage of the "Jenny Jones" case. At the individual level, reporters and columnists frequently took the show to task in the form of editorials, thereby providing an outlet for their own unfavorable views of the show and others like it.

The newspaper journalists covering the "Jenny Jones" case often seemed to have taken a "holier-than-thou" tone in their stories of Scott Amedure's death. It is possible the professional background of these reporters and columnists enabled them to view the talk-show host and producers as professionally careless in their attempts to achieve higher ratings via exploitative means.

At the routines and/or the individual level of influence, newspaper reporters often presented a relatively one-sided story via the sources they used in their stories. Some stories, while seemingly objective, contained a position simply by the use of some sources and not others.

It seems as if the "elite" newspapers relied on Thompson, the prosecutor, heavily because he provided a voice for the point of view that was presumed to sell more newspapers. Thompson readily blamed the "Jenny Jones Show, " Jenny Jones herself, and the talk-show producers for the murder. Numerous news stories quoted family members and friends of Schmitz in addition to psychologists and analysts hired by the defence team.

Furthermore, "elite" journalists were able to work many expert and official sources into their stories by relying on murder experts and psychologists who provided a rationale for Schmitz's actions and in some cases even took the blame away from Schmitz and placed more blame on the talk show.

Following Amedure's murder, several members of Congress also spoke publicly about the negative and violent content of television talk shows, and some even advocated removing the shows from television altogether.

The inclusion of these sources in the news stories was certainly justifiable, yet few stories provided the depth and analysis that would represent alternative views.

Initially, the "Jenny Jones" case did not receive the prominent news coverage of the other cases reviewed here. The murder was not considered newsworthy until the entertainment media were accused of helping to commit the crime. The story seemed to illustrate the routines of "status conferral" and of pack journalism.

As the story and its subjects became more prominent, it began to appear in more and more newspapers. Some newspapers devoted one story and several sidebars to the case for weeks and even months. Other newspapers ran stories for several days in a row, even though new information had not been uncovered or released.

While this behaviour may be standard practice in many newsrooms, it also illustrates the way news editors are often "forced" to allow more space for a story simply because the competition or national newspapers are running the story. From an ideological or hegemonic standpoint, blaming the "Jenny Jones Show" and its producers meant the "cause" for the tragedy was easily pinpointed.

American society could point its finger at the media, and

then, in a figurative sense, rest comfortably with the thought that the villain was identified. As de Mooij suggests, American culture strives for a source of blame, an identifiable cause, and views tragic events as a consequence of blame-worthy factors.

Blaming the media, in this case, helps maintain order because members of society do not necessarily have question the social forces that pit members of a dominant group (heterosexuals) against those from a non-dominant group (homosexuals) with potentially fatal consequences once the media have been isolated as the villain.

The underlying theme of the press coverage is that ordinary citizens do not have to fear for their safety unless they appear on a talk show themselves, rather than suggesting homophobia and hate are all too common in society. Initially, this well-publicized case may have temporarily heightened fear and feelings of uncertainty in members of society. With the elevated fear, they searched for a culprit, and once the talk shows were identified as the "cause," the fear subsided, and members of society, as well as those in the "elite" media, were able to feel more secure about their status quo social world.

It seemed much easier to blame the products of popular culture when the finger-pointers could step back and draw a clear distinction between themselves and those they were blaming for the tragedy. By making daytime television seem sleazy, trashy, and outlandish, the "elite" media improved their own image by comparison. However, the oversight seems to be that these same "elite" media were using similar stunts to draw in larger audiences themselves.

Case: Columbine High School Shootings. On April 20,1999, just before lunchtime, 18-year-old Eric Harris and 17-year-old Dylan Klebold, armed with guns and homemade bombs, opened fire on their classmates at Columbine High School in Littleton, Colorado. The siege lasted over four hours and ended with 15 dead, including the two gunmen, and several others wounded.

It was the bloodiest school shooting in the history of the

United States and was carried out with well-orchestrated and disturbingly cold and calculated precision-as well as visible glee on the part of the gunmen. The series of events and its aftermath left many to grapple with the difficult question of what had gone so terribly wrong that two young men would wreak such awful havoc on their peers.

This case study attempts to illustrate how the print news media covered this tragedy, with an emphasis on how journalists dealt with the task of addressing the issue of why the shooting occurred. In the course of investigating and discussing possible entities at fault, the news media quickly came to focus on popular-culture and entertainment-media products as causal contributors to the massacre at Columbine High.

Extensive quotes drawn from major newspapers around the world (searched via LEXIS-NEXIS) illustrate and also place into context the tendency of the news media to point the finger of blame at popular culture following this tragic event.

JUST THE FACTS

The very first accounts in the news media of the school shooting in Littleton, Colorado, followed traditional journalistic ideals of reporting on who, what, where, when, and how. The first day of coverage was a veritable news media frenzy, with blow-by-blow accounts broadcast live across the United States on the major radio and broadcast television networks and extensive coverage of gory details on cable news networks.

News that day featured terrified testimonials from students. Expressions of immense relief were broadcast as parents were united with their children. But above all, the view of a bloodied student escaping from a second-story window was perhaps the most memorable image, because of both its profundity and the number of times it was shown.

Quotes from print news media on April 20, 1999, document the tragic and frightening sequence of events and reflect the journalistic tradition of conveying the particulars (who, what, when, where, and how) of the event. The first newspaper articles on the topic came out before all the facts were known and thus included attempts to find out what exactly was happening inside the school, reporting the harrowing estimations of how many were killed, how many wounded.

From The Denver Rocky Mountain News, reporters Mike Anton, Manny Gonzalez, Kevin Vaughan, Charley Able, and Lou Kilzer, on April 20, 1999: At least 21 people were injured today when two or three gunmen dressed in black overcoats and masks opened fire inside Columbine High School in Littleton. Witnesses said the gunmen, reportedly students, appeared to fire randomly and set off explosives, possibly pipe bombs, laughing as they went.

From The Denver Rocky Mountain News, reporter Mike Anton, on April 20, 1999: Authorities said some victims were still inside the school as of 2:15 p.m. About 30 students were reported hiding in the choir room Seconds after the shooting began, hundreds of students and teachers poured out of the school while others sought refuge inside, hiding under desks and locking themselves in bathrooms Said another student "We were all under the table and the girl across the table from me was shot in the head right there."

A finger pointing of sorts occurred on this day, but served to merely answer the most pressing question at hand: who was responsible for this tragedy? Early blame was narrowly focused on those quickly identified as the gunmen, Eric Harris and Dylan Klebold. News stories traced the steps of the siege, its consequences, and its perpetrators.

POPULAR-CULTURE CULPABILITY

The next day, however, on April 21, 1999, the basic facts had largely already been gathered and disseminated. News coverage would now be dominated by placing blame and assigning responsibility to various people, institutions, and entities.

Exceptions to the blame-laying patterns that prevailed in the aftermath of the shooting were stories about vigils and grieving processes, connections made in communities around the country with those involved, and decisions to cancel sporting and other events in light of the tragedy.

Most other stories appearing for more than a month later attempted not to repeat the who, what, where, when, and how issues, but rather tackled the far more complex issue of why.

Instances of popular culture being blamed came quickly, on the day of the tragedy to help fill the broad expanse of time that cable news networks devoted to coverage, and in the days immediately following in print. The tradition of many news sources picking up the same angle or the same threads of the story was also readily apparent.

Wire reports appeared in newspapers across the nation, and the same shocking footage became less and less troubling as American television news viewers were exposed to it again and again. Once popular-culture products were introduced as culprits in early coverage, journalists across the world made a similar connection.

Those who pointed the finger of blame at media and popular-culture products in newspaper coverage largely fell into three categories: students at Columbine and other area schools, experts-typically professors, counselors, attorneys, and police officers-and reporters and newspaper editorial staff writers themselves.

Many popular-culture products were implicated as causal contributors to Harris and Klebold's violence. Movies (especially The Matrix), television, video games, the Internet, and recorded music were all scrutinized as antisocial influences on the gunmen.

In fact, though there is plenty of precedent for a single film or book, for instance, inspiring real-life antisocial behaviour, the Columbine shooting stands out as the one historical incident in which so many different popular-culture products were seen as responsible in so many different ways.

From The Atlanta Journal Constitution, reporter Mike Williams, on April 22, 1999: According to their friends, Harris, 18, and Klebold, 17, were part of a loose-knit group called the 'Trenchcoat Mafia' and often dressed in black, favoring leather and the long coats that have been featured in many violence-filled Hollywood movies.

The boys played violent computer games for hours, friends said Harris set up an Internet home page that spouted Nazi ideology and condoned violence. The shootings came on the 110th anniversary of Hitler's birthday.

From The Daily Telegraph (London), reporter John Hiscock, on April 22, 1999: The two laughing teenagers who shot and bombed their way though the halls of Columbine High School were members of a Gothic-style group known as the Trenchcoat Mafia.

Students at Littleton, Colorado, yesterday described Dylan Klebold, 17, and Eric Harris, 18, as "satanic individuals" who talked about Nazis and were fans of the "shock rock" star Marilyn Manson.

From The New York Daily News, reporter Helen Kennedy, on April 21, 1999: A Web page attributed to one of the members contained crude sketches of demons along with juvenile nihilism like "Anything I don't like sucks." There were song lyrics, from a German underground band called KMFDM an acronym for Kein Mehrfeit Fur Die Mitleid (No pity for the majority) including "What I don't like I waste," "I am your apocalypse," and "Chaos panic/no resistance/ detonations in the distance."

From The Daily Telegraph (London), reporter John Hiscock, on April 22, 1999: The Trenchcoat Mafia was born about three years ago when about a dozen students at Columbine started wearing black and listening to German techno music.

They often wore German slogans and swastikas on their clothes. Both were obsessed with the Internet-widely used by neo-Nazi groups-and computer games. Their favourites were Doom and Quake-violent fantasies where the aim is to kill everything you meet.

From The Denver Post, reporters Susan Greene and Bill Briggs, on April 21, 1999: "It appears you have a bunch of kids who've been into black metal music-Marilyn Manson-who basically have apocalyptic fantasies and (who operate under) a heavy code of neo-Nazism," said (Dr. Carl) Raschke (author of Painted Black, which explores violent youth culture).

From The Denver Rocky Mountain News, reporter Robert Denerstein, on April 22, 1999: In the enormously popular new movie The Matrix, Keanu Reeves wears a black duster and battles the forces of evil with two-fisted bursts of gunfire. He stages an attack on the conspiracy that has turned his life into a living hell.

The movie already is being mentioned as a possible source of influence on the Trench Coat Mafia, two of whose members entered Columbine High School Tuesday carrying weapons and wearing long black coats. It's not the first time movies have been connected with real-life violence

The above quotes demonstrate the wide variation in types of popular-culture products blamed, as well as the unique combinations of those entities that were viewed as responsible. They also demonstrate other aspects of youth culture, including hairstyles, body art, and means of dress, that were indirectly implicated in the news coverage of the Columbine shootings.

The entire nation was introduced to "gothic" culture in a manner that was at times valiant in its pursuit of value-neutral reportage. At other times "gothic" culture was implicated as a menacing desensitization to and even morbid fascination with death and dying that purportedly helped explain why Harris and Klebold acted with such utter disregard for human life.

The short amount of time it took to blame popular media and popular culture was partially explained by the relationship of the events that occurred in Littleton that day to other school shootings with young perpetrators in other areas of the country. It was an eerily familiar formula, and attempts at explanation linked Columbine to these other school shootings as sources and reporters struggled to make sense of the lot. In fact, one newspaper account used the media and popular culture to link the tragedy at Columbine to another recent high-profile student shooting. From The

Ottawa Citizen, reporters Bob Harvey and Christopher Guly, on April 22, 1999:

Just last week, parents of three girls killed in 1997 in Paducah, Kentucky, sued the makers of another film, The Basketball Diaries, starring Leonardo DiCaprio. The Paducah killer, Michael Carneal, said his decision to open fire on a school prayer group was influenced by that film.

EXONERATING POPULAR CULTURE/ SHARING THE BLAME

Certainly the media and popular-culture products were not the only entities blamed for the Columbine tragedy, though they were among the most frequent targets. Other sources of blame included poor parenting, unsafe schools, uninformed school and police officials, teen cliques, feelings of ostracism, and, perhaps the most frequent additional target of criticism-the prevalence and accessibility of guns. Some of those who assigned blame in the Columbine shootings chose to focus on only one of these culprits, while others argued that these factors acted in concert to explain the tragedy that had occurred.

Some took the position that other societal factors outweighed the role of popular culture in contributing to the tragedy. Others seemed to feel that those entities should share the responsibility. From The Los Angeles Times, reporter Josh Getlin, on April 22, 1999:

The shooting also brings up an old question. How much responsibility does the culture bear for images of violence and retribution, which fill movies, TV, video games, the Internet, recorded music and even the most elementary cartoons today? "We've seen a steady escalation of violence as entertainment, and it reaches people in disturbing ways," (Joyce) Appleby (American history professor) said. "Billions of people watch these pictures around the globe, but somewhere a handful of boys weren't horrified, they were fascinated."

From The Ottawa Citizen, reporters Bob Harvey and Christopher Guly, on April 22, 1999: Those especially vulnerable to violent media messages are individuals-like the two gunmen in the Denver suburb Tuesday-who are "separated away from the mainstream," said Mr. (Andrew) Osier (media professor at the University of Western Ontario), who researches media and violence at the university's Faculty of Information and Media Studies.

A few reporters and experts alike voiced concern that media and popular-culture products were serving as scapegoats in the wake of Columbine, possibly masking other, ostensibly more important causal factors. Articles defending these entities, however, were in the minority and tended to occur in response to the preceding typos of popular-culture accusations. From The Chicago Sun Times, reporter Richard Roeper, on April 22, 1999:

It's impossible-and unfair-to point to a band or a movie or a TV show and say "That was the cause," and then to turn to a slaughter and say, "This is the effect." If that's the way it worked, how can it be that hundreds of thousands of fans the world over have been exposed to the spine-thumping music of KMFDM without turning violent?

From The Los Angeles Times, reporter Josh Getlin, on April 22, 1999: "The media influences people, but you don't march into a school armed with guns and grenades and kill 13 people overnight. It doesn't come from nowhere," he (Todd Boyd, an author and professor at the USC School of Cinema and Television) added.

From The Denver Rocky Mountain News editorial, on April 21, 1999: What, many Americans wonder, is going on? We don't profess to know, yet surely part of the answer is a relatively simple phenomenon: unbalanced, resentful kids imitating the highly publicized actions of other unbalanced kids. Most other explanations-the influence of violent entertainment, for example, or too-easy access to guns-suffer from the weakness of having long predated the recent trend of gun-toting students invading their schools with guns.

Do news accounts merely blame the content of popular entertainment media without assessing the media companies and the production and distribution processes that create that content? The answer in this case appears to be yes. Noticeably absent in coverage of the Columbine school shootings was a larger, more macroscopic context for popular-culture blame.

Newspaper articles that mentioned either the corporations involved in the production of the content that many found objectionable or the commercial structure of American media that de-emphasizes social responsibility in the creation of content were noticeably rare.

Indeed, though many an allegation was made against popular-culture products for their role in this shooting, most blamers did not accuse the producers of these products but rather just the products themselves. This seems to suggest media and popular-culture content were "naturalized," perceived as a given in this case.

Most accounts did not tend to acknowledge that there were people making decisions that dictate what types of content we see in entertainment media and popular culture. Though very rare, we will share the few exceptions in which producers of the objectionable content were blamed. From The Boston Globe, reporter John Ellis, on April 22, 1999:

The television networks, the major movie studios, record companies, video game software producers, print and other media are spending hundreds of millions of dollars every year to adapt children to this diet of violence and carnage. Once addicted, they'll want more of it, which can and will be provided at a slightly higher price.

From The London Independent, reporter David Aaronovitch, on April 22, 1999: Film-makers who allow violence to seem cool and attractive should examine their consciences. And we should criticise them more. Organisations like CNN, who offered "uninterrupted live coverage" of events at Columbine High School, should consider whether that isn't exactly what the avenging dweebs want.

Some news accounts were acutely aware of the blaming tendency and viewed it as a defence mechanism, for coping with the tragedy, also noting that at the most fundamental level, there truly was no sufficient explanation for a tragedy of such magnitude. These atypical news articles drew the most macroscopic picture possible, speculating on broad problems at issue in society or simply conceding that an accurate and fair assessment of blame was impossible. From The Arizona Republic editorial, on April 21, 1999:

Whatever that elusive answer may be, it is no longer enough to simply wag our fingers at the usual suspects. This time, we can't allow ourselves to simply scowl at the National Rifle Association. Or at disintegrating families and bleak, cynical television that trivializes life. We can't simply rage at bloody video games.

From The Boston Globe, reporter John Ellis, on April 22, 1999: We have surrounded ourselves with violence. It is everywhere we turn. It is in our music. It is on our televisions. It is in our movies. It is on our video games. It is prominently featured in print media and on popular Web sites. If it bleeds it leads and it leads because it sells. Tuesday's massacre at Columbine High School in Littleton, Colo., was not an aberration. It was and is a fact of modern American life.

From The Denver Rocky Mountain News editorial, on April 21, 1999: But as we said, we don't know what the explanation is and don't care to speculate right now. The moment is too solemn, the bloodletting too extensive for the mind to even grasp. For the time being, our thoughts remain focused solely on those who lives now will never be the same.

UNIQUE ELEMENTS

The role of popular culture in the Columbine school shooting is a rather complex phenomenon. In addition to the basic and pervasive tendency to blame popular-culture products (films, television, video games, recorded music), there were three additional sources of media-related blame in newspaper coverage.

First, many questioned the role of the local news media-universally picked up by the national news media-during the tragedy, in that their actions may have inadvertently jeopardized the safety of the students in the school. Others blamed the news media for being unnecessarily sensationalistic, insensitive to the trauma experienced by those involved, and inordinately intrusive into the lives of members of the community. (It is important to note that still others applauded the local news media for accurate and compassionate reporting, though those accounts are not reported here as they do not involve blame.) These quotes also demonstrate the way in which some news organizations differentiated themselves from others in order to elude blame by association. From The Atlanta Journal Constitution, reporters Don Aucoin and Drew Jubera, on April 21, 1999:

In the heat of the moment, missteps occurred. At one point, the information was broadcast that one youth was trapped inside the schools' "choir room," a potentially risky step if the gunmen were watching TV inside the school.

From The Chicago Sun Times, reporter Phil Rosenthal, on April 21, 1999: From ground zero of the melee at Columbine High School in Littleton, Colo., a student hiding under a table with his cell phone called to alert others of his predicament.

His call went not to his parents or police, as some did. It went to Denver's KUSA-TV, which broadcast his report live in Denver (and nationally via CNN, MSNBC and CNBC), oblivious to the fact the school had TVs in every classroom and that the inside information might be aiding the gun-toting assailants behind the siege.

From The Boston Herald, reporter Monica Collins, on April 22, 1999: On television yesterday, it was a mop-up operation after Tuesday's horrendous live coverage of the massacre at Columbine High School in Littleton, Colo. Bigfoot network reporters arrived, interviewing shell-shocked student survivors.

Sobbing parents who awaited their children's corpses at a nearby elementary school were not spared from the intrusive lenses. Viewers still shudder at the memory of those macabre, unfiltered visions captured at the height of the evil event Second, many critics of the news media also speculated on the possibility of copycat instances following the very extensive coverage the news media gave the event.

Critics mentioned the unwitting tendency of the news

media to elevate the perpetrators to cult celebrity status, which may, in turn, encourage similar behaviours from young people elsewhere. One might expect newspaper reporters to omit such instances in which news media were implicated, albeit indirectly, out of self-interest.

However, sources consulted for the stories often thrust this angle into the news discourse about the event. Furthermore, newspapers were able to protect their own interests by emphasizing local strategies to avoid hypercoverage that may lead to copycat phenomena.

From The Atlanta Journal Constitution, reporter Phil Kloer, on April 21, 1999: As the sheriff spoke to reporters, news helicopters circled overhead. He was immersed in a sea of reporters, their microphones all lined up in concentric circles, pointing inward. "We've had a lot of media attention of these kinds of situations," the sheriff said, "and you don't know how much that gives other people the idea to do it."

From The Boston Herald, reporter Monica Collins, on April 22, 1999: Detective Sgt. Margot Hill, the Boston police media relations director who helped hammer out the pact (setting standards for the airing of live tragedies) with Boston broadcasters, says "There's no value in airing live. If you air live, you're ghouls and you'll probably create a copycat within a week. We've become a nation of voyeurs."

From The Columbus Dispatch, reporter not listed, on April 22, 1999: "Media attention has given a star quality to such incidents," (Richard) Hazier (a professor in Counselor Education at Ohio University) said. "Kids now have the thought in their minds that it is possible to bring guns into school and get revenge that way," he said"That's why copycat issues are such a concern today."

Third, another subtopic of media-related blame involved Harris and Klebold reportedly learning how to make pipe bombs on the Internet. From The New York Daily News, reporter Kevin McCoy, on April 22, 1999:

A Colorado prosecutor confirmed the cybersearch yesterday as new details emerged about violent imagery and pipe bomb assembly instructions on a Web site linked to gunman Eric Harris. "The Internet is very involved in this case," Jefferson County District Attorney David Thomas said when asked whether Harris and Dylan Klebold used computer expertise to plot the rampage.

From The London Independent, reporter David Aaronovitch, on April 22, 1999: Ah yes, but Eric and Dylan also had home-made pipe bombs. Where did those come from?

Almost certainly from the pages of the Internet, where Randy from Idaho, or the Urban Terrorist's homepage, will give any teenager all the information he needs to know to blow up his enemiesPerhaps they were rendered immune to the reality of what they were planning to do as a consequence of long, crepuscular hours spent at the keyboard, blasting punks and decapitating jerks to earn record scores. After a while, real flesh may become confused with pixellated gore and guts in the adolescent mind.

CONNECTIONS WITH THEORY

The quotes from the newspaper coverage of the Columbine tragedy demonstrate many of the theoretical foundations outlined earlier in this chapter. Just as Pauly and Eason discuss in essays about Rupert Murdoch and the news story "Jimmy's World," respectively, analysis of the press coverage of the Columbine school shootings reveals rather ingrained, idealized notions about the nature of journalism.

Journalists reporting on Columbine seem to deem themselves above the fray, even when discussing the apparent mistakes made by fellow journalists in covering the story, such as being too intrusive or insensitive or having coverage that is so extensive it could inspire a copycat shooting.

In fact, some of the stories-either through the comments of sources or the words of journalists themselves-suggest disdain on the part of "serious" journalists for their more sensationalistic or entertainment-oriented counterparts. Rarely was a distinction between "serious" journalism and more "frivolous" and presumably "harmful" entertainment media content made explicitly by a reporter in the story.

Rather, the distinction was made implicitly in the tone of the stories, in the words and phrases chosen, and in the angles pursued in the telling of the story. The distinction that we argue is made here is similar to the one discussed by Bird in her analysis of tabloid newspapers and their relationship to "serious" journalism.

In the case of Columbine, the distinction may, in fact, be easier for newspaper reporters to argue because the medium is often different, with newspapers or print journalism seen as "serious," informative, and helpful, and video games, recorded music, television, and movies seen as more "frivolous" and "harmful."

The same types of assumptions that Jensen argues underlie major strains of media criticism are apparent here. There is a sense of protectionism that borders on elitism on the part of those who criticized popular media in major newspaper coverage of the Columbine shootings, with the notion that the newspapers provide what is good for the public, and entertainment media provide what is bad.

The newspaper's role is one of savior. By pointing out the evils of the popular media that Dylan Klebold and Eric Harris enjoyed, newspaper coverage can help save other impressionable youth or raise a warning flag for their parents. The newspaper coverage of the Columbine school shootings can also be examined in terms of Shoemaker and Reese's levels of influence on media content.

On the individual level, for instance, the tone of the coverage suggests that the journalists may have shared the sadness and outrage of the American public and were thus inclined to point the finger of blame as a way of coping with and trying to make sense of the tragedy.

In fact, the immediate deaths of Klebold and Harris served to remove them as a target for continuing feelings of grief and anger. Assigning responsibility to an ongoing social institution such as the popular media provides both reporters and their readers with an enduring target at which they can vent their anger.

The individual reporters and their editors may also have

chosen this angle because it corresponds with their own personal values or opinions regarding popular culture and media influence. The quotes that imply disapproval or the ones that adopt a moralistic tone would support this as one factor shaping coverage.

Also on the individual level, reporters and editors at the newspapers whose coverage was examined may have felt a "holier than thou" attitude toward entertainment-oriented popular media. This influence bridges the theoretical structure of Shoemaker and Reese with that of Jensen, Bird, Eason, and Pauly.

On the media routines level, the routines regarding the selection and use of sources as well as the traditional emphasis on localism were apparent in coverage. For example, schoolmates and area residents were often called upon for first-hand accounts of possible popular-culture blame, and experts such as police officers or college professors were often utilized for verification.

The coverage also evolved from reporting "who, what, where, when, and how" to also including "why," the latter leading to the popular-culture blame explored here. Finally, the routine of providing simplified, uncomplicated explanations for events was followed in some of the coverage of the Columbine shootings that advanced one particular or more compelling explanation for the tragedy (often popular culture) rather than discussing multiple and complex factors.

In either the organizational or the extramedia level as defined by Shoemaker and Reese, ownership issues and the chain of command may have influenced coverage of the Columbine shootings. With such a broad range of media and popular-culture products implicated, a conflict of interest was possible because of growing cross-media ownership.

A newspaper owned by the same company that owns a record label whose recording artists or types of music were criticized for their role in the shootings may have been disinclined to emphasize the possible effect ofthat music on the shooters because of pressure from the top.

On the other hand, a newspaper relatively free of those

direct connections with the popular media being implicated (or with holdings in competing media that would benefit from a possible boycott of the particular popular media criticized) may be more likely to point the finger of blame.

In the case of Columbine, it is possible that manufacturers and distributors of popular-culture products that advertise in newspapers would be displeased with coverage that implicates those video games, the Internet, television, or movies in such a high-profile tragedy. For instance, the newspapers from which we have quoted may carry lucrative advertising inserts for retail outlets offering or even specializing in media-driven products (TV sets, DVD players, video game consoles).

Perhaps popular-culture culpability would havo been even more extensive or scathing if it were not for this influence that may have trickled down from the owners and managers in the newspaper's organizational structure. Also on the extramedia level, the sources used to cover the Columbine tragedy helped shape the content.

The students of Columbine High School were quick to report the violent and nihilistic media and popular culture content that attracted Klebold and Harris, as is apparent in the quotes from coverage above. This early angle may well have helped define the story from that point on.

Similarly, the efforts of other media organizations to establish the popular-media culpability angle, including the hometown Denver newspapers who had the earliest and most extensive coverage, may have set the tone that other media organizations followed. Finally, influences found at the ideological level may have shaped coverage of the Columbine shootings, as well.

For instance, in many of the quotes from newspaper coverage outlined above, occasional resistance to assign blame to producers of content is evident, as writers relied instead on accusations against media content itself as divorced from those who created it.

This may have been, consciously or not, a defensive strategy on the part of the newspapers to deflect criticism from their possible role in creating "a culture of violence" by helping to obscure the connection between the decisions and approaches of creators of content from content itself.

Also evident in the language used to implicate popular media are the lines of distinction implicitly drawn in coverage of the Columbine tragedy between the news media who covered the event and the entertainment media who were blamed.

The emphasis was often on the blood, gore, and generally antisocial content of particular music lyrics, video games, and movies, and the apparently disturbing notion that this is what is used to entertain young people in our society. Thus, responsibility was placed firmly at the feet of media who are merely entertaining the masses rather than the news media who are providing a public service by informing them.

In the case of Columbine, there exists an underlying assumption that something is dreadfully wrong with the people who tune in to violent media fare and that the news media are trying to save them by pointing this out. Also at the ideological level, blaming the media for the Columbine tragedy could help maintain comforting notions of social order and reassure the public of social stability.

The discomfort that comes with leaving such a tragedy unexplained is evident in the very few editorials that expressed that they were mystified by the tragedy and admitted this created a disquieting sense of chaos. It is also evident in the majority of newspaper stories that did, indeed, offer the popular-culture culpability argument as an explanation.

As de Mooij suggests, Americans are comforted by a sense of rationality and order, of things occurring for a reason. Advancing the popular-culture culpability attempts to bring rationality to the otherwise senseless nature of the tragedy, compounded because of the young age of the assailants and victims, the seemingly safe setting, and the apparent glee with which Klebold and Harris perpetrated their crimes.

This study uses three high-profile cases to investigate conceptions regarding the moral consequences of popular media in contemporary soci-ety. In analyzing the discourse generated in news coverage of the three events, the theme of popular media's moral culpability was quite apparent.

Whether it was for the car crash that claimed the life of Princess Diana, for the shooting that followed an apparently incendiary taping of the "Jenny Jones Show," or for the multiple-weapon assault enacted on Columbine High School, newspaper coverage included the assignment of blame to popular media and popular-culture products for these tragedies.

Analysis of the news discourse surrounding these events points to a number of themes regarding cultural and social practices. First, we can examine views and perceptions of "the media" as having potentially different readings and carrying quite disparate critical connotations depending on one's perspective.

Some conceptualize "the media" as a relatively homogeneous and powerful force in the contemporary social structure with only slight, if any, important differences based on news versus entertainment content. This view holds that each media outlet exists for the purpose of profit and seeks that profit by appealing to audiences of specific sizes or characteristics.

Differences between news and entertainment are seen as minimal and shrinking, in a time in which "infotainment" abounds and the "news hole" in newspapers and on television is diminished by the amount of space or time allotted to weather, sports, and "light" features.

Yet, the discourse examined in newspaper coverage of these three events shows a very different view of "the media." Rather than assuming similarities between news and entertainment and rather than newspapers sharing a sense of responsibility for a "culture of violence" or sensationalism such as is criticized in these cases, "the media" is seen as a heterogeneous collection of very different types of organizations with very different functions.

Implicit distinctions are drawn between those "serious" journalists whose function is to inform the public of important information related to their health and well being and those producers of popular media who allegedly instead jeopardize public health by irresponsible practices and the transmis sion of potentially harmful content.

The notion of irresponsible practices can be seen in the condemning tone in newspaper coverage that discusses the paparazzi in the case of Princess Diana's death and talk show producers and creators in the case of the "Jenny Jones Show" murder.

The notion of harmful content is also an explicit element of the news discourse surrounding sensationalism, sex, and violence in talk shows as related to the "Jenny Jones" murder and antisocial and violent themes in popular media as related to the Columbine shootings.

Thus, there are some parallels to the theoretical argument made by Jensen. Jensen would argue that the view of the media described first above, as a homogeneous force, is an example of modern media criticism that may better be viewed as a criticism of modernity.

Yet, she would presumably also object to the defensive strategies embarked upon by the newspapers whose coverage we examined because of their underlying assumptions regarding popular preferences and morality. These lines of distinction between "serious" and "popular" media comprise the second major theme revealed in this analysis.

As mentioned in the case studies, the distinction between "us" and "them" was not always made explicitly in the news coverage of the events. However, in the pursuit of the popular-culture culpability angle, in the disapproving tone of sources turned to or in reporters' own words, and in the lack of connection established between the newspaper itself and the other forms of media criticized, the distinction appears as an underlying assumption.

The assumption of a stark distinction between the "elite" press and other media forms is tenuous at best. As Bird andPauly suggest, those who position themselves as "serious" journalists and those who are viewed as "tabloid" journalists (and even those who create and disseminate entertainment media content) have more similarities than differences in terms of practices and goals.

Yet, even when the connection between the accuser (the newspaper) and the accused seems most obvious, as in the discussion of excessive news coverage paving the way for a copycat following the Columbine tragedy, no elements of the discourse suggest similarity or recognize potential involvement on the part of the accuser.

Rather, the newspapers reported from a presumed position above the fray, akin to an omniscient and impartial observer, who then adopts an interpretive role to further the public good by helping to cure social ills. This not only reveals a privileged position for "elite" journalists but also suggests an artificial, unrealistic isolation of the newspaper from surrounding society.

At the centre of the issue of what makes a media professional "serious" or not is an assumption about the nature of the audience. The analysis of news discourse provided here shows further evidence of a protectionist, somewhat elitist view of audiences as being drawn, like moths to a flame, to content that is bad for them.

Whether one blames the producers of such content or the audience members themselves for this assumed preference, the premise is the same: audience members must be encouraged to see the error of their ways in their enjoyment of or tolerance for violent, sexual, sensationalistic, and intrusive media content.

Some of the quotes we have cited from newspaper coverage of these three events appear to adopt the position that deaths such as these are the price we pay for the moral decline evident in the popularity of certain types of media content. Others reveal a tone of warning for local communities to prevent similar tragedies from occurring or recurring.

Still others call directly for greater governmental regulation, stricter parental control, and more responsibility on the part of the media industry. All such angles suggest a need for those wiser and more moral-led, in this case, by the "serious" journalists - to help save audience members from themselves. Underlying the blame of popular media and culture in the media discourse examined in our study is the "serious" journalists' notion of audience members preferring what is "easier to digest" or more appealing (popular media and culture) rather than what is good for them. What is good for them, in the case of our study, is presumably more "elite" media and culture, including the reading of newspapers such as those that are blaming their more populist counterparts.

By focusing on the aspect of each story that involves the purportedly appealing qualities of the popular media criticized, "elite" newspapers can capitalize on those qualities (e.g., violence in the case of Columbine, sex in the case of "Jenny Jones") at the same time that they implicitly draw a distinction that separates them as more "tasteful."

Shoemaker and Reese's theory of influences on media content also provides insights about situated, particular practices of news professionals, constraints and traditions in news gathering, and the interplay of producers, content, and public. Of the five spheres of influence identified by Shoemaker and Reese, we would argue that media routines were among the most likely to have a direct and measurable impact on how these three events were covered in the news.

Routines including news values, ideas of what makes a "good" story, and traditional practices and constraints of news reportage are also presumably the influences that would most likely be listed by journalists themselves if asked what factors affect how events are covered, because of their practicality and concrete nature.

The other, more microscopic spheres of influence are slightly less compelling in this context. For example, though many journalists would welcome a work environment in which their own preferences, opinions, and values could dictate coverage, few achieve this degree of autonomy and write articles that run unchanged by higher-ups in the organizational structure.

We believe the more macroscopic factors of extramedia influences and ideology also play a crucial role, but one which is less apparent and more insidious. It is this element of the

Shoemaker and Reese theory that can be linked to the theoretical contributions of Jensen, Bird, Pauly, and Eason. Though these forces are not always obvious, we argue that the factors comprising them are among the most potent in shaping news content in general, and coverage of these events specifically.

The influence of ideology encompasses cultural elements such as the cause-and-effect paradigm that de Mooij suggests is expected in American culture. This cultural norm is readily apparent in news-media discourse surrounding each of these three events, evident in the attempts to answer "why" the tragedies occurred in a simple and straightforward manner.

The ideological level also encompasses the issues of journalists (and others) holding rather unflattering perceptions of audience members and espousing a somewhat idealized role of the "serious" journalist as watchdog in contemporary society. In this scenario, there is a protectionism that borders on elitism.

A key element interwoven throughout these theoretical foundations is hegemony. A revered and respected role reserved for "serious" journalists assures their position in society. Economics also play a crucial part. Newspapers tell stories in a certain way to sell copies in order to sell space to advertisers.

Popular-culture culpability, by its very populist nature, is a virtual guarantee of public interest. Yet, the public may be surprised to find the news discourse generated is one of shame, guilt, and danger associated with popular media. We would like to caution our readers, however, about assumptions that underlie this research endeavor. Our aim here was not to blame the "serious" news media for, in turn, blaming more populist news and entertainment media because we feel that blame is not deserved.

On the contrary (and perhaps contrary to the position Jensen would adopt), we do believe there are irresponsible practices and potentially harmful content in tabloid news and entertainment media that may have contributed-though certainly not as the sole culprit-to these three tragedies, and to other events as well. Our purpose here was to examine how this blame took shape, to illuminate forces and factors that led to the pursuit of this blaming as a common angle, and to elucidate the implicit strategies to keep "serious" journalists above blame.

It is this distinction that is made between accuser and culprit in the news coverage we examined, when the distance between the two is arguably quite small, that we suggest is the most interesting finding from our study.

Chapter 3

Usage of Various Electronic Media

On the one hand, there have been huge investments by the educational sector on the establishment and maintenance of educational media for students. On the other hand, there has been very little and sporadic knowledge about the usage of such media in education. There is a need to understand the opinions of the target group on the functioning of the educational media and to elicit their suggestions towards the improvement of educational media in terms of content, duration, timings and methods available through them. Media had to be viewed on a comparative note in order to identify the more effective ones among them.

While the growth of the electronic media of radio and TV in terms of reach, popularity and variety has been phenomenal, there has not been a corresponding growth in their education-related usage. Lack of publicity about the contents and timings of the programs, inability of one's electronic equipments to receive the signals and lack of interactive nature of their programs have contributed to the under-utilization of these educational media.

In the case of internet, the problem has been one of access and affordability. Rural students are said to have less familiarity on the availability and contents of various media inputs. Similarly, the students of distance education and regional language medium classes also have been facing limitations in their utilization of educational media resources compared to regular streams and English medium classes.

The objective of the study included identifying the variations among the students of different demographic characteristics in terms of their media usage. As part of the study on various media usage patterns among the students of the state, the researcher carried out an extensive review of literature to identify the various issues and perspectives with regard to the area of focus. Radio is playing a significant role in reaching, informing and educating people.

Radio is still a dominant medium with wide access. Computers and internet have started influencing the way we learn. All these media are very powerful to reach, teach and enrich. But learning from them is quite different from reading a book according to Singhal and Rogers (2001). Reports confirm that educational Radio programs have been tried out in a wide range of subject areas in different countries.

In Thailand, the radio is used to teach mathematics to school children Galda and for teacher training and other curricula Faulder; In Mexico, radio was used for literacy training and other programs Ginsburg and Arias-Goding; In Nigeria, radio was used for management courses for the agriculture sector Shears; The Philippines used the radio for nutrition education Cooke and Romweder; The Dominion Republic used radio in support of primary education White; Paraguay used radio to offer primary school instruction according to the Academy for Educational Development.

Radio in education can provide useful answers with diverse learners to solve easily, according to McLeish. Mason has stated that radio can be valuable in distance learning milieus ranging from schools, colleges and universities, from commerce and industry to public sector organizations. Moreover, radio programs can provide flexibility and openness, and easy accessibility to knowledge as well as better higher-order thinking and skill improvements with high-tech learning environments.

Radio can create new distance milieus in which learners are able to take greater responsibility for their own learning and constructing their own knowledge according to Resta. Moore and Tait, focusing on the use of new communication technologies in distance education systems such as e-learning, stated that educators and trainers give up working with radio as a low-tech educational tool. Radio has a unique power to create better interactive distance education environments itself than do emerging communication technologies, which can empower the capacities of radio when being used together in distance education systems.

Radio, moreover, provides life-long learning, professional updating, in-service training and community education from a cradle-to-grave position, which is independent of not only place but time as well.

Mason Learners, for that reason, can gain knowledge about themselves without feeling any digital diversity to share and exchange their experiences with others to promote their understanding with other learners from different culture. Learners can share and exchange their ideas, beliefs, opinions, knowledge, and information with others in interactive distance educational radio programs synchronously and/or asynchronously according to Crisell.

Also, learners and instructors can collaborate with any experts and learners from any places in the world. Synchronous education allows all distance learners taking their educational session at the same time, and interactivity occurs at same time. Synchronous communication in interactive distance radio programs allows live interactions among learners, instructors, experts, resources, etc., as per the views of Bonk and Cunningham.

With the technology growing in leaps and bounds, education does not stop at the borders of the campus and Television (TV) offers another way to reach out into homes and serve people where they live Reddi. Where TV is supposed to be the most effective one. Mohanty and Rath made an appraisal of Country Wide Class Room (CWCR) TV Programs.

Among other things they found that the knowledge objective has been realized to a great extent in all the programs whereas understanding and application objectives have been realized to a great extent in 60% and 52% of the programs respectively. Jaiswal and Goel (1991), referring to the CWCR programs suggested that different pedagogical fields such as methods, media, techniques, devices, aids and formats have to be well selected.

There are several pointers to suggest that television, if used appropriately would be one of the powerful educational media. "Tests showed that students did significantly better when they viewed the lessons that demonstrated planned visual continuity, contained visual reinforcement, and had been the result of a team approach to make effective use of the TV medium." Chu and Schramm.

Without the ITV technology students would have limited access to courses" said Garland and Loranger (1996). According to Ranganathan (2002) watching TV is popular among students and not all of them watching TV for entertainment alone. Considerable numbers among them are on the look out for useful and usable information.

They seek information that will enhance their general awareness and help them in their educational pursuits. Among the TV viewers there are some who watch CWCR occasionally. Ways to hold on to the existing viewer ship by enhancing viewer interest in our programs and attract others by extending the scope of programs should be found out. It is imperative that the programs are different and contain something special to get noticed among the plethora of programs offered by various channels.

The focus ought to be not on undergraduates but all the information and knowledge seekers. It is necessary to produce need based programs such as preparatory courses for those who take the competitive examinations at various levels. Promotion of CWCR through cross channel publicity is absolutely essential.

TV expansion in years has been phenomenal. TV covers over 85% of the country's population. Cable TV is largely used for entertainment but it has great potential of being used for education as well according to Yadava (2000). Saiprasad (1991) carried out a study to elicit opinions and expectations of students and teachers on CWCR programs.

The results implied that there is a need to be conscious of the entry skills of the target group, to produce programs which require student participation and to integrate the CWCR programs into the collegiate education. According to a study Saiprasad (2001), higher education students seek information on education, career guidance, career advancement and a host of other areas through the internet.

Research has indicated that computerized learning motivates students to invest more time in a subject-area (time-on-task), in particular when the student can work according to his own pace and time schedule, as described by Worthen, Van Dusen and Sailor.

This also happens when the system creates extra possibilities for the student to communicate with other students (through e-mail, bulletin boards and computer conferencing). The enthusiasm of students working with the WWW is a clear illustration of these research findings. Research has shown that using computerized learning can reduce the necessary learning time of students to two-third of the time needed in a conventional course, as per the observations of Kulik and Kulik.

Internet enables citizens to have access to anything and everything of their choice - books, news, bank accounts, shopping, databanks, friends, peer groups and interest groups - and at a time of their choice without stirring out of the comfort of their homes with a flick of buttons on their remote control and computer keyboard.

Voice-activated signals may even do away with all this trouble of pushing buttons. But one may have to pay tolls for using internet. 'Unparalleled and unlimited human connectivity and interactivity without stirring out of homes, is set to transform intellectual, cultural, economic and political life' says Yadava (2000).

Internet-based emerging communication tools, such as e-mails, bulletin boards, etc., provide more reflective and useful interactions among learners, instructors and resources according to Picciano (2002). The researcher found that, in the field of education, TV has assumed immense importance not only in terms of its reach but also in improving the quality of education at all levels and promises to play a major role in educational endeavors, towards upgrading as well as enrichment.

Web-based course delivery offers a complex learning and teaching environment. A vibrant learning community can be created using different teaching strategies, activities, and technologies. Thus, review of literature suggests that the number of educational courses that depend on modern educational media, more so in case of distance education. Education has become media technology enabled worldwide.

Methods play a major role in research. This study has adopted the survey method and descriptive research design. The universe or population of the study consisted of the entire set of student population in the graduate level in the state of Tamilnadu. According to the statistical handbook 2005, a total of 7.02 lakhs students are studying of under-graduation (UG) in various colleges in Tamilnadu.

A total of 14,000 respondents (2%) of the universe have been covered as the sample. The sample for this study was selected from among the UG students of regular - distance mode and urban - rural students. Samples were drawn from different type of colleges like Arts, Science, Commerce, Engineering and Technology, Medicine and Agriculture.

Totally 14 places were selected for this study including seven major cities and seven small towns. Data were gathered using a self-administered questionnaire prepared specially for these purpose. Over 1,000 questionnaires were collected from each place.

Based on the average of incomplete responses, the researcher has taken up 840 respondents from each place for the final analysis. The data was collected during the period from January 2005 to March 2006. Total numbers of respondents whose responses were taken up for analysis were 11,760. The chi-square test, simple percentage, Friedman's two-way anova and cross-tabulation were used for the analysis of this study.

DATA EXPERIENCES

The researcher observed that many of the students had

come to know for the first time, about some of the media opportunities available, only at the time of research, by going through the questionnaire. The students expressed regret about the fact that no one had briefed them about the need to use various educational media.

The researcher also found that management bodies of many colleges were quite averse to the idea of researching media usage among their students. A notable facet that was exposed during the data collection was that many Principals and faculty members were ignorant about the latest educational media and programs available.

USAGE OF VARIOUS ELECTRONIC MEDIA

The ensuing part of the article presents the demographic details of the respondents in terms of their place of living, gender, age and academic details like the courses pursued by the candidates and their modes of study.

SAMPLE COMPOSITION

Students of regular mode of study and distance-education mode are likely to differ on several characteristics such as time of direct interaction with faculty members, employment status, time available for education and opportunities to keep oneself up to date in their field of study.

Considering these differences, the researcher thought it necessary to consider viewing the two modes of study as separate groups for further analysis of their responses. There have been exactly equal numbers of respondents from regular as well as distance education streams. Exactly 50% were students in regular mode of study while the remaining 50% were in distance mode. Thus, it may be seen that the mode of study has been taken as the prime parameter for the stratification of respondents.

There have been more male respondents than female. (56.90% were male while the remaining 43.10% were female). This percentage, though unequal in numbers, could be stated to reflect the same proportion of men and women enrolling themselves for studies in the universe of the study.

Needs and wants of people tend to differ with their age in general. Further, age factor could heighten the level of exposure a person is likely to have. Since all the respondents were students, a vast majority of them would belong to a narrow range of age group, namely 17 to 30.

Hence their age groups were grouped at narrow intervals. 6146 (52.26%) belonged the age group 17 - 20, while 4438 (37.74%) belonged to the age group 21 - 25 and the remaining 1176 (10%) were above 25 yrs. Thus it may be seen that the study has covered more of undergraduate students, reflecting their relative proportion in the actual student population.

The researcher felt the need for diversity of respondents in terms of the courses they pursue, so as to bring in the pluralist perspective on the usage of media. Out of the total, 28% have their course of study as B.A. while 33.33% have their course of study as B.Sc., and the rest of them pursued B.E, B.Com and other courses.

More than nine of ten respondents 93.33% have had English as the medium of instruction while 6.67% have Tamil as the medium of instruction. Of the respondents, 50% belonged to Institutions located in rural area. While the remaining 50% belong to Institutions located in urban area.

POSSESSION OF VARIOUS ELECTRONIC MEDIA

Educational Media could take multiple forms. They could be either mass-based or personalized, containing materials in audio or visual formats. Using them regularly would require the personal possession of the instruments appropriate for each.

A comparison of possession patterns with respect to different instruments shows that the costs involved in owning an instrument is inversely proportional to the number of people owning them, the only notable exception being TV, which occupies the second position among the instruments owned closely following the radio sets, despite involving a higher initial investment compared to tape recorder or telephone, which are owned by fewer respondents.

The appeal of TV as a media could be understood from

the emerging analysis. It is noteworthy to find that 90.24% possess radio, 86.43% possess tape recorder and 96.31% possess TV while 71.90% possess telephone. Merely, a 35.24% possess Personal Computer as compared to 61.31% who possess Satellite/Cable connection, 20.95% who have access to Internet and similarly, 49.64% who possess CD player.

USAGE PATTERN OF RADIO

Distribution of Students by Listening To Radio From the radio listening group 35.71% of the respondents listen to radio everyday a week, while 5.12% listen to radio 4 to 5 days a week, 8.93% listen to radio once a week and 12.86% rarely listen to radio. It is found that 18.10% never listen to radio.

Combining the segment listening to radio every day and at least 4 to 5 times a week, it may be stated that the majority of respondents tend to be frequent radio listeners. However, there remains to be a sizeable segment of nearly one third of the total respondents whose radio usage is almost non-existent to produce any impact.

APPROXIMATE TIME SPENT ON LISTENING TO RADIO

While 30.36% listen to radio less than 30 min., 27.74% listen to radio 30 - 60 min., 18.10% do not listen to radio, 13.57% listen to radio 60-120 min. and 10.24% listen to radio above than 120 min.

With regard to the time spent on listening to radio, the emergent data shows a divergence among respondents, with respondents' time ranging from nothing to two hours a week, which could be interpreted to be offering a considerable scope for increase.

PLACE OF LISTENING TO RADIO

Summing up the responses, it is found that 87.35% listen to radio at home, 23.11% listen to radio at friends place. Others listen to radio at their office; place of study or at cyber cafes. Data indicate that home is the place where most of the respondents have been listening to radio, thereby suggesting that timing of the educational programs through radio should match with the time when people are at home.

LISTENING TO RADIO PROGRAMS

With a view to ascertain the purpose of listening to radio, respondents' listening patterns were further enquired. It was found that 37.06% listen to radio for education, 84.30% listen to radio for entertainment and 29.07% listen to radio for Science. 5.23% listen to radio for purpose other than those mentioned above.

Analyzing the data on the purpose of listening to radio, there seems to be scope for improvement as the majority of respondents have reported that they do not listen to radio for education or for Science programs.

INTERPRETATIVE ANALYSIS ON RADIO

LISTENING TO RADIO AND MODE OF STUDY

Hence it can be concluded that there is a significant relationship between listening to radio and mode of study. This means that the two streams would differ in their usage of radio, as they have similar syllabus but dissimilar teaching-interaction process.

LISTENING TO RADIO AND AREA OF INSTITUTION

Urban and rural milieu of students tend to differ in the available levels of exposure to co-curricular events, access to educational services like counseling and library services. In the absence of multiple forms of educational assistance, there is a greater likelihood of students becoming dependent on the mass media as a one-stop source for the fulfillment of their educational needs.

It was with this assumption that the researcher endeavored to examine the association between place of study and the patterns of listening to radio. It was concluded that there is significant association between area of institution and listening to radio.

The result of this analysis could mean that media planners would have to focus on the target audience according to their place of study. Programs might have to be tailor made to suit the specific needs of the two categories of students.

LISTENING TO RADIO AND MEDIUM OF INSTRUCTION

The medium of instruction in higher education in most of the cases remains to be English, while the mass media offer contents both in regional languages and in English. In order to identify the possibility that mass media like radio caters to students with concerns about the medium of instructions, chi-square analysis was done to find out if there is any association between the two variables.

It can be concluded that there is significant association between medium of instruction and listening to radio, which could indicate that language plays a vital role in out-of-classroom learning. Media planners need to carefully address the issue of medium of instruction used in radio as well. With the help of primary data, it was also concluded that there is significant relationship between course of study and listening to radio.

The relationship could be interpreted as arising out of the differing requirements between various types of courses. Whether these differences are also affecting the time spent on listening to radio, is to be analysed further.

APPROXIMATE TIME TO LISTEN TO RADIO

Having established the fact that radio usage is unmatched with the supply, the researcher has undertaken to analyse the various factors that could further influence the increase or decrease in the usage patterns. This analysis is carried out in order to find clues that could be valuable in making students listen more actively to the medium.

There is significant association between mode of study and approximate time spent on listening to the radio. The implication of this finding might be that different strategies would be necessary to address the distance and on-campus learners, as far as improving the time spent on listening to radio. Also there is significant association between the area of institution and the approximate time of listening to the radio.

Rural and urban students spend different amounts of time listening to radio, and within the attention spans of each of the categories, programs should be able to convey the important messages. In the same manner it was concluded with the help of chi square analysis that there is significant association between medium of instruction and approximate time to listen to radio.

Hence it is felt necessary to look into the familiar lingua franca of the local population if the average duration of listening has to be increased. The study also proved that there is significant association between course of study and approximate time to listen to radio. This implies that the media planners should conduct audience research and find out the subjects for which the demand for radio programs are higher and broadcast them accordingly.

USAGE PATTERN OF TV BY HIGHER EDUCATION STUDENTS

DISTRIBUTION OF STUDENTS BY WATCHING PATTERN ON TV

TV tends to occupy a coveted position among the media because of its audio visual presentations. The analysis portrays the respondents' viewing patterns.

FREQUENCY OF WATCHING TV

Data on viewing time suggest that 65.36% watch TV every day in a week, 12.74% watch TV 4 - 5 days in a week, 5.83% watch TV once a week and 5.48% watch TV rarely and 4.64% do not watch TV. From the data on TV viewership, it may be observed that majority of the respondents watch TV every day in a week and that it is a very small segment which abstains from watching TV totally. This response pattern reiterates the general perception about the popularity of TV among people.

TIME SPENT ON WATCHING TV

In order to verify the dependence on TV, respondents were requested to provide data on the time spent on watching TV. The analysis brings out the data on this question.

Since media planners and analysts have divided TV slots into durations closer to 30 minutes, this duration was taken as the minimum period. 20.60% watch TV < = 30 min., 29.17% watch TV from 30 min - 1hour, 21.07% watch TV for a duration between 1 to 2 hours, 16.90% watch TV from 3 to 5 hours and 7.62% watch TV for more than 5 hours.

A closer look at the data presented shows that the majority of the viewers' spend not less than an hour on an average and this would imply that educational TV programs should also time their programs accordingly.

PLACE OF WATCHING TV

With regard to the place of watching TV, the response pattern has shown a striking similarity with that of radio. A vast majority of 86.64% of the students watching TV at home, 25.22 % watching TV at friends place and the rest of the people watching TV at other places like study place, office or at cyber cafes.

PROGRAMS WATCHED ON TV

Analyzing the purpose of watching TV, it is seen that 69.91% watching TV for news, 35.08% watching TV for education, while 78.40% watching TV for entertainment, 3.50% watching TV for other than those mentioned above. The pattern of data shows that viewing TV for education purposes should be enhanced among the majority of the students.

TYPES OF MATERIAL/CONTENT WATCHED BY STUDENTS ON TV

Respondents expressing opinions on the contents watched on TV were sought with options for multiple responses. Results showed that, out of the total respondents, 68.12% watched subject-based programs on TV, 38.12% watched scientific programs and expert lectures, 46.77% watched interactive programs, while 58% watched career guidance, higher education information on TV. Interactive video can improve student attitudes and results in increased participation.

Distribution of Students Watching University Grants Commission - Country Wide Class Room (UGC - CWCR) Among the educational programs, a pioneering initiative under the aegis of the UGC was its CWCR. Respondents were enquired on their usage of these unique programs. Of TV watching respondents, 14.61% watch UGC CWCR while 85.39% do not watch UGC CWCR.

The results show that a vast majority of the respondents do not watch the programs, even though there are specific programs to suit every student group's needs.

Frequency of Watching CWCR

17.95% stated that they watch UGC on DD1 every day in a week, while 11.11% stated that they watch UGC on DD1 4-5 days in a week, 14.53% stated that they watch UGC on DD1 2-3 days in a week, 13.68% stated that they watch UGC on DD1 once a week and 42.74% stated that they watch UGC on DD1 rarely. It is seen that even among those who watch the programs, majority of them do not watch even twice a week. Only a very small segment is deriving benefits out of the programs, about which there should be some form of interventions from the telecasters.

Reasons for not Watching CWCR

A segment of respondents who stated that the reason for not watching CWCR; opine that they were not interesting. 1063 stated that reason for not watching CWCR as inadequate interaction. 48.15% stated that reason for not watching CWCR was that they received no signal. As high as 74.90% stated that reason for not watching CWCR was lack of periodic information about it.

Knowledge About Gyandarshan (GD) and Receiving

Among the students covered by the study, as large a segment as 82.38% stated that they do not receive GD programs on TV. When compared with other educational programs offered by the Government, very similar results are found with regard to the GD programs. It is evident that there is little awareness about the telecast of GD.

Since the percentage of population using the various educational telecasts is small, the focus of the analysis is shifted towards understanding the opinions of the small segment of users, about the effectiveness of these programs. As the programs have rich and varied contents, all the users might not need all the inputs. Hence the respondents were asked to estimate the percentage of programs which they found GD to be helpful.

Reason for Not Accessing GD

A total of 1112 stated that they do not access GD due to non-availability of signal while 10684 stated other reasons for not accessing GD.

Format of Presentation Followed Mostly in GD

Expressing opinions on the content of programs, a sizeable segment (44.59%) stated that format of presentation followed in GD is mostly lecture based only. A perceptible section of 33.11% stated that format of presentation followed in GD is mostly lecture with demonstrations only. 4.73% stated that format of presentation followed in GD to be other than those mentioned above.

From the data, it is obvious that the major form of presenting lessons has been lecture, which has been vouched as a dependable method for disseminating large quantity of information in a short period of time. However the programs watched by the respondents were apparently confined to lectures not complemented with value enhancing presentations.

Not accessing GD is an area of concern as it could render the investments made in producing educational programs and the costs of telecasting them as unproductive. The reasons for not accessing as stated by the respondents were analysed, to know if it is due to any faults in the contents of the programme. The analysis and results discussed so far have shown that mass media's reach is yet to expand in a significant way among students.

INTERPRETATIVE ANALYSIS ON TV

WATCHING TV

While both TV and radio are mass media, their audiences tend to differ in terms of their reach and extent of usage. Therefore, respondents' views on television were sought with regard to the same indicators of usage such as frequency, duration and perceived usefulness of the media, as used in the context of radio.

It can be concluded that there is significant association between the modes of study and watching TV. This association is found to be very much similar to that of radio usage.

Watching TV and Area of Institution

Association between area of institution and watching TV is significant. In respect of this variable too, there is similarity between radio and TV. Consequent to further analysis, it was concluded that there is significant association between medium of instruction and watching TV. Analyzing the result in the light of earlier findings, it is seen that there is inter-media consistency among radio and TV and hence a common approach could be adopted in planning and striving for greater effective usage of the two media.

The study also resulted in the conclusion that there is significant association between mode of study and approximate time spent on TV watching. The difference could possibly be the result of unstructured or inadequate time availability to students belonging to any one of the two modes of study.

Analysis of data showed that there was significant

association between the area of institution and the approximate time spent on watching TV. Comparing the results with that of earlier findings, it is seen that differences do exist between the areas of institution on almost every parameter taken up for measuring usage patterns of both radio and TV.

There is significant relationship between medium of instruction and approximate time spent on watching TV. This result adds to the general belief that there must be separately designed programs meant for students belonging to different medium of instruction, rather than merely translated versions.

Watching UGC CWCR

The present study took up the task of examining the viewing practices in Tamilnadu between regular and distance mode, rural and urban areas. There is significant association between mode of study and watching UGC CWCR. Similarly there is significant association between area of institution and watching UGC CWCR.

Further, among the respondents viewing the programme very frequently, there are more urban students than their rural counterparts. Hence efforts are to be directed towards popularizing the programme among rural audience too.

Also there is significant association between medium of instruction and watching UGC, CWCR. From the figures, it is seen that there are disproportionately higher levels of students studying in English medium than the regional language.

However the frequency of Tamil medium students watching UGC CWCR is more than their expected frequency. Hence there is a great need to fill the gap by supplying programs in the local language.

Watching UGC CWCR was also significantly associated to the course of study pursued by the students. In terms of the frequency, no clear picture can be said to have emerged among the courses as their relationship has not been linear. Initial negative attitude towards educational TV is likely to lessen over time and become more positive or neutral.

RECEIVING GD PROGRAMS

Mode of study can largely be differentiated in terms of the average age groups benefited, the level of expenditure on education and a host of other grounds. However, to eliminate bias, the researcher assumed that there is no significant association between mode of study and receiving GD programme on TV.

That there is significant association between mode of study and receiving GD programme on TV. This reinforces the initial surmise that the two modes would differ on maximum variables used in the study. Receiving GD programme could largely depend on the area in which the place where the respondents mostly watch TV.

Earlier the analysis on place of watching TV showed that home is the place most of them used for TV watching. However, in order to verify the data, the relationship between the area of institution and receipt of GD programs was examined.

Hence it can be concluded that there is significant relationship between area of institution and receiving GD programme on TV.

There is also significant association between medium of instruction and receiving GD programme on TV. In this regard too, the emerging data is similar to that of CWCR and TV in general. It also can be concluded that there is significant relationship between course of study and receiving GD programme on TV.

The programs are not labeled to be meant as exclusively for students belonging to any particular mode of study. Hence it was assumed that the two are not seen as closely related. On a comparative analysis of the various results discussed in relation to watching educational programs CWCR or GD, it is seen that there have been significant relationships established between this dependent variable and all other independent variables taken up for the study such as the place of the institution, the mode of study and the medium of instruction.

The results seem to stress the importance that is to be

accorded to these variables while planning and implementing educational programs in various media.

USAGE PATTERN OF INTERNET BY HIGHER EDUCATION STUDENTS

DISTRIBUTION OF STUDENTS BY INTERNET USAGE

Internet being a media of recent origin has evoked the interests of educational researchers and media professionals alike. The various parameters of assessing the reach of this medium, such as favorable opinions on the medium, number of people using it, the frequency at which they use it and the time spent on Internet are analysed.

EVER USED INTERNET

As large as 92.86% have used Internet while 7.14% have not ever used it. Since a vast majority of the respondents have effectively utilized Internet at least once, one could be optimistic about the potential for its growth in the future educational efforts. Internet could be accessed at ones' convenient times.

FREQUENCY OF USING INTERNET

It is seen that the usage frequency is widely dispersed, with majority of the users browsing not less than twice a week. Internet usage is unlike that of others. A user is not an owner and is merely allowed access on payment of charges.

The frequency of usage could have been influenced most by the interest levels of the respondents followed by the costs involved in using them. 19.36% use Internet everyday in a week, 14.87% use it 4 - 5 days in a week, 21.28% use it 2-3 days in a week, 28.85% use it once in a week and 15.64% use Internet rarely.

APPROXIMATE TIME SPENT TO USE INTERNET

In using the internet, searching takes a sizeable time. 1hour, 18.33% use it approximately for about 1-2 hours, 5.51%

use it approximately for about 2 - 3 hours, and 4.63% use it approximately for more than Shours. The emerging data shows that majority of the respondents have used the net for the optimal time. As the browsing pattern shows that just a small segment comprising of 24% are using it less than 30 minutes, the statistical mode of browsing time is the duration of 31 to 60 minutes.

A summary of the analysis on indicators of browsing standards would be that the quantum of browsing within the initial decades of browsing in India could be described as in the right direction. However, the adequacy and quality of browsing would depend on the individual and the connectivity available.

PLACE OF ACCESSING INTERNET

Institutional provision of browsing facilities is still in a rudimentary stage. An ideal situation for education related browsing would be before or after the class room sessions, in which case the place of browsing is a significant influence in the benefits of browsing.

22.56% stated that they browse at home. 62.56% stated that they browse at cyber cafes, 29.36% stated they browse at friends places, 41.28% stated that they browse at institutions and 3.21% stated that they browse at other than those places mentioned above.

PURPOSE OF USING INTERNET

Browsing could be done for different purposes and education is one of them. Majority (59.74%) of browsers answered that they use Internet sometimes to send mail and 24.74% use Internet always to send mail.

With 16.41% having stated that they don't use internet for the purpose of seeking information about education, 41.92% use it always to seek information about education. While 20.26% stated that they don't use for the purpose of gathering information about study, 40% use it always to gather information about study.

Whereas 25% stated that they don't use for the purpose

of fun and entertainment, 27.44% use always for fun and entertainment, 27.86% stated that they don't use the internet for the purpose of chatting with friends, while 22.34% use rarely for chatting with friends and 21.95% use it always for chatting with friends.

INTERPRETATIVE ANALYSIS ON INTERNET

FREQUENCY OF USING INTERNET

Through the chi-square test there is significant association between mode of study and frequency of using Internet. It is also similar to the association between area of institution and frequency of using internet. This could be understood in the context of unequal spread of internet in India.

Frequency of using internet and medium of instruction were also found to be significantly associated. The predominant language medium of the vast majority of web sites would be English. Further, it was concluded that there is significant association between gender and frequency of using internet. There is significant relationship between course of study and frequency of using internet.

It can be concluded that there is significant association between year of study and frequency of using Internet. As years go by, a student tends to be more independent and moves towards a wide range of experiences according to personality theorists like Chris Argyris.

Approximate Time Spent on Internet

There is significant association between mode of study and approximate time spent to use internet. Also there is significant association between area of institution and approximate time spent to use internet.

This result could be viewed in relation to the findings of another study described below in which educational media have been found to benefit the rural students than the urban students. Rural students, tested against rural control groups, benefited more than urban students tested against urban control groups as per the writings of Galda & Searle.

The project evaluators hypothesized that radio lessons were particularly effective in raising the level of knowledge of those who knew least, which in this case were the rural students. The findings of the present study could be understood in the light of the earlier finding.

Similarly there is significant association between medium of instruction and approximate time spent on Internet. Approximate time spent to use Internet and course of study were also significantly associated.

The analysis resulted in the conclusion that there is significant association between course of study and approximate time spent to use Internet.

A comparative analysis of all the suggestions provided by respondents through their answers to the open ended questions reveals noticeable commonality among the suggestions to the various media, they are the need felt for greater subject-orientation, enhanced exposure to scientific advancements, examination-centreed contents, need for user-interface and contribution and the like.

As suggestions, the users have provided opinions that more visual, movable content should be available with the facility of interaction. Educational media, when used in classrooms are likely to produce maximum learning then using them elsewhere. This has been the theme of the variables analysed. While data on viewing time suggested that 65.36% watch TV every day a week, 35.71% of those who listen to radio do it everyday a week, only 19.36% of those using internet, do it everyday a week. Majority of the respondents tend to be frequent listeners of radio and TV, while TV has more regular audience than radio.

A vast majority of respondents possess radio sets as well as TV sets. It was found that 37.06% listen to radio for education, 35.08% watch TV for education, while 40% use internet always to gather information about study. Data indicate that home is the place where most of the respondents have been listening to radio, while vast majorities of 86.64% of the students watch TV at home; only 22.56% stated that they browse at home.

41.28% stated that they browse the internet at institutions, whereas only a negligible segment of students use radio and TV at their institutions. Among the less interactive media, 61.62% answered that they need interactive programs in radio, while only 21.86% have answered that interactive programs are needed for educational purpose on TV programs. Majority 66.90% use Internet, which, in comparison to the fact that very few owned computers, is a significant achievement of media planners in higher education.

Media planners would benefit by basing their interventions based on the comparative standing of various educational media as understood through the viewing patterns presented with the help of the findings of the study.

It is suggested that measures be on to improve the viewership, listening frequency, the priority being on the latter, which is found to be the least frequently used educational media among the students in the area of study.

Since majority of the respondents have not used any of the media for educational purposes, the top priority is to be given to strengthen the educational usage of the powerful electronic media. Use of electronic media at educational institutions is found to be low. The usage needs to be enhanced in order to facilitate the increased usage of the media for educational purposes, as indicated by the previous suggestion. Creation of awareness among students about educational media should be taken up on a massive scale with a sense of urgency. Local inputs and interaction should be made a regular feature in the educational radio.

Programs and contents in regional and locally understood languages should be featured for more duration and frequency than it is being done at present.

In order to achieve localization of educational contents of the electronic media, well-equipped media centres carrying out research and producing need based programs should be created in each University. Campus based electronic media systems could be introduced to produce and present programs of specific educational needs.

Chapter 4

Comparing the Internet and other Nontraditional Media with Traditional Media

Elections have witnessed the traditional media's monopoly on campaign communications threatened as candidates relied on a host of nontraditional media such as the Internet, radio and television talk shows, morning talk shows, MTV, and late night talks shows to present their message directly to the American people-much to the chagrin of the mainstream press.

Reporters from the mainstream media chastised candidates for relying on the nontraditional media of talk and interview shows in the 1992 and 1994 campaigns, charging that appearances on venues such as Larry King Live and the morning talk shows allowed candidates to sidestep the tough grilling they could expect from the traditional media in favour of "softball questions" designed to boost their image.

However, studies indicate that questions posed by the audiencc members in call-in programs often focused more on issues than those asked by journalists, who tended to focus on the strategy of the candidates. Others have suggested that the nontraditional media have improved the public's issue knowledge by providing more opportunities for citizens to see candidates and to hear them discuss issues.

In addition, the nontraditional media allow voters to speak directly to the candidates or host which might increase campaign interest among those previously indifferent about the political process. Venues such as talk shows may also humanize candidates and improve their image in the eyes of the public by allowing them to appear directly before the public unfiltered by the traditional news media.

Although the rise of the talk shows in 1992 represented a new strategy for employing existing broadcast media, the introduction of the Internet into the media mix in 1996 represented the birth of a new medium. While supporters argue that the Internet may eventually alter the dynamics of the election process much like television did when it overcame newspapers' campaign dominance, the emergence of the Internet only produced muted criticism from reporters.

Some press pundits charged that the Web provided another high-tech means for candidates to bypass the traditional press, and that while information on candidate Web sites appeared objective, it was the product of the candidates' spinmeisters. However, reporters did not heap as much criticism on the Internet as they did on talk shows four years earlier for at least two reasons.

First, journalists recognized that candidates' Web sites were rich, albeit slanted, sources of information about their issue positions as well as for up-to-date news on the campaign. Second, all the major news organizations rushed to put their own sites up with more indepth and up-to-date information than in their own publications. These sites paid dividends; media and other nonpartisan Web sites were swamped with people trying to log on to get the most recent election returns while network ratings plunged.

While several observers have commented on how the rise of the nontraditional media has influenced how candidates conduct their campaigns and how the traditional media cover them, less attention has been paid to the influence of the "new media" on the public's image of the candidates and their knowledge of the candidates' issue positions.

Studies that have examined the differences between the effects of traditional and nontraditional media on political attitudes and behaviours have produced conflicting results. Previous studies were also conducted before the Internet emerged as a means to reach voters as well as to attract campaign volunteers and funds.

This study will examine the extent to which heavy users of the Internet and other nontraditional media differ from heavy users of traditional media in their knowledge of the issue stances of Bill Clinton and Bob Dole after controlling for demographic and other political variables. This study will also examine whether nontraditional media users differ from those who use the mainstream media on images they hold of Clinton and Dole.

The Nontraditional Media in the 1992 Presidential Campaign Although politicians have relied on nontraditional media to present their views directly to the American people at least as far back as the 1930s when Franklin Roosevelt addressed the country through his "fireside chats," the candidates' use of such media was unprecedented during the 1992 campaign.

The three candidates made ninety-six appearances on Larry King Live, Donahue, and the three network morning shows alone in the year preceding the election in an effort to court voters. The candidates' appearances on nontraditional media produced some of the most vivid and lasting images of the campaign: H. Ross Perot coyly announcing on Larry King Live that he would run for president if he received a mandate from the American people; candidate Bill Clinton donning dark sunglasses and a flower tie to play the saxophone on the Arsenio Hall Show; and Clinton being queried whether he wears boxers or briefs on MTV's Choose or Lose.

Furthermore, the candidates' reliance on "new news" has been credited, at least in part, with boosting voter turnout to its highest level since 197210 and for spurring the traditional media to focus more attention on the issues. The Nontraditional Media in the 1996 Presidential Campaign

The 1996 election, however, should have allayed fears that reporters would become irrelevant to the campaign process because candidates' use of nontraditional media decreased sharply. Clinton relied on more traditional means of campaigning in order to appear more presidential. While Dole made some appearances on radio talk shows, he largely avoided the talk show circuit after he attacked Today Show co-host Katie Couric and the rest of the media for questions about his statement that tobacco was not addictive. The candidates allowed their surrogates to campaign on nontraditional venues.

For instance, Elizabeth Dole rode in on a Harley with Jay Leno to begin the Tonight Show, and the challenger's wife also offered a Top 10 list to David Letterman on his talk show. Neither candidate made extensive use of talk radio either, although Dole warmed up to the medium near the end of the campaign.

However, Congressional candidates crowded the airwaves and during the Republican primaries, candidates such as Pat Buchanan relied extensively on talk radio to reach potential voters at little cost. This study, then, will also allow a comparison between the effects of the nontraditional media in an election like 1992 when they were used extensively to 1996 when they were not.

THE INTERNET IN THE 1996 PRESIDENTIAL CAMPAIGN

The Internet emerged as the dominant "new media" in the 1996 campaign, one that indeed represented the birth of a new medium rather than simply a different strategy for using an existing one. All the major candidates running for president in 1996 created their own home pages, cyber campaign offices that featured speeches, position papers, pitches for funds and volunteers, and, in some cases, audio and video clips.

While a political Web page presently receives less exposure than a single television commercial, it is hardly ignored. The Republican National Committee reported that more than 8,000 people signed the site's guest book in the first few months of operation. More important, the home page of their candidate, Bob Dole, received more than 3 million "hits" during the first six months it operated.

More than 10,000 joined the campaign e-mail list, and 1,700 registered to vote. Similarly, Bill Clinton and Al Gore bragged that their site receive 1 million hits in its first ten days. While the candidate sites might be onesided and sanitized, many news and nonpartisan organizations have created their own sites of political news and issue stances of the candidates.

The Internet is also increasingly becoming an important part of political reporters' beats to find updated news and candidate issue positions as well as to "listen" in on discussion groups to get a sense of the public's attitudes toward issues and the candidates.

Political observers predict that the Internet will transform the election process in the near future away from TV soundbites toward more substance as the sheer volume of news and issue information on the Web will allow voters to readily compare candidates' stances on issues and determine how issues will directly affect them.

Proponents also claim that the Internet will shift the locus of power away from corporations and special interest groups as individuals can lobby policymakers directly through e-mail and download information for themselves, bypassing the traditional media.

Also, grassroots organizers can become "hightech colonial pamphleteers" by creating home pages or electronic newsletters to distribute information to like-minded individuals or to spread their message through e-mail or discussion groups. Critics are far less sanguine, arguing that the Internet is likely to reinforce the existing political structure by providing a new, powerful tool for lobbyists and entrenched interests to influence government.

Also, because the poor will have little access to the Information Superhighway, the Internet may actually increase the gulf between the "haves" and "have nots." Some experts predict that the Internet will be a primary way candidates campaign in the future-perhaps as early as the year 2000.

The 1996 election served as the test-drive year for politics on the Internet as candidates struggled to learn how to use the new medium to best reach voters. Therefore, the Internet served as added exposure for candidates, rather than the main avenue for campaigning. As media critic Edwin Diamond noted, "It's a man with a belt wearing a pair of suspenders. It ain't the pants, and it ain't the belt."

NONTRADITIONAL MEDIA AND POLITICAL KNOWLEDGE

While few political observers would argue that the emergence of the nontraditional media altered the nature of campaigning, they differ on the effects of the "new media" on political attitudes and behaviours. Specifically, past studies are divided about whether the nontraditional media contribute or hinder the acquisition of political knowledge with results often depending on what medium is examined.

Recent studies have disputed the notion that talk radio listeners come from the lower socioeconomic strata and that talk radio has little impact beyond creating or reinforcing social isolation. Talk radio listeners are those who perceive they have the most at stake in the political system: the wealthy, white Republican male.

Consequently, talk radio listeners report greater interest in politics than nonlisteners, and they voted in greater numbers over the past four elections. Studies have consistently found that talk radio is linked to political knowledge and participation, even after controlling for other factors.

Frequent talk show listeners are not only more politically knowledgeable, but they also think they are better informed than other citizens. Listeners also say they attend to talk radio to keep up with news and to gain information they cannot find elsewhere.

Researchers are split on whether television talk show use contributes to political knowledge. On the one hand, research by Lemert and associates disputed the notion that the talk-show audience was composed of "helpless souls, unable to evaluate independently what they were seeing and hearing."

Heavy viewers were highly educated, had strong feelings of internal efficacy, and were generally interested in the campaign. More important, heavy viewers knew more about the views of the candidates than light viewers. Finally, while voters were more likely to view talk shows as a more helpful source of campaign information than all traditional forms of media except for debates, heavy talk show viewers were also heavier users of more traditional media such as television and newspapers.

The talk shows supplemented, rather than replaced, more traditional forms of campaign information. However, several studies have found little relationship between talk show use and political knowledge.

For instance, Miller and associates found that viewing daytime talk shows such as Donahue and Oprah tended to be negatively related to political knowledge, suggesting that those who watched daytime talk shows showed little interest in political information and thus did not seek out more conventional sources of information.

Similarly, McLeod and associates found that talk shows were not significantly related to issue accuracy among a cross section of voters and negatively related to issue knowledge in their panel study. However, like the Lemert study, talk show viewing was linked to high political interest, internal efficacy, and use of more traditional media.

Similarly, Waluszko, Weaver and Drew, Price and Zaller, and Hollander found that television talk shows were unrelated to gains in political knowledge. The discrepancies on the links between nontraditional media use and political knowledge may result, at least in part, because of different definitions of what constitutes nontraditional media.

For instance, Waluszko restricted "new news" to radio and television talk shows while Hollander examined talk shows, late night talk shows, and MTV. Miller and associates expanded the definition of nontraditional media to include entertainment content such as daytime talk shows like Oprah, comedies like Saturday Night Live, and situation comedies such as Murphy Brown, while McLeod and associates considered debates, polls, and ads as nontraditional media. Indeed, Hollander and Chaffee and associates discovered that the influence of nontraditional media on political knowledge depended on which medium one examined.

While watching talk shows was linked to increased campaign knowledge, MTV and late night talk show viewing was negatively related to campaign knowledge. While there seems to be no agreed-upon definition about what constitutes nontraditional media, scholars suggest that they entail presenting public affairs information in forums in which the message is unfiltered by a mediator and the public becomes a participant by being able to directly interact with the public official or with a host, or, in the case of the Internet, with other individuals.

For the purposes of this study, "nontraditional media" is defined as talk shows like Larry King Live, radio talk shows like Rush Limbaugh, MTV, and late night talk shows. While the political Web site on the Internet also qualifies as a nontraditional medium, it will be analysed separately because it represents the birth of a new medium rather than simply a new strategy for employing an existing one.

NONTRADITIONAL MEDIA AND CANDIDATE IMAGE

Studies suggest that the nontraditional media may have a greater influence on candidate image than on political knowledge-at least for certain candidates. Pfau and Eveland Jr. found that nontraditional media influenced perceptions of the candidate's competence and image.

Similarly, Elliott and Wickert found that nontraditional media use was positively related to images of both Clinton and Perot, although it had no influence on attitudes toward Bush. However, McLeod and associates only found that talk shows influenced images of, and feelings toward, the candidate who relied most on nontraditional media: Perot.

Results, then, suggest that the nontraditional media can have different effects on different candidates, with the effects being the most pronounced for those candidates who rely more on such media. Previous results suggest, then, that the influence of the nontraditional media depends on what political attitudes and behaviours one examines and which medium is examined.

The nontraditional media appear to have more influence on affective attitudes such as image than cognitive ones such as political knowledge. Also, "new media" that is heavier in information content, such as radio talk shows, will increase knowledge more than entertainment-oriented forums such as late night talk shows or MTV. This would suggest that the information-rich Internet could produce larger information gains than the talk shows that dominated the 1992 campaign.

INTERNET AND POLITICAL ATTITUDES/ BEHAVIOURS

Only recently have scholars examined the extent to which the Internet is linked to knowledge gain and other political attitudes and behaviours. Several recent studies have dispelled the notion that the Internet is "a haven for isolated geeks who are unaware of important events occurring outside their cavelike bedrooms." Internet users are more politically knowledgeable than the average citizen.

In addition, Web users are politically interested and active, report high levels of political efficacy, are more likely to vote, and more likely to seek out information from the media than the general public. Furthermore, politically active Internet users score higher on these measures than general users. However, no studies could be found that examined the relationship between Internet use and images of candidates.

While evidence is just beginning to accumulate on whether Internet use does increase political knowledge, evidence suggests it should. If the ability of a medium to produce knowledge gain is increased by its information content, then those who regularly visit political Web sites should be high in political knowledge.

Political observers tout the sheer volume of campaign information available on the Net through candidate Web sites, nonpartisan sites such as PoliticsNow, and online publications, contending that it could transform media coverage away from sound bites toward more substance and produce a generation of "cybergenic candidates" where issue stands will matter more than good looks and soundbites.

While the large volume of Internet information is only seen by a fraction of the voter-the Pew Research Centre found that about 12 percent of the voting age population used the Internet for political information in the 1996 election and about 3 percent listed the Internet as their primary source of informationS—those who do rely on the Internet may be highly motivated to seek out political information, and information found there may influence their voting decisions.

Studies by the Freedom Forum suggest that people who have visited politically oriented Web sites are political junkies, watching CNN, Sunday public affairs programs and C-SPAN, and reading more newsmagazines than the average voter. They are also more than twice as likely to have read a political book in the last year.

Political Web site users are more likely than the average voter to have graduated from college and to earn a high income, two characteristics associated with high political knowledge as well as likelihood to vote. This study will examine the influence of nontraditional vs. traditional media on knowledge of issue stances and images of candidates through a survey of 320 Jackson County, Illinois, residents conducted by trained undergraduate and graduate students as part of a media and politics course in July 1996.

The sample was drawn from local exchanges using random digit dialing procedures. Independent Measures. "Nontraditional media" use was defined as relying on talk shows such as Larry King Live, late night talk shows, MTV, and radio talk shows like Rush Limbaugh for information on the 1996 presidential campaign.

Using political Web sites on the Internet will be treated as a separate nontraditional media because it represents a new medium rather than simply a new use of an existing one. The traditional media examined were newspapers, television network news, radio news, news magazines, news programs like Meet the Press and more "elite" broadcast outlets such as CNN, C-SPAN, and National Public Radio.

Respondents were asked two sets of questions examining use of both new and traditional media, one that explored frequency of use64 and one that examined attention to the media. Both questions were asked of each information source examined in this study. Demographic and political attitude and behaviour measures were also included as independent variables. The demographic variables employed were income, education, age, gender, and race.

The political attitude and behaviour measures were likelihood to voting, political interest, strength of party support, and amount of political discussion. To measure likelihood of voting, the survey asked respondents to indicate on a 0 to 10-point scale the chances they were going to vote this year. Similarly, they were asked on a 0 to 10 scale their interest in the national election.

Participants were first asked to indicate whether they were strong Republicans, lean toward Republicans, independents, lean toward Democrats, or strong Democrats in order to gauge strength of party support. Answers were recoded into a 3-point scale of independent, lean toward 1 of the 2 parties, and strongly support 1 of the 2 parties.

Political discussion was measured by a 5-point question: "On a scale of 1 to 5 where 1 indicates nothing at all and 5 indicates a great deal, how much have you heard about the 1996 presidential campaign within the last month or so through discussions with other people?"

DEPENDENT MEASURES

The dependent variables are knowledge of Bill Clinton and Bob Dole's issue positions as well as images of the two candidates.

Political knowledge was gauged by totaling the number of correct responses to questions examining President Clinton and Bob Dole's stances on six issues: a constitutional amendment banning abortion, affirmative action programs for minorities, a ban on assault weapons, providing welfare benefits for illegal immigrants, term limits for Congress, and the North American Free Trade Agreement.

Image of the candidates was measured by asking respondents to evaluate Clinton and Dole on a 1 to 10 scale on several characteristics: friendly, warm, likable, honest, trustworthy, and leadership. The variables were combined into indices measuring images of Clinton and of Dole. The Cronbach alpha test for internal reliability was.88 for images of Clinton and for images of Dole.

Data Analysis. The data were analysed in three stages. First, frequencies were run on the media use and attention variables to compare how much respondents relied on the "new media" versus the traditional ones. Second, Pearson Product Moment correlations were run between the independent variables and the knowledge and image measures." Finally, hierarchical regression was used to measure the predictive power of each of the media measures.

The predictor variables were entered in five blocks: demographics; political attitudes and behaviours (campaign interest, likelihood of voting, strength of party support, likelihood of voting, amount of political discussions); use and attention paid to traditional media (newspapers; television network news; news magazines; radio news; news programs; and elite broadcast media such as CNN, C-SPAN, and NPR); use and attention paid to political Web sites on the Internet; and use and attention paid to nontraditional media (television talk shows, late night talk shows, MTV, and radio talks shows).

The "new media" measures were entered last to test their influence after other possible predictors, including traditional media, were statistically controlled for.

TRADITIONAL VS. NONTRADITIONAL MEDIA USE

Political observers suggested that the "new media" of talk and interview shows had partially supplanted traditional media as information sources in the 1992 election. However, results from the 1996 media demonstrate the continued dominance of traditional media.

Those surveyed said they paid more attention to each of the traditional media than to the "new news." Respondents were more than three times as likely to say they used television news as the most popular nontraditional medium, television talk shows. Those surveyed were even less likely to use late night talk shows and radio talk shows-15% and 10% respectively.

Scores were even lower for attention to these information sources. MTV and the Web sites on the Internet were all but ignored as sources of political information with only 5% and 2%, respectively, regularly getting political information from these media. The results also suggest the dominance of broadcast media as a source of information.

People relied on network television news the most for political information, and elite broadcast news sources such as CNN, CSPAN, and NPR challenged newspapers for second. Scores for media use tended to mirror media attention, although respondents were more likely to say they used television news than to pay attention to it.

CORRELATIONAL ANALYSIS: POLITICAL KNOWLEDGE

Past research has been split on whether nontraditional media contribute to increased knowledge of candidate issue stands. This study found that while traditional media were correlated with knowledge of Clinton and Dole's issue positions, only 5 of 20 nontraditional media measures were linked with knowing candidate issue stands.

Both use and attention to television talk shows correlated with knowledge of Dole's position stands, while talk show attention was linked to Clinton issue knowledge. Late night talk show use also correlated with Dole issue knowledge while radio talk show attention was linked to knowledge of Clinton issue positions.

On the other hand, use of all the traditional media-newspapers, television, radio, news magazines, news programs, and elite broadcast media-correlated with issue knowledge, with news programs and elite broadcast media such as CNN and C-SPAN posting the strongest correlations. Similarly, attention to all the traditional media except television news correlated with knowledge of the candidates' issue stands.

Again, attention to news programs and elite broadcast media recorded the strongest correlations, although attention to radio news was also strongly linked to knowledge of Clinton's issue stands. Generally, attention correlations were stronger than use ones.

Correlational Analysis: Candidate Image. Earlier research suggested that the nontraditional media may be more strongly correlated to candidate image than knowledge. Indeed, "new media" variables were more strongly linked to candidate image than the traditional ones; 7 of the nontraditional media were correlated with candidate image compared to only 2 of the traditional media measures.

Radio talk show use and attention were both strongly linked to images of Clinton and Dole, with heavier users viewing Dole favorably and holding negative images of Clinton. Television talk show use and attention also correlated with positive perceptions of Dole, although MTV use was negatively related to Dole's image.

Clinton fared better with the traditional media as television news use and attention were both correlated with positive images of the president. No other traditional media were correlated with images of the two candidates, and the Internet variables also failed to post significant correlations.

Regression Analysis: Political Knowledge. The hierarchical regression analysis revealed nontraditional media use and attention did not predict increased issue knowledge-but traditional media did not fare much better.

No nontraditional media variable significantly predicted knowledge of the candidates' issue stands, although attention to radio talk shows was negatively related to knowledge of Dole's issue stands. In 12 of 20 cases, including all 4 Internet measures, "new media" tended to be negatively related to candidate issue knowledge.

Nontraditional media use contributed about 4% of the variance to knowledge of Clinton's issue stances and 5% to Dole knowledge gain. But traditional media did not prove a strong predictor of issue knowledge either. Only one measure proved significant: attention to news programs like Meet the Press predicted knowledge of Dole's issue positions.

In addition, radio attention predicted knowledge of Clinton's issue stands before the "new media" media variables were controlled. Like nontraditional media variables, the traditional media explained only about 5% of the variance in issue knowledge.

Standard demographic and political measures, however, were strongly related to issue knowledge, explaining more than 25% of the variance for both Clinton and Dole. Being male and highly educated were linked to knowledge of issue stands as was political interest. Likelihood of voting predicted knowledge of Clinton's issue stands, but not Dole's.

Surprisingly, support for a certain candidate did not mean higher knowledge of his issue positions. In fact, the likelihood of voting for Clinton or Dole was negatively related to knowledge of their issue stands. Strength of party support and amount of political discussion with friends were also unrelated to knowledge of issue stances.

REGRESSION ANALYSIS: CANDIDATE IMAGE

While nontraditional media variables better predicted candidate image than knowledge, they only weakly influenced candidate images after controlling for other factors. Two nontraditional media measures, Internet use and attention to political Web sites, predicted images of Clinton, and talk show attention fell just short of significance.

However, Internet attention proved negatively related to Clinton images, and the block of "new media" variables did not significantly increase the variance in Clinton's Image. Only radio talk show attention predicted images of Dole, and in 6 of 10 cases, nontraditional media use was negatively related to images of Dole. Internet and other nontraditional media explained about 3% of the variance for both Clinton and Dole images.

Traditional variables had even less impact on candidate image. Attention to television news and newspaper use predicted images of Clinton, although newspaper use was related to negative images of the president. Only newspaper use significantly predicted images of Bob Dole, and the relationship was negative.

Demographic variables did not fare much better. High income was related to positive images of Clinton. Age was the only significant predictor of Dole's image, with older voters expressing the most positive images of Dole. Political variables explained almost the entire variance in images of both candidates.

Not surprisingly, intending to vote for a candidate influenced whether respondents had a positive image of him. Similarly, strength of party support was related to positive images of both candidates. However, likelihood of voting in general was negatively related to images of both candidates. On the other hand, the politically interested had positive images of both candidates.

Post-mortems of the 1992 election raised the specter of whether public officials would sidestep the traditional media and largely conduct their campaign through the nontraditional media of talk shows and entertainment programming.

New York Times reporter Maureen Dowd pondered, perhaps only partly in jest, whether presidential press conferences would be replaced by presidential call-ins on Oprah, whether the State of the Union message would be delivered on the Arsenio Hall Show, and whether Clinton would sell his agenda for change with an MTV campaign called "Rock the Deficit."

The Arsenio Hall Show did not survive to see the 1996 campaign, and the role of the nontraditional media in general was greatly diminished. Candidates made few appearances on nontraditional media venues, leaving such campaigning for their surrogates.

Not surprisingly, then, relatively few individuals said they had read or heard much information about the campaign on nontraditional media sources. Respondents were more than three times as likely to say they had seen a great deal about the campaign on television news as on the most prevalent nontraditional media source, television talk shows. Political Web sites and MTV were almost ignored as information sources.

Past studies have been split on whether "new media" contributed to political knowledge. They suggested, however, that more information-rich sources were most likely to be linked to political knowledge. This study offers little evidence that nontraditional media influence political attitudes and behaviours.

Three measures, use and attention to television talk shows and late night talk show use, correlated with knowledge of Dole's issue positions. Attention to radio and attention to television talk shows were positively linked to Clinton issue knowledge. However, once the nontraditional media variables were entered into the regression equations, none significantly predicted knowledge of candidate issue stands except radio talk show attention, which was negatively related to Dole issue knowledge.

Twelve of the 20 relationships were negative, including all 4 Internet variables. The poor performance of the Internet in improving voter knowledge does not mean that its proponents' hopes that the Web could transform media coverage and campaigns away from soundbites to substance are wrong, but simply premature.

Only 2% of respondents said they got a great deal of information from political Web sites, numbers that parallel other studies that suggest about 1% rely on the Web for political information. But the Internet is in its infancy as a political tool; the majority of people in this country have yet to go online, and politicians are just learning how to employ this technology to reach citizens. As Bimber notes, in terms of both number of users and its influence on the political process, the Internet of today is much like television of the early 1950s.

Television did not significantly influence the political process until the 1960s and 1970s, so it may take a decade or more for the Internet to achieve some of the lofty goals predicted of it. Researchers will need to wait until at least the year 2000 to assess the influence of the Internet on the political landscape.

This study supported earlier ones that suggested that the nontraditional media had a greater influence on images of candidates rather than political knowledge. In fact, the influence was greater than for traditional variables. Correlational analysis found radio talk show use and attention were positively related to images of Dole, while radio talk show listeners harbored negative images of Bill Clinton.

Talk show use and attention were related to positive image of Dole. However once other variables were controlled for, only 3 of the 20 relationships were significant and 1 of the significant relationships was negative. Not surprisingly, while radio talk show use and attention were positively correlated to images of Dole, they were negatively related to Clinton's image.

Unlike other new media variables that cut across political ideology, studies indicate that radio talk show listeners are overwhelmingly Republican. For instance, a Media Studies Centre poll found that Republicans outnumbered Democrats among regular political talk radio listeners by a 4-1 margin. Internet use was positively related to images of Clinton, while attention to the Internet was negatively linked to Clinton's image.

The negative relationship between Internet attention and Clinton images may reflect characteristics of the politically interested Web user. Experts suggest that "netizens" tend to be libertarian and to be disconnected from Washington unless the government is actively attacking the Internet. Dedicated Internet users perceive Clinton as an enemy of the Internet because of his positions on cryptography, pornography, and copyright on the Net. In addition, studies find that Internet users report high levels of political distrust.

Dole's ability to benefit more from nontraditional media than Clinton reinforces previous studies that suggest effects are greater for those candidates who rely more on nontraditional media. As noted earlier, Clinton largely campaigned through the traditional media to appear more presidential.

While Dole did not rely heavily on new media, he did warm up to radio talk shows late on the campaign and used surrogates such as his wife to campaign for him on talk shows like Jay Leno and David Letterman. Overall, then, results suggest that the nontraditional media had less influence in the 1996 election than 1992 in part because its use by the candidates has declined considerably from the last election.

Although the correlational analysis indicated nearly all the relationships between the traditional media and political knowledge were significant, the traditional media, surprisingly, had even less influence than the nontraditional media ones once other factors were controlled for. Only one variable, attention to news programs, was connected to any of knowledge gain measure and only attention to television news was positively linked to image of either candidate.

Several factors could account for the lack of impact of traditional media, many of which would also apply to the nontraditional media. Probably the main reason for the limited influence of traditional media was methodological. Media variables were entered into the regression equations after demographics and political ones.

Demographics and political variables accounted for close to 30% of the variance in knowledge and more than 50% in images of Clinton as well as a significant variance in Dole measures. This conservative test of the research questions meant that the media variables had a limited opportunity to influence knowledge and image. Other studies of both the presidential campaigns employing hierarchical regression also found the media had limited influence after controlling for demographic and political factors.

Another methodological limitation was that not all of the variables were normally distributed, so they had a reduced ability to influence the political attitudes. But campaign-related factors might also explain the weak relationships for traditional media. First, this study was conducted during the lull between the primaries and the national convention when little was happening in the campaign. The candidates were not feverishly campaigning, and the media were not covering the campaign extensively. Consequently, fewer than half of those surveyed said they were paying attention to the campaign on television news; scores for other media were lower.

However, a study conducted later in the campaign using the same traditional media measures found both new and traditional media had even less influence on political knowledge than they did in July, suggesting the time when the survey was conducted was not a major factor.

Second, the political climate was much different in 1996 than in 1992. Despite motor voter and other innovations to stimulate turnout, voter turnout fell below 50 percent, the lowest level since 1924.

Several scholars and political observers lamented that the major issue in the campaign was not the economy or health care, but the "sheer crashing boredom among the electorate." Indeed, a Pew Charitable Trust poll revealed that 73 percent of the respondents said they were bored by the 1996 campaign, and only 24 percent of the public paid close attention to the 1996 campaign, down from 42 percent four years earlier.

Dissatisfaction with the major candidates ran high; almost two-thirds of respondents to a September 1995 poll said they supported the formation of a third party. Public confidence in elected officials continued to slide, and public optimism for the future of this country was even lower in 1996 than when Richard Nixon resigned in 1974.

In this poisoned atmosphere of voter alienation and apathy, it is perhaps not surprising that the public would express little interest in the campaign and would pay little attention to it. The media's ability to influence candidate knowledge is greatly reduced in a campaign when relatively few people express interest in it.

The rise of the alienated and apathetic voter in campaign '96 might also explain why the likelihood of voting for a certain candidate would be negatively related to issue knowledge about that candidates" and why likelihood of voting in general was negatively related to images of the candidate.

Results from this study, then, suggest that the nontraditional media, as well as the traditional press, had limited influence in a 1996 campaign which may be remembered less for the voters sending Bill Clinton on to a second term of office than an alienated electorate that stayed away from the voting booth in droves.

This study was conducted during a lackluster campaign and at a time when the Internet was getting its "test drive" as a new campaign medium. Campaign interest is bound to increase in the 2000 election. The race will not feature an incumbent, making it likely the public will witness a more competitive race.

Future studies should compare results from the 2000 and 1996 election to determine the degree to which campaign competitiveness influences the degree to which the media impact political attitudes and behaviours. Future studies should also perhaps focus on the Internet and its ability both to increase candidate knowledge as well as to reconnect voters to the political system.

Chapter 5

A Demand-side View of Media Substitutability

Competition among media for audiences and advertisers is fierce and unrelenting. In both local and national markets, with weapons ranging from prepackaged contests and promotions to drastic overhauls of talent and management, media wage war with one another to attract audiences to sell to advertisers. Often underlying these intermedia battles is a simple, if unproven, assumption: that mass media are interchangeable, competing in the same market for the same advertising dollars.

In this chapter, we report results of a two-stage study conducted to explore the media interchangeability assumption as it relates to national advertising. The study specifically addressed the question: What are toplevel advertising managers' judgments about the degree to which cable TV, broadcast TV, radio, newspapers, magazines, billboards, and place-based media are substitutable for one another in national media schedules?

Advertiser opinions were collected in two stages. In the first stage, we mailed questionnaires to a sample of 402 chief advertising managers with the leading 100 national advertisers. In the second stage, we personally interviewed another sample of 34 national advertising managers to validate and extend the survey results. As detailed in the following paragraphs, both practical and empirical observations about media substitutability and national advertising guided our research approach.

According to Picard, media substitutability may be more evident in the market for advertising than any other media demand area. However, there are both practical and empirical reasons to suspect that media will not be seen as completely interchangeable by advertising managers. Based on these reasons, we predict that:

HI: For national advertising campaigns, advertising managers perceive little, if any, substitutability among traditional media options. Practical Considerations. As any advertiser well knows, different media provide different access to different kinds of audiences, which in advertising terms are defined as target markets.

Media for all advertising are typically selected based on a host of factors, including product consumption patterns, media usage patterns and habits, market size and location, vehicle cost efficiencies, specific media qualities (i.e., time and space availabilities, mechanical characteristics, delivery patterns, support services, etc.), and audience characteristics (i.e, demographics, lifestyles, psychographics).

Advertisers and their representatives, agencies, independent buying services, and in-house media planners, take these factors into consideration when planning advertising, seeking the media mix that best serves particular communication needs before specific media buys are negotiated and finalized. Therefore, for practical reasons, we predict that traditional media options will not be seen as completely interchangeable for national media schedules by advertising managers.

EMPIRICAL CONSIDERATIONS

A few researchers have empirically examined the question of advertising media substitutability. For the most part, these studies have been confined to local advertising and to the newspaper medium relative to local media options. One study found that print media are the most likely replacements for newspapers; others suggest that other media are also considered by local advertisers.

Sentman found that when a local newspaper goes out of

business in a market where more than one newspaper is available, local advertisers are more likely to substitute the other newspaper in their media schedules than another medium.6 In two related studies, Smith found that the majority of local advertisers believe small dailies compete with other media, not just other newspapers, for local advertising dollars.

According to the Smith studies, more than three-fourths of the surveyed ROP advertisers said they would look to another medium if newspaper ad rates increased by 20 percent; about 40 percent said they would substitute another form of print media for newspapers, while more than one-third said they would use a broadcast medium as a replacement; and insert advertisers indicated that direct mail and a combination of other print would be appropriate substitutes for small dailies.

A study by Cameron, Nowak, and Krugman found that direct mail is seen by local advertisers as the primary substitute for advertiser dollars, although cable TV and yellow pages could be considered. Ferguson, in a study of newspaper advertising rates and competition for advertising dollars in a market, found that an increase in the number broadcast stations is associated with lower newspaper advertising rates, but that presence of a competing daily newspaper was not significantly related to newspaper advertising rates.

Work by Dimmick and Albarran adapted niche theory from the field of ecology to examine the displacement of existing media by newer media forms. Neither study specifically asked advertising experts about substitutability among media options. Nevertheless, the work is relevant to our study because the results are suggestive of patterns of substitutability in advertising media planning.

Niche theory suggests that the more similar two media are perceived by advertisers and consumers, the more likely they are considered replacement options for one another. In one study, Albarran and Dimmick combined niche theory with a uses and gratifications approach to explore how niche breadth, overlap, and competitive superiority apply to the video entertainment industries. The study found a great deal of overlap among types of video media.

In a later study, Dimmick suggests that the approach helps explain the "video revolution." According to Dimmick, advertisers are proficient observers of changes in consumer media and audience compositions. As new media emerge that meet the same needs as already existing media, the two media overlap or compete.

Advertisers react to media overlap by altering their ad placement patterns. The medium that is considered superior on the gratification dimension is the one that attracts more advertising dollars. The study most relevant to our investigation was conducted by Busterna. Although there are arguably methodological grounds to question the absolute validity of Busterna's findings, his conclusions are suggestive, if not conclusive, and predicative of our hypothesis.

Spurred by definition disputes and conceptual inadequacies in the published research literature, Busterna used secondary industry data to determine which media are in the same market with newspapers for national advertising. Specifically, he tested the concept of cross-elasticity of demand, using price sensitivity to define market boundaries: "In simple terms the cross-elasticity of demand measures the relative change in quantity demanded of a given product or service in response to a change in price of another good or service.

If two products or services exist as reasonable substitutes, then an increase in the price of one will result in an increase in the quantity demanded of the other." Demand functions for five media were tested: television (network and spot), consumer magazines, newspaper supplements, radio (network and spot), and outdoor.

Regression analyses revealed that "cross-elasticity of demand between newspapers and other media is consistently nil across all media," meaning that none of the tested media resides in the same market for national advertising dollars. From the results, Busterna drew two conclusions:

First, it is clear that advertisers do not possess significant price sensitivity between newspapers and other media to consider newspapers a viable alternative for advertising that was intended to be placed in other media. Second, claims of significant competition between newspapers and other media often come from those who have a newspaper industry (seller) perspective rather than an advertiser (buyer) perspective.

Focus of the Study

Our study goes beyond Busterna's examination of newspapers as a substitute for other advertising media, as well as the previous studies of media substitutability in local advertising. As described more fully in the following methodology section, we asked two samples of top-level managers of national advertising programs to evaluate the interchangeability of seven media options against one another, not just newspapers against other media.

The study was designed and executed to accomplish three objectives: (1) to provide more evidence on the question of media substitutability in national advertising; (2) to re-examine Busterna's finding about the substitutability of newspapers in particular; and (3) to augment Busterna's price-sensitivity-based "buyer perspective" with perceptual data like that reported by Dimmick and Rothenbuhler and Lacy.

RESEARCH METHODS

Stage 1: Survey of Advertising Managers. To test the study's hypothesis, we first conducted a mail survey of top-level advertising managers, the individuals with large American companies who are responsible for spending national advertising dollars.

Following Busterna's suggestion, we wanted to avoid the sampling error of studies conducted by Dimmick and Rothenbuhler and Lacy. In their studies, the researchers sampled executives with media organizations (i.e., supply-side representatives) on the assumption that media are active agents in deciding what advertising will be scheduled.

However, as pointed out by Busterna, the active agent in advertising media planning is the advertising executive, not the media executive. Therefore, we sought buyer judgment of media substitutability rather than seller judgment since it is the buyer of advertising, not the seller, that fuels intermedia competition.

Sample and Mailing Procedure. Advertising Age's list of "100 Leading National Advertisers" and the Standard Director of Advertisers were used as the sampling frame. Four hundred-two individuals listed as the chief advertising officer (i.e., brand manager, advertising director, vice president of marketing, marketing communications, or advertising) for each of the 100 advertisers' corporate, division, and/or subsidiary organizations were selected as survey participants.

A notification postcard was sent to each of the 402 advertising officers one week prior to the mailing of questionnaires. The postcard informed the individuals of the nature of the study, requested their participation, and informed them that questionnaires would be arriving in seven to ten days. One week following the notification, the questionnaires were mailed.

Each questionnaire was accompanied by a cover letter and a postage-paid return envelope. Three weeks after the initial mailing, a second mailing was sent to nonrespondents. Four weeks later, a third mailing was executed. The third mailing was followed two weeks later by a reminder letter. A copy of the questionnaire was not included in the fourth mailing.

Of the mailing of 402, a total of 91 completed, usable questionnaires were returned: 43 from the first mailing, 16 from the second mailing, 22 from the third mailing, and 10 from the reminder mailing. Eleven questionnaires were returned incomplete and/or unusable, 42 were "returned to sender," and 19 were returned with notes of refusal, for an adjusted individual response rate of 28%.

The 91 usable questionnaires were completed by individuals with 50 of the 100 national advertisers, for an advertiser response rate of 50%.

The individual response rate is consistent with other surveys of advertising managers. A sampling of studies published in the Journal of Advertising, journal of Current

Issues and Research in Advertising, and Journal of Advertising Research between 1981 and 1996 found that reported response rates ranged from 21% to 33%io, with an average of 32%.

Questionnaire Construction and Pretest. An eight-page questionnaire was used to collect the survey data. The questionnaire was modified from one used in a past survey of agency media specialists. That questionnaire was stringently pretested with five advertising specialists located in New York, Chicago, Cincinnati, and Atlanta and produced a return rate of 54%.

The questionnaire contained seven sections, three of which are relevant to the focus of this study. The other four sections asked questions about media selection criteria and media-provided advertiser services.

National Advertising Definition. Included in the survey instructions was the following definition: "National ad accounts are accounts for brands/ services that are distributed or available in most or all of the U.S. The advertising for these accounts need not be national. Coverage may be regional."

The definition was developed from interview information collected in the aforementioned advertising media survey and a search of basic advertising texts. The definition was provided to frame the construct for the respondents in an effort to reduce potential response variance.

Respondent Qualification. The first section asked one question: "Do you feel qualified to voice opinions about the appropriateness of media (i.e., TV and magazines) for national advertising campaigns?" The question had two closed-end options, yes and no, and was included to screen out respondents who felt unqualified to answer questions about national advertising and media substitutability.

MEDIA SUBSTITUTES

The fifth section contained seven traditional advertising media options, cable TV, broadcast TV, radio, newspapers, magazines, billboards, and place-based, formatted in a matrix with "media to be replaced" listed ina vertical column and "appropriate media substitutes" listed in corresponding horizontal rows.

The respondents were asked about media substitutability in the following manner: Sometimes because of factors beyond advertiser control, one media type must be substituted for another in national campaign planning. The list in the left-hand column below contains several media options.

For each medium in this list, please indicate those media that you believe are appropriate and reasonable replacements from the list of substitute media provided. Please indicate your belief by circling each medium you consider to be an appropriate substitute.

RESPONDENT BACKGROUND

The final section of the questionnaire contained six questions designed to collect background information from the respondents about their age, gender, education, present title/position, and years of advertising experience. Education information was collected on a categorical basis. Open-ended questions were used to gather the other background information.

QUESTIONNAIRE PRETEST

Although a version of the questionnaire had been pretested previously, we pretested the modified version because it contained three additional items: the respondent qualification question, the media substitutability measure, and several additional respondent background questions. Three advertising managers with Chicago- and Atlanta-based advertisers agreed to participate in the pretest.

The pretest was conducted using both mail and personal interviewing techniques. First, agreement to participate was secured by telephone contact. Pretest questionnaires were then mailed and returned completions were followed up by phone calls to discuss any identified problem areas.

No serious problems were uncovered. However, the format of the media substitutability measure was slightly modified to facilitate the response task (i.e., spacing was changed to enhance readability). Before final printing, the format change was cross-checked with the three pretest participants.

Stage 2: Personal Interviews with Advertising Managers. Using the same directory sources as the survey stage of the study, 50 additional advertising managers with large national advertisers were identified and contacted by telephone. Thirty-eight officers agreed to be interviewed; however, interviews could be arranged with only 34 of the 38.

Ten days prior to the scheduled interview, each participant was mailed a copy of the data analysis, with instructions asking them to consider and explain what the results indicate relative to their professional experiences. All interviews were conducted by the same procedure and protocol: the study's purpose was reiterated and the participant was asked to interpret patterns in the survey data and to explain what the patterns suggest about the question of media substitutability for national advertising accounts. Following are profiles of the two sets of respondents and the results of both the survey and interview stages of the study. Wherever appropriate, the survey and interview results are integrated.

RESPONDENT PROFILES

The majority of advertising managers who participated in the survey were male (73.6% male vs. 26.4% female) and under the age of 45 (57.3% under 45 vs. 42.7% over 45). Nearly all were college graduates (96.7%), with 56% having a graduate degree. Almost half had more than 15 years of professional advertising experience (48.4%io), either on the agency or client side of the advertising business. Just over one-fourth of the respondents had more than 20 years of professional advertising experience.

The profile of the 34 interviewed managers mirrored the characteristics of the survey respondents. Male managers outnumbered females (76.5% male vs. 23.5% female). The majority were under the age of 45 (55.9% under 45 vs. 44.1% over 45) and nearly all were college graduates (97.1%), with half having a master's degree. Fifty percent of the interviewees had more than 15 years in advertising, and almost one-quarter had more than 20 years of advertising experience.

QUESTION OF MEDIA SUBSTITUTABILITY

Not surprisingly, all 125 ad managers considered themselves competent to consider the issue of media substitutability and national advertising. The 91 respondents who returned useable questionnaires answered yes to the qualifying question about ability to judge media for national advertising campaigns. The 34 interviewees responded yes when asked about their abilities to consider the question during the opening phase of the interview session.

Each medium was perceived an acceptable substitute for another in national advertising planning. Analysis of the response frequencies and mean ratings revealed interesting patterns in the ad managers' judgments.

Consistent with the frequencies, substitutability among the six media is suggested by the means: every medium, on average, had at least one substitute mentioned and all but placebased were identified as a substitute for at least two other media. Cable TV had the highest mean number of mentions as a replacement (2.44) and placebased had the lowest (.83).

The mean number of mentions of cable TV as a substitute was significantly higher than those of the other five media, whereas the mean mentions of radio as a replacement was significantly higher than the means of three media: magazines, broadcast TV, and place-based media. The broadcast TV mean was significantly higher than the mean mentions of place-based media.

The interview results were consistent with the survey results. The consensus among the interviewed managers is that media are replaceable in national advertising schedules. All of the managers told us that they considered both media and audience characteristics when trying to determine national media schedules. They acknowledged that there are clearly times when one medium will do a better of job of communicating a message than another medium. However, in many cases, availabilities in geographic markets, timing considerations, media costs, and other conditions force managers and their representatives to consider substitutes.

As two managers put it: Though we prefer not to substitute, there are circumstances which dictate a change of direction in media planning. If you can't afford ABC, CBS, then you consider what we can do with a combination of magazines and USA, TBS, ESPN, or whatever other cable options are out there. The key is trying to deliver a message to a certain audience at a certain place and time, with effective exposure in a cost efficient manner.

Media are interchangeable, not in that they are all the same, but in the fact that it's audience delivery, message exposure, and cost which drive the typical national ad schedule. Yeah, there are options; there is an option for every medium because it's not media per se. It's what is being delivered by the medium that counts, and that what is the right audience.

Media is a negotiated process. The ideal often differs from what is planned for and what results. The issue of replacement comes down to a simple point-audience delivery. If you can't get it with a television schedule, then you back up and look at other combinations.

It's difficult to talk about it, but when you get down to it, media provide access to audiences-some deliver a specific audience better than others. From my experience, while not preferable, there are always acceptable substitutes in some combination. Sure national media are replaceable or substitutable for each other.

Every competitor can't be in TV at the same time. You've got to look for other media to break through TV clutter, to out smart the competitor in another medium. Costs, audience, and message impact they are the factors that determine national media schedules, not media types.

One interesting factor mentioned by several of the ad managers was value-added opportunities, promotional incentives offered by media as inducements for media space and time sales. As suggested by two managers, these inducements sometimes persuade planners to took beyond time and cost when comparing media options.

We work with media to service our needs in ways beyond running our ads. Merchandising, joint-marketing efforts are important to us in stretching our promotional dollars. If a magazine comes to me and says I'll feature your product in a special section on house repair or gardening, and I'm considering buying TV spots, I'll try to do a cost analysis.

The extra offered by the magazine might offset a higher actual cost between different media. Like in any situation, cost is a relative thing. In today's planning environment, media extras are important. If a newspaper group comes to me and says they can get us premium space with a large retail chain in X number of cities, then I'm gonna listen. The same is true of media that offer to tiein our line with contests and special programs, for example, radio.

Rates are important, yes. But, unless there's a tremendous difference in total schedule cost, sometimes the "extras" offset money differences. The whole process is more complex than comparing CPMs, and media incentives play a big part. Same is true with consumer incentive programs; advertisers are the consumers targeted by media sellers.

From the frequencies reported, it is apparent that not all substitutes are perceived alike; there are patterns in the responses which suggest that certain media fall into specific categories of substitutability. There is substantial agreement among the managers about the substitutability of both forms of television advertising.

Cable and broadcast TV are considered highly appropriate substitutes for each other, with nearly 8 of 10 managers having judged one medium an appropriate and reasonable replacement for the other. Other combinations were identified as acceptable at the 40% to 50% range. Five of 10 managers judged newspapers and magazines acceptable substitutes of each other (52.8%/56.2%).

Radio was seen as a reasonable replacement for newspapers (53.9%), and cable TV an acceptable substitute for both radio (56.2%) and magazines (49.7%). Four of 10 thought billboards and place-based media were acceptable substitutes for each other (41.6%/39.3%). The same percent judged newspapers an acceptable substitute for radio (42.7".io), and radio a reasonable replacement for both cable TV (41.6%) and billboards (41.6%).

Thirty of the 34 interviewed managers agreed with the survey respondents-that is, media fall into specific replacement groupings. The most interesting and common explanation offered for categorization is the belief that creative decisions drive media decisions.

You have to understand once a creative approach is decided upon, then media are planned around that approach. Media are considered, but they are secondary in my view. Look at it in terms of give and take. Once creative is determined, there is no replacement. Sure media differ in how they deliver and impact messages, but they can be interchanged to some degree. Creative can't.

TV for TV, print for print. What's surprising about that? A point of fact is creative and media work hand-in-hand - they are like hand and glove. In my experience, creative drives the process, and when it comes to media If you can't get network broadcast spots, you're going to look at cable. Same is true in print, and in reminder type ads - billboards.

We often prefer to buy network TV spots because of coverage and message delivery impact allows us to demonstrate our brands at a pretty cost effective level. But if we have to we go with cable advertising in markets where we can't get the numbers with network Or because the spots aren't available We look to cable.

Cable is relatively cheap, you can buy lots of spots at different times, on different networks. I certainly understand and agree that television is substitutable for TV. I see the same situation with print and out-of-home reminder media, like outdoor in store, or whatever.

A similar observation about magazines and newspapers was made by 9 managers. Said one manager: Look, when you are trying to run a print ad there's a reason— you want to deliver a specific type of message to a particular type of audience. Suppose you want those people to spend sometime with what you are saying to control exposure.

For whatever, if I can't get a magazine in a particular market-let's say a business mag-I'm not going to TV? A whole different ballgame there. No, instead, I'm going to look at newspaper options, particularly the business pages. Another example that comes to mind is a business magazine like Business Week or Fortune

The ability of cable TV, newspapers, and radio to transcend media form was attributed to the fact these media are sometimes looked upon as secondary options in national advertising planning.

Radio is a great medium, especially for local advertisers. I think what you see is this radio is generally regarded as filling gaps in a national schedule building audience coverage, increasing total impressions when time can't be purchased in TV. It's a secondary medium for most national advertisers, a fall back option.

Other managers explained it this way: We use radio and newspapers to fill in holes in our schedule. We like magazines because of their specialization and extras. If we buy radio or newspapers, we are supplementing. I suspect that the same is true of users of cable TV. Cable is used to supplement network schedules and spot buys Why is radio a reasonable replacement for cable TV and billboards?

Simple. Radio is not a primary option for most national advertisers. If you can't schedule enough TV or print to meet your market-by-market objectives, you fill in with radio if creative allows it. Radio is secondary in national ad planning, not primary.

Contrary to our hypothesis, these results suggest that there is a degree of "perceived substitutability" among traditional media options for national advertising planning. The results also call into question the absoluteness of Busterna's finding that newspapers do not reside in the market for national advertising dollars with television, magazines, radio, and outdoor.

It appears from our data that national advertising managers put traditional media in certain boxes, at least perceptually, when considering schedule substitutes. These findings are not particularly surprising if it is true advertising experts place media into national and retail boxes as well.

As for newspapers in particular, our findings suggest that newspapers compete directly with magazines and radio for national advertising expenditures. Though we would agree with Busterna that newspapers do not compete with every medium, the medium is not perceived by national advertisers in isolation, separate and distinct from other media options.

Considering the evidence provided in our depth interviews, we would argue that the issue of substitutability in national advertising comes down not to the issue of media type per se, but to other considerations such as audience delivery, communication effectiveness, and value-added opportunities.

As suggested in the interviews, media are replaceable in national advertising because of similarities in form and function, that is, the physical and qualitative properties of each medium. Apparently in national advertising planning, when the first option is not available or too costly, then, the second option is considered on the same principle as the medium of choice-the ability to deliver the largest percentage of the targeted audience at the right time with the most frequency and the greatest communication impact.

In his economic analysis, Busterna focused on one factor of media selection-space and time costs. Our findings indicate that cost is not the only factor that plays a role in the decision to select a medium, including the decision to replace one medium with another.

For a variety of competitive and creative reasons, a medium may be used in a national media schedule even though it is more expensive on an overall cost basis. Actual media costs are important; however, unique communication qualities of a medium, delivery of a target audience (which would make a medium more cost efficient even though it is more expensive), value-added opportunities, as well as other factors certainly affect the relative cost of a medium as much as time and space cost.

In fact, surveys of how advertising specialists choose media for both national and retail campaigns convincingly demonstrate that, while media costs are essential to the media selection process, selection decisions are driven by a medium's ability to effectively reach a specific audience.

Even cost-per-thousand data, a better measure than overall cost data adjusted for inflation (constant dollars) in determining the value of a medium because the measure considers the relationship between cost and audience delivered, overlook the effects of such factors as added-value opportunities, creative considerations, and audience characteristics.

All things considered, we suggest that differences between the newspaper-specific findings of the two studies are attributable to the temporal nature of Busterna's media data. From his analysis, Busterna concluded that leaving the large rate differential between national and retail ad rates in newspapers makes sense from a managerial view because advertiser demand for newspaper space is somewhat inelastic.

Hence, he advised newspaper executives not to expect to get increased advertising business from advertisers in other media with national rate reductions. The problem with Busterna's recommendation is that during the time period of his data, 1971-1985, national newspaper advertising made up a small percentage of total U.S. advertising spending; it declined steadily from 4.96% to 3.53%. There was very little variability in the amount of national advertising in newspapers.

It is possible that the slope of the demand curve for newspapers would have been flatter (i.e., a sign of more inelastic demand), with more variation in 1971-1985 data, if national newspaper ad rates had been lowered significantly during the period. However, it is quite possible that trade-offs between media options already existed as the result of relative cost considerations; perhaps national advertisers were using newspapers less than magazines and radio on the basis of relative cost versus actual cost, for example. Those advertisers who were consistent users of newspapers during the 1971-1985 period might have found them an effective and efficient way to reach their target audience, despite the national/retail rate differential. If our findings accurately reflect advertising manager perceptions, we suggest that a reduction in the national/retail rate differential may have attracted national advertisers from magazines and radio to newspapers during 1971-85.

There is also reason to suspect the relative price variation between newspapers and magazines may have been more dramatic than reflected in Busterna's data as the result of differences in another non-cost factor, valueadded opportunities. During the period, magazines became much more specialized and the number of magazine options offering specialized audiences increased dramatically.

According to the MPA Handbook, the number of domestic consumer magazines which accepted national and broad regional advertising increased from 874 in 1970 to 1,492 in 1985. By 1995, the number of domestic consumer magazines increased to 2,454. As these magazines became more specialized, they also increased the number of value-added opportunities to national advertisers.

Newspapers were much slower to jump on the value-added bandwagon. In addition to rate reductions, it is possible that newspapers may have attracted more national advertising dollars if the medium had countered magazines with its own value-added opportunities during the 1971-85 period.

PRACTICAL AND RESEARCH IMPLICATIONS

The implication of our findings for the practice of advertising is that media should be sold against other media, but not in the straightforward, one-for-one manner of selling one medium against every other medium. Rather it is suggested by these findings that sales representatives pitch their time and space directly against.media perceived as acceptable substitutes among national advertisers.

For example, national ad sales pitches for newspapers would be more productive by focusing on magazines and radio as the competition, not on television. Pitches for billboards would work best against other out-of-home options, not against print or electronic options.

Sales programs for radio would be more effective if positioned against newspapers, cable TV, and billboards, whereas sales efforts for cable TV would be more productive targeting broadcast TV, radio, and magazines. In each case, sales efforts should not concentrate exclusively on "absolute" cost differentials to sell media options.

National advertisers are interested in relative cost as much as absolute cost, and media must compete on non-cost competitive factors such as impact of message delivery, creative fit, and value-added opportunities.

For researchers, the implication of our results is that questions of substitutability and other comparative inquiries must be asked of buyers, not just sellers of media. As with any one-shot survey, our study needs to be replicated among another sample of media buyers. While the acheived response rate was in line with other relevant industry studies, the rate was less than desired. Replication would confirm and enhance interpretive validity

Other studies on agency buyers, media sellers, and perhaps marketby-market comparisons are needed to flesh out our findings. To extend our findings beyond the seven studied media options (e.g., syndicated TV, spot TV, network TV, internet), localized and specific market comparisons are needed to "tease" out differences and to expand the scope of the findings from general media options to specific market-based options.

Others studies are needed to examine, among other things, (1) the relationship between what national advertisers try to accomplish with their advertising and how media substitutability is affected by different creative approaches, and (2) the effects of over-time variation in factors such as actual media cost, valueadded opportunities, and new media introductions on patterns of media usage and substitution.

It would also be worth studying additional forms of advertising media, including new media options such as Internet advertising and direct mail advertising, and other categories of advertisers such as localized or retail advertising to compare and contrast opinions of media substitutability among national advertisers.

In the final analysis, these findings add to what is known about national advertiser opinions of substitutability among seven traditional media options. However, many other questions about advertising media substitutability need exploration, from many methodological viewpoints. Until those studies are conducted, we suggest that media, including newspapers, are substitutable to a certain degree and compete with each other in specific patterns for national advertising dollars.

Chapter 6

Operationalizing and Analyzing Exposure

Measurement or manipulation of exposure is the foundation of research examining effects of mediated information such as news, music videos, Internet sites, and advertising. It is equally fundamental to studies of intentional influences on that environment such as behaviour change communication campaigns.

Our ability to test theory and to establish media or campaign effects is a function of our ability to successfully manipulate or measure exposure to mediated communication, and to analyse effects of that exposure. Exposure, in principle, is a straightforward concept.

McGuire's information processing model, for example, distinguishes exposure as the prerequisite for subsequent attention, comprehension, and retention. Accordingly, we may define exposure as the extent to which audience members have encountered specific messages or classes of messages/media content. However, operationalizing such a definition is a messy business.

This definition says exposure refers to a person's merely encountering the messages, whether or not they are noticed enough to be remembered. After all, noticing the relevant messages in the communication environment is almost certainly confounded with variables that may predict attention to the content of that message, such as prior knowledge or involvement with the topic.

It is also quite possible that exposure may leave an

affective if not a cognitive impression of some kind, even if the messages have not been attended to well enough to be remembered.

However, if messages are not processed thoroughly enough to be recalled, how can exposure be self-reported? As a result, operations for exposure either take the conservative position of estimating exposure from the possibility of exposure, absorbing the error associated with not actually encountering the messages of interest, or use various techniques to obtain self-reports of exposure, and then use various strategies to control the effects of selective attention due to prior knowledge or involvement which would otherwise undermine causal claims.

Each available approach involves significant trade-offs and uncertainties. Some of these strategies have recently been evolved or incorporated into studies of exposure, making a critical review of methods used to study exposure effects timely.

USING SELF-REPORT MEASURES OF EXPOSURE

The most straightforward way to assess people's exposure to mediated communication is to ask them. Given the thousands of messages and other mediated content to which an individual is exposed in a month, the accuracy of such recall is often problematic. Since exposure to messages and media is, outside of the research lab, volitional and self-selected given prior knowledge, involvement, and other variables typically associated also with outcomes of interest.

The direction of causality is also problematic. The task of the media effects researcher using self-report measures is to minimize these problems insofar as possible. The issues with respect to such operations are well-recognized and will therefore be only briefly reviewed here.

Global Self-report. One may simply ask respondents how often they watch the news, play "first-person shooter" video games, or listen to conservative talk-show radio programming. Perhaps the best-known, though widely criticized, example of such analysis is found in early cultivation research in which amount of television viewing was correlated with fears concerning crime and violence.

Problems include the lack of specificity regarding the actual content of media exposure represented by global self-report,Which would result in underestimates of effect sizes and lack of control for third-variables and reverse causality.One strategy to address effect size problems is to increase specificity of exposure measures.

Asking about frequency of watching specific crime dramas and reality cop shows is more precise than asking about overall TV viewing if one is interested in effects of violent TV content.Specificity of media exposure measures should include separate measurement of media types (such as television, radio, and newspapers) as well as of media content.

Another approach to obtaining detailed information about specific media use is media diaries. Respondents are asked to record all of their use of specified media over some time frame. Problems include motivating respondents to provide complete and accurate record keeping, and the time-consuming task of coding and entering data from such diaries.

A primary weakness in the use of global self-report measures is the inevitable uncertainty concerning the exact nature of the relevant content of the media to which respondents report exposure. This uncertainty can largely be removed when content analyses of those media are conducted in conjunction with the survey of exposure self-reports.

Such content analyses permit quantification of specific elements of media content, such as valence of coverage, sources used, and ethnicity of people portrayed. This should facilitate more precise theoretical specifications of mechanisms as well as increasing predictive power.

The claim that one has characterized the content of a medium is only convincing, however, insofar as one has successfully defined a corresponding population of messages and has randomly sampled or taken a census of those messages.

Recall and Recognition. More precise than global

exposure self-reports, but also more resource-intensive, are exposure self-reports that involve the recognition or recall of specific messages. In recognition measures, messages (or sometimes verbal descriptions of specific messages) are presented to the respondent. In recall measurement, the respondent is asked to describe content of messages that he or she has seen, which then must be analysed by coders to assess the accuracy and completeness of recall.

To use these methods, one must have a relatively small population of messages from which to sample test messages (for recognition measures) or against which to compare open-ended recall measures. Such approaches, then, are typically more appropriate for the evaluation of specific media-based campaigns than for studies of the existing media environment, unless one is interested in the impact of specific programs, articles, or other messages.

In general, recognition measures appear to be preferred over recall for several reasons. Coding of free or cued recall is time-consuming, difficult, and error-prone. More important, people who process messages with relatively little attention are likely not to remember them in the context of a free recall task, but are more likely to recognize them.

Therefore, recognition measures are probably less confounded with variables related to attention such as prior interest in the topic than are recall measures, and therefore are closer to the conceptual definition of exposure. One of the principal problems of recognition measures, however, is the tendency of people to report recognizing messages that they in fact have never seen.

The primary reason is probably respondent uncertainty: people are exposed to a great many messages on most topics, and it is easy to mistake a message presented in a recognition task with other rather similar messages that one may have seen. Other possible reasons include social desirability-the belief by a respondent that he or she "should" have seen the message-or simply response set when other messages in a test group are in fact recognizable.

A simple strategy for handling this problem is through

use of foils or ringers. These are messages that could plausibly have been of the type being tested, but were never shown and are different enough from messages actually shown that legitimate confusion is unlikely.

Recognition of foils can be used as a statistical control for response set and social desirable response bias; analysis of foils in a treatment/control design also suggests that simply using a "might have seen" response category, and coding it as "never seen," can reduce error due to false recognition.

Analysis of foils/ringers and "maybe" responses are useful for reducing the impact of false recognition, social desirability, and response set, but they do not address underlying problems concerning direction of causation, third variable explanations, and selective exposure.

THE DOSE-RESPONSE PROBLEM AND USE OF COVARIATES

As Hornik points out, the relationship of amount of exposure to media effects is a key applied question, on which the expenditure of many millions may depend. Establishing a "dose-response" relationship between exposure and outcomes also goes a long way towards validating the effect of a class of messages. Unfortunately, in field contexts amount of exposure is self-selected, not manipulated.

Exposure is typically a mediating, rather than a truly exogenous, variable: It may be substantially influenced by both baseline scores on an outcome variable and by many possible third variables (also known as endogeneity). Baseline scores can only be effectively controlled in longitudinal research.

Use of statistical controls or covariates can manage third variable problems-to the extent that they are well-measured, that all relevant third-variables are identified and incorporated into the model, and that no variables are mistakenly included as covariates when in fact they are mediators of effects. This ideal scenario can only be approximated, and there is always a substantial degree of uncertainty concerning the appropriateness of one's choices of control variables. Moreover, large numbers of covariates make for cumbersome models that use up degrees of freedom and statistical power (overparameterization), and can only accurately account for variables with a linear relationship to the outcome variable.

One statistical method recently applied to exposure studies in the evaluation of the National Youth Media Anti-Drug Campaign is the use of propensity scoring. This was done because this government-sponsored campaign was national in scope and begun before the evaluation began.

Absent control groups, control over exposure levels, or a baseline, evaluators were dependent on assessing dose-response effects while trying to control for all the many variables that might predict variation in exposure to campaign advertising.

Propensity scoring involves building a statistical model predicting the likelihood of a given level of exposure from a variety of exogenous variables that are likely to be related to exposure. A single vector can be calculated from this model and applied to adjusting the outcome of interest for this propensity to be exposed.

This strategy has a number of desirable statistical qualities. Analyses are not encumbered with a long series of control variables-even if hundreds of covariates are incorporated in the model used to create the propensity score, only one propensity weighting must be used in adjusting a given analysis. Moreover, propensity scores do not assume a linear relation to the outcome as covariates do, and can be balanced over levels of the outcome variable.

Propensity scoring, then, addresses the degrees of freedom and linearity problems with covariate analyses, but remains as dependent as traditional covariate analyses on identifying all key third variables and measuring them with a minimum of error. Moreover, researchers using propensity scoring may be especially prone to inadvertently using mediators as covariates, because there is no price paid in statistical power or model complexity by adding in additional variables to the propensity score model.

A critical assumption when covariates are used is that they are all exogenous-that is, none of them in fact serve as mediators of exposure effects. For example, in political communication, one might want to use political discussion as a covariate, under the assumption that it might predict exposure to political coverage in the media as one seeks out information to use in such discussions.

However, if effects of political coverage are mediated by political discussions (which might, for example, encourage incorporation of new information learned from the media into knowledge structures), then its use as a covariate or as part of propensity scoring might help eliminate media effects that in fact are present.

Managing Problems of Causality Using Longitudinal Analyses of Exposure. Causality and Endogeneity. The problem of reverse or reciprocal causality (or the endogeneity of exposure) is, as noted above, a fundamental challenge in most media effects questions.

Research in selectivity suggests people are likely to seek out, process attentively, and remember information that interests or is relevant to them. These selectivity m echanisms, then, are likely to increase self-report of exposure to a given type or class of messages.

For example, consumer research shows that people who have an interest in a type of product are more likely to report having seen such advertising, more aggressive youth are more likely to seek out violent media content, and more politically involved people process mediated information with more attention.

One cannot ascertain in cross-sectional data whether exposure items are measuring exposure, or salience of the type of information conveyed to people predisposed to seek out and recall such information. For example, in political communication, cross-sectional studies that link exposure to political knowledge may inflate the strength of such relationships. People who have an interest in and are knowledgeable about politics are probably more likely to seek out and recall mediated information, as well as having such mediated information increase their knowledge. Conversely, youth exposed to an anti-drug advertising campaign may be more likely to notice and recall such messages if they are experimenting with or using drugs, which would militate against finding favorable impacts of exposure in cross-sectional data.

In fact, one might state as a general principle that cross-sectional analyses that assume unidirectionality exaggerate the relationship between exposure and outcomes when the messages are consistent with the outcome, and underestimate it when the messages-as in many health prevention contexts-are intended to decrease a behavioural or attitudinal outcome of interest that may in turn be predictive of attention to the message.

The true relationships cannot be estimated with confidence. Structural equation models or instrumental variables may be used with cross-sectional data to estimate reciprocal paths. Causal models of cross-sectional data can provide useful initial evidence regarding the relative strength of reciprocal relationships, but can hardly be regarded as providing definitive evidence.

LONGITUDINAL ANALYSES, SELECTIVE EXPOSURE, AND CAUSALITY

One approach to reducing these problems is to use longitudinal data analysis. Studying longitudinal effects of exposure on change in political knowledge or marijuana use, controlling for prior levels of knowledge or use, is more convincing with respect to causal influence than are cross-sectional analyses, as one can control the time-ordering of effects and the influence of prior scores on the outcome measures; in other words, one is testing the effects of exposure on change in the outcome variable.

The simple use of lagged prediction, however, may not go far enough; the contribution of selective exposure may be to some extent controlled (insofar as it is captured by the influence of baseline scores on the outcome variable), but it is still not understood unless it is explicitly modeled. Use of longitudinal data permits comparisons, for example, of nested structural models positing selective exposure effects versus selective exposure plus media effects paths.

In such models, model fit for a stability model plus the lagged selective exposure effect can be assessed. Fit can then be reassessed with the lagged media effect path added, and a chi-square difference test computed to ascertain whether adding the media effect path or paths to the selective exposure paths resulted in a statistically significant improvement in model fit.

Cross-lagged panel regressions, however, have been criticized as being statistically inferior to growth curve models. Growth curve models focus on analyzing individual respondents' developmental trajectories in a longitudinal data set, and identify coefficients for averaged trajectories that can serve as variables in a regression or structural equation model.

Multi-level growth curve models can also separate out effects of "trait" and "state" components of predictor variables, which can be important in analyzing effects of media exposure. For example, the author and colleagues used multi-level growth curve models to test the "downward spiral" hypothesis that while aggressiveness in adolescents tends to increase use of violent media content (selective exposure), this exposure would reinforce that aggressiveness (media effects).

Use of the multi-level model made it possible to look in particular at effects of variation in aggressiveness over time and not simply at aggressiveness as a trait, which is less likely to be subject to media influence. By modeling both selectivity and media effects, using either growth curve or more familiar cross-lagged models, one can move beyond simplistic discussions of competing causal directions and specify ways selectivity and effects of exposure to media content may reinforce each other or cancel effects out.26

INSTRUMENTAL VARIABLE APPROACHES

Still another approach to improving causal inference in pre-post and other longitudinal designs is to utilize instrumental variables, a technique widely used in econometric analyses. Instrumental variables in the present context are variables that are associated with exposure but not with the outcome of interest.

A classic hypothetical example (described by Hornik) would be an international development effort in which some members of the population are blocked from receiving a radio broadcast because of a mountain blocking radio reception.

Area of residence-if not confounded with income, social status occupation, and so on in ways that might also be related to outcomes of interest-can then serve as an instrumental variable estimating relationships between exposure and outcome, and exposure-outcome relationships can be estimated using two-stage least squares methods, irrespective of possible reciprocal relationships between exposure and outcome.

The problem is that it is often difficult or impossible to identify variables strongly predictive of exposure that are conceptually and empirically independent of the outcome of interest. As a result, exposure studies using instrumental variables to control endogeneity are at best a rarity.

THE PROBLEM OF LAGGED EXPOSURE EFFECTS

There are significant challenges to analyzing exposure using lagged longitudinal analyses, besides logistical issues such as cost, confidentiality, and respondent mortality. Effects of message exposure may be short-lived.

If so, longitudinal lags (typically one-half year or more) may be too long to detect lagged effects of message exposure, especially for a message processed incidentally and with little attention, such as with advertising.

A more sensitive way to capture the effects of message exposure, especially regarding short-lived effects as in the case of advertising, is to use time-series analyses.

Such analyses, however, are most effective when exposure measures are not dependent on self-report, and therefore are discussed later.

EXPOSURE AND ATTENTION: CONCEPTUAL AND ANALYTIC ISSUES

McGuire's information-processing model of persuasion highlights exposure and attention as the two prerequisite conditions for message influence. Some media effects research treats these variables as additive, controlling for exposure before analyzing the effects of attention.

Other research argues that effects of exposure should be weighted by attention,The latter argument is attractive at first glance. Certainly, it is likely that the degree to which exposure affects an individual is a function of the amount of attention that individual pays to the message. However, this is also methodologically problematic.

Attention is inherently confounded with the prior knowledge, interest, and attitudes that give rise to attention. Such prior variables might independently be related to the outcome of interest independent of exposure. Weighting exposure by attention might produce effects that are primarily due to attention's antecedents, not exposure.

Moreover, there are serious statistical questions raised by using multiplicative terms without using the additive terms in the same model. If such an approach is to be explored, use of the main effect terms as well as the weighted term is to be recommended.

ESTIMATING EXPOSURE FROM THE POSSIBILITY OF EXPOSURE

An alternative to exposure self-report measurement is to identify or manipulate the possibility of exposure to a set of messages in a given population. The classic way to do this is through experimental manipulation in a laboratory setting or in the field. Experimental manipulation, however, is not the only way to study possible exposure.

One may use instead reach and frequency, using the traditional media planning terminology. Studies of advertising can take advantage of data concerning amount, type, and placement of advertising available (at non-trivial cost) from Nielsen and other market research firms. If one is working in cooperation with advertisers, as in the evaluation of a counter-advertising campaign, one can use media buy records to identify levels of possible exposure. Conceptual and methodological problems with respect to using each of these methods to operationalize exposure are discussed below.

EXPERIMENTAL MANIPULATIONS OF EXPOSURE

Of course, the only certain way to demonstrate causal relationships between exposure to media content and subsequent effects is through experimental designs. There are good reasons, though, that such studies do not fully dominate the media effects field.

The following briefly reviews the problems and opportunities associated with experimental manipulations of exposure. Laboratory Experiment. Experimentation is well understood by social scientists, but it may be useful to note issues that have particular impact in research on effects of exposure to mediated messages.

For example, the complexities of selective exposure, information clutter and competition, the casualness with which much information is processed in real-world settings, the social contexts in which messages are received and discussed, and the cumulative effects of exposure to many hundreds or thousands of messages over a period of years cannot typically be reproduced in the laboratory.

Experiments build theory and help elucidate processes, but these theories and models must be tested in the social environment as well.

The choice and presentation of message stimuli to which research participants are exposed in particular pose difficult problems.There has also been considerable debate over how possible it is to cleanly manipulate message variables, and the appropriate ways to analyse message differences in an experiment.

Several researchers have argued that the key distinction is between true manipulation of a message (e.g., varying the source attribution) and operationalizing a message variable by presenting participants with various exemplars of different types of messages, such as humorous versus fear-inducing advertisements.

There is some consensus that in the latter case at least random effect models are appropriate, as the message variable has been operationalized through selection of examples rather than through a crossed experimental manipulation.

Use of random sampling to create a pool of experimental stimuli to be used in an experiment more closely approximates the real media environment, and results in a more ecologically valid operationalization of exposure than would otherwise be the case.

Manipulation of exposure can be made a little less artificial by providing people messages outside of a laboratory environment. For example, some market research firms maintain panels of people who have agreed to serve as research respondents.

Respondents can be sent experimental stimuli, thus providing a high degree of control over exposure outside of a lab setting. Similar me the Internet and then randomly assigned to experimental conditions.

FIELD EXPERIMENTS AND QUASI-EXPERIMENTS

The gold standard for any study of media or campaign effects is the group randomized trial, in which entire communities are randomly assigned to media treatment and control conditions. The strength of inference such studies make possible is impressive.

Communication effects are studied in "real world" community settings, with all the complexities of audience selective exposure and attention, multi-step flow, and community process intact.Communities are in many respects a natural unit of analysis for exposure to mediated communication, as broadcast areas for radio and television, and circulation areas for newspapers, largely correspond with physical communities.

Media markets typically become the necessary unit of randomization in field experiments in which broadcast media or newspapers are involved. As noted earlier, this approach assumes that research participants have been adequately exposed to the message simply because they reside in a media treatment community.

Such an assumption makes for a conservative test, given the degree to which exposure depends on access to specific forms of media and selective attention to the messages provided.The primary difficulty, though, is that the gold standard requires lots of gold.

The expense of community intervention trials, such as those using media markets as the unit of randomization, has increased tremendously with the recent expectation that community trials be analysed using clustered or nested analyses in which the primary unit of analysis is the community.

This represents a very serious challenge for researchers. Communication interventions typically have small effect sizes. Such effects are non-trivial given the ability of such campaigns to reach much or most of a population. However, an expectation that such studies should be analysed at the community level of analysis reduces power to detect effects considerably.

The costs of community-level media intervention studies precludes in most cases obtaining an adequate number of communities to assure reasonable power. For example, the author and colleagues are currently analyzing results from a field study of 16 communities to test the effects of using media in communities and schools to reduce teen substance use.

Effects on virtually all attitudinal and behavioural outcomes are significant or highly significant when analysed at the individual level (with an N over 3,000); some outcomes of interest, though, no longer remain significant analysed at the community level (N = 16), though fortunately major intention and behaviour treatment effects remain statistically significant even at the community level.

Effect sizes even for outcomes that go to non-significant, though, are relatively robust relative to typical campaign interventions.Group randomized trials, then, have a substantial risk of resulting in Type II error that might mitigate against socially important findings.

Sophisticated journals will accept analyses of studies where treatments are applied at the community or institutional level (e.g., schools) that do not conduct a full hierarchical analysis of the data, but normally expect that these analyses are statistically adjusted for community-level or other clustering effects using procedures such as generalized estimating equations.

CROSS-OVER DESIGNS

Another model-the cross-over quasi-experimental design-has the potential to permit field experimentation in which media markets are used to manipulate exposure, but at a much lower cost than community-randomized designs.

Cross-over designs, in which a control group is given the intervention treatment after post-test is completed on the original treatment group in the expectation that an effective treatment should replicate effects on the control group, are commonplace in biomedical research. Indeed, such designs are standard when withholding the treatment entirely raises ethical problems.

Such cross-over designs are, unfortunately, a rarity in media effects research. One example is a recent study of anti-marijuana advertising that compared two similar communities in Kentucky and Tennessee, one community exposed to the advertising, one the control. This would hardly have been considered a publishable design, but for the use of the cross-over procedure.

Successful replication of treatment effects in the control community eliminates many alternative explanations for treatment effects, such as uncontrolled variability between communities or history effects.

It is conceivable that history effects might have generated experimental effects first in the experimental community and then in the erstwhile control community, while simultaneously lowering effects subsequent to exposure in the original experimental community-but the probability of such a pattern seems small indeed. As noted below, the explanatory power of this cross-over design was also enhanced by the use of time-series data collection.

Cross-over designs using only a few communities exposed and unexposed to a media treatment do not rise to the same unambiguous evidentiary standard as the community-randomized designs described above.

However, they provide an attractive alternative to community-randomized designs to explore important research questions that would otherwise be impossible to study rigorously in the field given resource constraints, or when ethical or political considerations require that communities receive equivalent treatment exposure.

TRACKING STUDIES AND OTHER TIME-SERIES ANALYSES

Another technique in the cross-over study of anti-marijuana advertising was the use of rolling cross-sectional data collection and interrupted time-series data analysis to assess exposure effects. Rolling cross-sections involve collection of data at regular, closely spaced time points, such as every week or every month, typically over at least 30 or more points in time.

Interrupted time-series can be used to statistically test for the effect of an intervention in changing the slope of the outcome behaviour as plotted against time. Such analyses can also potentially be used to estimate the "half-life" of message effects and, if carried out long enough, can identify confounds such as seasonality effects that might otherwise lead to misinterpretation of longitudinal findings.

Face validity of intervention findings are much enhanced when time-series analyses show that desired effects closely follow increasing distribution of and exposure to the messages of interest, and that these effects decay predictably when message exposure is withdrawn.

Rolling cross-sectional data collections and the resulting time-series data sets are known in the advertising industry as tracking studies. Tracking studies take advantage of a unique aspect of paid advertising campaigns: precise knowledge, on a week-to-week basis, of advertising placements and the consequent reach and frequency, or possible exposure, of the communication effort.

Typically, tracking studies have modest objectives, testing for ad and brand recall and recognition to ascertain whether expenditures are achieving expected levels of awareness. However, such studies can also be used to assess impacts on self-reports of attitudes and behaviours.

Causality in such analytic models is relatively unambiguous, as exposure can be measured exogenously, using Gross Rating Points (GRPs) or other measures of exposure inputs, and not through exposure self-report. It is also possible to use self-report measures of exposure in time-series analyses; however, assertions about causal direction are much weaker when self-report measures of exposure are used than when reach and frequency measures operationalize exposure.

The assumption that messages placed were actually seen is an uncertain one, but should lead to conservative estimates of effects free from selectivity and other confounds. Another approach to the use of time-series analyses to investigate exposure effects has been pioneered by David Fan. Fan and others using similar techniques assume exposure, and link rolling cross-sectional outcome data with rolling cross-sectional content analyses.

The latter poses significant logistic challenges, which have been addressed through computerized content analytic strategies using key terms to identify stories on a topic and the valence of the story.

AP wire stories represent the media environment. Time-series analytic techniques are applied to test the association of fluctuations in amount and valence of media coverage with fluctuations in relevant public opinion polling that is carried out in an on-going way.

Such an approach has limitations. The AP wire is an imperfect indicator of all U.S. media coverage. There is no measurement of individual-level exposure to such news as a mediator of coverage effects on attitudes or behaviour-again, this method focuses on possible versus actual or self-reported exposure.

It is possible that third variables may drive both coverage and behaviour (though this possibility can be tested through examination of evidence for a slight lag in exposure effects on outcomes).

Many of these limitations, however, should increase conservativeness of findings. The more serious limitation is that these techniques can only be employed for exposure to media for which on-line sources over time are readily available, and for outcomes that are tracked regularly through on-going surveys.

When such studies are an option, however, they permit exceptionally robust inference concerning real-world effects of media exposure on national populations.

The array of designs and analytic techniques available to study effects of media exposure permits convincing inferences when results triangulate across methods. This is illustrated in particularly concise and dramatic fashion in a recent meta-analysis of media violence studies, in which studies are separated by method, variation in effect size by method indicated, and the overall convergence of effects shown.

Media effects theories are theories of process, of cause and effect. Longitudinal designs that permit modeling of process over time or field experimental designs that permit unambiguous causal tests are where maturing theories must find their supportive evidence.

Longitudinal designs also permit-indeed, they demand-explicit theorizing regarding the role both of selective exposure and media effect.

In the realm of media campaigns, rolling cross-sections and time-series analyses offer researchers the opportunity to evaluate campaign impact with a precision that has previously been unattainable, and cross-over designs may increase the viability of quasi-experimental studies.

Simple cross-sectional surveys and small-scale

experiments provide excellent opportunities to ascertain if theoretical propositions and hypothesized mechanisms are viable and worthy of further exploration. They are insufficient to test whether these mechanisms operate as hypothesized in the larger social world. Expanded use of more sophisticated designs and methods is necessary if the media effects and campaigns research area is to continue to advance.

Chapter 7

Phenomenological Medium Theory

For in the piece, besides addressing the problems concerned with Marxism in late, reflexive modern, neoliberal democracies, Derrida conjures a number of these specters, ghosts, spirits—hauntings—which he deals with through this logic of the ghost, hauntology. The word itself is, of course, a Derridean invention which plays at once on the subject of the spectral and the essence of Being. Medium theory, most often in the phrase "the medium is the message," has had a contentious history vis-a-vis media and cultural studies. This chapter argues that, along with that of Karl Marx, the spirits of Harold Innis, Marshall McLuhan, and Martin Heidegger haunt us on a regular basis in media and cultural studies.

If they already exist in ghostly form, perhaps by exorcising them through the logic of the specter, we can allow them to comingle with the living via historical materialism, Marxism, and phenomenology, along with a Heideggerian "questing for technics."

Daniel Czitrom once noted that "for the most radical and elaborate American media theory, one must look to the work of two Canadians, Harold Adams Innis and Marshall McLuhan."

Innis's central claim regarding media and power as having been ossified in the political economy canon is surely without question, cemented into thousands of bibliographies as firmly as anyone else in Canadian historiography. Beyond the field of political economy, however, there has clearly been some renewed interest in Innis's place within the media studies canon in recent years.

In his introduction to the 1994 rerelease of Understanding Media, Lewis Lapham wrote that Marshall McLuhan makes sense now more than ever, and, though he made this proclamation over a decade ago, little has changed. That was just following Wired magazine's 1993 launch, whereby they labeled McLuhan their "Patron Saint" on the masthead.

And beyond these examples, there is no denying the signs that abound, indicating the presence of McLuhan in contemporary discourse. For many, his pseudo-prophetic conjectures are now only beginning to show their clarity with regard to the "Internet Age." This is to say that Innis and McLuhan are a presence; they haunt us, to be sure.

By placing medium theory in this historical context, it will be shown that its epochal history of communication demands to be dually understood in terms of Marxian materialism and phenomenology. The final section will discuss Martin Heidegger's "technological question" with relation to the Derridean deconstructive, hauntological apparatus, in order to juxtapose both the parallels and incongruities of these disparate philosophical tendencies.

EPOCHAL HISTORIES

To adapt Todd Gitlin's famous comment regarding the overzealous application of Gramscian hegemony theory, if medium theory explains everything, it explains nothing. And while this is a shortcoming of a field that is all too inclusive (cultural studies, I feel, suffers this same malady), the historical possibilities medium theory provides are still worth noting, for, as grand theories go, they don't get much grander.

Medium theory, specifically in the historical work of Innis, McLuhan, and Ong, has such an impressive scope that it draws upon the entire history of humanity, complete with its "social upheavals" and its "growth of languages, techniques, inventions, arts, and sciences". Each lays out an epochal history with nuanced classification.

For example, for Innis, all communication media were

biased in terms of time and space, thus creating what he termed "monopolies of knowledge" for the dominant culture. Time-biased media are durable and difficult to transport, whereas spatially biased media are light and can be moved across space with relative ease, speed, and accuracy. Following Innis's lead, McLuhan divided human history into three distinct eras based on the dominant medium of communication that characterized the period.

Thus, mankind may be seen as having three epochs: the oral tradition, which stretches from the moment man first acquired speech to the beginning of literacy roughly five thousand years ago, the literate era, which extends from the invention of writing to the creation of the electric telegraph, and, lastly, the era of electric communication, beginning at the first telegraph usage in 1844 through today.

Walter 1. Ong, heavily influenced by McLuhan (who was Ong's teacher and master's thesis advisor), doesn't simply recapitulate the work of his forebear, however. Rather, he sees the history of man as divided into four stages of communication and culture—orality, chirography, typography, and electronic orality, or what he refers to later as "literate orality" and "secondary orality" to describe the complex and contradictory blend of old and "new" found within the media environment.

From within this paradigm, we can begin to see that media are not conduits, rather, they are active agents of cultural and psychological change. And while I have only provided a perfunctory gloss of the historical and theoretical uses of medium theory, a simple perusal of this theory's grand theorists clearly emphasizes the breadth and scope that becomes incorporated.

It also becomes clear that this approach is historical materialist (not dialectical materialist) in nature. If we take the power that a particular medium might hold over its niche within the historical context, we might term its underlying biases as a kind of dominant ideology, though its "effects" might not be relationally understood without the benefit of hindsight.

The dominant ideologies at work in the biases of these communicative forms would thus incorporate subordinate technologies and their uses, rendering them politically quiescent and overshadowing alternative modalities via the concealment of reactionary social realities.

Thus, the mechanics of dominant communicative forms are inherently powerful enough to bypass social contradiction and reify its position within the social, political, and personal consciousness. Underlying this technological manifestation is, of course, a specter in itself: the classic thesis from The German Ideology.

Historical materialism is the theory of social change, developed by Marx and Engels, in which history is divided into a series of epochs (or modes of production), each characterized by a distinct economy and class structure. Historical change in this view is fueled by the progressive expansion of the productive capacity of the economy, as well as the development of technology and the forces of production.

This becomes manifest in class conflicts and revolutions. ne of the reasons the historical materialist approach works so well in both Marxism and medium theory is that it shows that ideas actually come from somewhere and gives an agency. Ideas and social change don't fall from the sky, and the appeal to this is clear in both schools of thought.

Dialectical materialism, in Marxist terms, encompasses those aspects of its philosophy beyond its theory of history (such as metaphysics, ontology, and epistemology). The term wasn't used by either Marx or Engels, but later became the dogmatic philosophy of the Soviet Union, building on works such as Engels's Dialectics of Nature.

Dialectical materialism, for our purposes here, might be characterized by its materialism and rejection of skepticism. The material world, in this view, is held to have a primacy over the mental, so that the material is a precondition of one's consciousness (which would seemingly make sense for someone like Innis, McLuhan, or Edmund Carpenter). The material world is then knowable through the realm of empirical studies. Beyond focusing solely on its materialism, the philosophy itself is dialectical, in that it sees reality in its ever-changing state of development, arguing not simply that change exists in the world, but rather that the reality of that world is characterized by varying properties and their emergence.

THE "BIAS" OF INNIS

Innis's research can clearly be classified as both idealist and materialist, with an evident emphasis on the latter. As William Westfall notes, "Instead of recounting the gradual unfolding of an idea or series of ideas (such as political liberty, responsible government, or autonomy) it turned history toward the ongoing ramifications of a body of material factors in a geopolitical and economic setting."

For obvious reasons, this parallels Marx's notion of the economic base, supporting a historically derived superstructure. Innis, however, avoided Marxian theory and "he certainly did not truck with socialism". In a 1948 essay, he makes clear the limits of Marxism and its approach and claims to be utilizing "the Marxian interpretation to interpret Marx".

While this would seem a worthy undertaking, Innis never really fulfills the promise in any of his published writings. It is worth pointing out, however, that he uses the term "Marxian," as opposed to "Marxist," which implies the source, rather than the tradition that sprang from it. Class-consciousness and any sort of concept of ideology, both of which are mainstays of Marxism, are glaringly absent in Innis's staple research (such as his work on fur or cod, etc.), which is why I am not linking him on that level. What is very present are the material conditions of production, and a sense of the cyclical nature of history (which Marx inherited from Hegel). Interestingly, Innis's later work, which valorized the oral tradition, is quite similar to Marx's notion of primitive communities.

The centrality of Innis's presence in critical communication and media studies is his focus on what he termed "bias." What began for Innis as a very specific problem (how does form influence power?) ended with what was almost an overarching theory of social and cultural analysis, the notions of spatial and temporal bias as the dominant way of understanding communication and, thus, power.

For Innis, the world that one studies could not be positivistically regarded as a conglomeration of facts that one could objectively analyse according to the traditional methods of the social sciences. For Innis, these "facts" all reflect a series of values; a certain level of cultural factors that were ontologically subjective in nature thus biased all facts. Further, the social scientist was him- or herself biased by the cultural assumptions of the environment in which they were immersed.

One of the reasons for Innis's turn towards the study of "biases" inherent within particular communicative forms as an enabler of empires/networks of power is that, from a broader perspective, this problematic is but one of a larger philosophical and methodological issue—the shortcomings of rational empirical science, particularly in regard to the historiography of religious phenomena—that a number of disciplines were attempting to confront at the time of Innis.

He, like so many others, had to deal with this on levels both abstract and personal. He sought to establish some kind of methodology which would allow the social sciences to explore the world objectively, and he tried to find a way for the social scientist to escape the gravity of the social environment so that he or she might gain some measure of freedom in order to deploy what Innis was trying to develop.

For Innis, the problem of bias itself needed to become part of the solution, thus making necessity a virtue. He would accept the fact that both sides of the subject—object dialectic were shaped by the bias, but it would be the bias itself that would become the subject matter for his social scientific analysis.

For Innis, there were patterns that would become apparent, when looking historically, in the way that bias influences particular cultures (such as whether or not a medium is time-biased or space-biased). Thus, for Innis, by examining the patterns and elements of history via their continuity and predictability, one could essentially construct scientifically sound statements. Hence, to "rescue objectivity, one should study the shape of subjectivity: The only element in society that was not relative, Innis seemed to argue, was relativity itself".

For Innis, the patterns of bias were themselves ecological reflections of the relationships that were tied to social processes, all of which could be studied empirically. We might, then, begin to understand Innis's representation of the social order as being a system of hierarchies with social reality on the surface and a system of bias on a level just below.

Beneath everything was what Innis often referred to as "primal cultural factors." The contemporary world, for example, is biased towards a certain attitude regarding time that is directly correlated to a system of communication (i.e., the world might be considered smaller now than ever before). And for Innis, in the last major project of his life, with the bias of communication as a starting point, one can begin to conceptualize the entire history of mankind.

Rereading McLuhan and Innis Through Marxism and Phenomenology In the following section, I wish to render problematic the theory of medium of communication, as expressed in the work of Innis and McLuhan, in two ways.

Beyond a traditional reading which might stem from structuralism and political economy, I wish to offer an alternative interpretation, which I believe to be truest to the epochal historiographies of Innis and McLuhan, and which might be called Marxist and phenomenological.

For both thinkers, central is the notion of space and time, and the conditions by which they are experienced (in the widest phenomenological sense) within a given social/historical condition, thus constituting a position within that history's hierarchy of production through the media of communication (in the Marxist sense). For Innis and McLuhan, media (or communication) are key in constituting the limits of what is humanly experience-able.

But key to understanding these limits are the manners in which they are experienced, thus locating power in the realm of social formations (as laid out by Innis in his studies of empire). In other words, the medium institutes a system of social order, based on biases that are both spatial and temporal, that is constitutive of life itself.

While Innis is clearly concerned with the social influences of the materiality of communication (though his history is far more pluralistic than would be a Marxist revision), it is in McLuhan where we find the concept of the media environment pushed to its (il)logical conclusion by claiming that media (no matter what form they may take) have no intrinsic qualities whatsoever, but the characteristics they hold are distinctly dependent on their relationship with the media environment as a whole and the given translations of experience between media forms.

This, I would argue, is an implicitly Marxist and phenomenological stance, though McLuhan would probably have argued it as a purely rhetorical posture, whereby media maintain a social influence only through an originating matrix beyond the medium in question. This is why, for McLuhan, media have no intrinsic content as such.

But while this might help us in establishing a line of phenomenological enquiry in the Innis-McLuhan genealogy (to incorporate Foucault's idiom), how can we begin to rethink media of communication in terms of historical materiality from a Marxian vantage point?

If we are to follow McLuhan's conjecture that media of communication should be understood as extensions of the corporeal system whose kinaestheses (or bodily motions/ expressions) consist of representative modes of expression and interface with the unseen media environment, we are then pushing McLuhan into the realm of pure reification. I wish to locate this interpretation in its opposition with the tendency to theorize the materiality of communication media through a focus on the commodification ritual as seen by orthodox Marxist approaches to a medium.

Rather, I would note that the key difference in this

dichotomy has already been combed over by Marx himself in his infamous "Theses on Feuerbach" wherein he distinguished the reference of his historical materialism to "human sensuous activity, [or] practice" from the "materialist doctrine that men are products of circumstances and upbringing, and that, therefore, changed men are products of other circumstances and changed upbringing" as proposed by Feuerbach.

In this sense, media of communication (from language itself to literal channels of discourse and desire) can thus be experienced as active rather than simply descriptive and representative, or referential, of an already constituted object/experience. So while the message may have meaning, it is ultimately overshadowed by the medium as message itself.

It is in the critique of McLuhan by Raymond Williams (Television) where these worlds converge. Here we find an instructive confrontation between McLuhan's modernist sensibilities, his essentially postmodern theory of media, and Williams' Marxist theory that explicitly recognizes the constitutive power of media.

In European thought, the critique of modernity in the twentieth century was primarily developed via the phenomenology of Husserl and Heidegger and the negative dialectics of the Frankfurt School, converging on questions of technology and the instrumentalization of reason within modernity. I call McLuhan's theory ultimately postmodern in that it does not situate the media environment within a larger totality, but uses the plurality of media itself as the impetus for any investigation of culture. Communication media are thus a manifestation of culture itself—not the other way around.

For Williams, on the other hand, media (or the material expression) of communication are purely a force of production. Williams felt that a failure of traditional Marxism was the relegation of issues concerning communication to the superstructure (removing it from the base and turning it into a second order process), thereby "missing the inherent role of means of communication in every form of production".

Therefore, analyses of the role of media (and the medium of communication) must be understood within the larger totality of the capitalist mode of production.Hegel once said, "Every philosophy can be nothing but its own epoch comprehended in thought" (qtd. in Korsch). To unpack this in terms of McLuhan and Innis's medium theory, we are left with a crystallization of interest, which then becomes the way in which we understand our period in relation to history.

Through philosophy (and I would argue all of this is a philosophically discursive approach to the ontology of media) we can define the conflicts and the dominant interest of an era. This is what it means to conduct a philosophical analysis and this is why medium theory needs to be understood in reference to both its Marxist and phenomenological underpinnings. For if we are to begin to understand the materiality of our media environment, we must think outside of the discourse of "effects" and construct a new philosophical, critical theory of communicative constitution and representation.

It is also worth noting some of the similarities between Innis and McLuhan for the purposes of relating them to a Marxian concept of history. Although the lineage and legacy of the McLuhan-Innis connection has been discussed ad infinitum, one thing remains controversial: Who was more important (as if this is a question worth asking)?

The problem that has risen from McLuhan's notoriety is that much of what Innis had to say in his major challenges to the future of communication studies has been overlooked (generally) in the process of separating his later work (such as Bias and Empire) from the ways in which they were discussed by McLuhan. For example, it is important to stress that McLuhan and Innis diverge sharply when Innis's critical quality and his social consciousness become the focal point.

Both shared a common "bias" about how to approach communication historiography; both manifest a keen interest in the classical tradition and its importance to both the humanities and the social sciences; both relate communication to culture as a value-laden term; both view the mode of communication as the formative process in the growth of structures of knowledge production, as well as structures of feeling within a culture; both would insist that there is an inherent aesthetic factor in the development of communication theory; both had a profound distrust of contemporary mechanization; and both wrote their histories with a sense of irony (Theall). I will now to turn Heidegger and technology to examine the place of deconstruction within communication.

HEIDEGGER/SPECTRALITY/PRESENCE/TECHNE

Derrida, in his turn to hauntology, examines the spectral (or ghostal) effects in any sensorial experience or interaction (communication, mediation) in order to illustrate that what appears present is always already contaminated, infected by what is absent (for Derrida this phenomenon is and must be associated with the general function of signs and their iterability).

With Spectres, he argues that the past can never be fully exorcised from the present. Today we live in a world haunted by multiple specters of Marx, for example, in terms of the political and philosophical landscapes.

From the specters of communism and totalitarianism to the articulation of class distinction and consciousness, from the millennial tensions of evangelicalism to those standing against the rising tide of neoliberalism, these ghosts haunt continually even as the contemporary moment superficially appears to be moving past Marx and towards what Fukuyama has termed the "end of history."

What we must remember about these hauntings, however, is that they are examples of erasure in action. The Union of Soviet Socialist Republics no longer exists in a material sense, yet the politics of memory are such that its flame is perpetually rekindled. Like a corpse, the remains remain.

In French hantologie sounds the same as ontologie because of the silent "h." This is part of Derrida's infamous play of differance, which I would argue has an extremely medium-centric attitude. Since the differance is an impossible possibility, it cannot exist outside of its communicative form. Differance can be read, thus privileging writing, and can only exist in speech as a possibility.

As McLuhan would say, the medium, is of course, the message. Hauntology is an offering to us, an offering of an alternative, not an opposition, to ontology. Its homonymic emphasis, then, is the nonpresent presence it presents the specter posing a fundamental challenge to ontology.

By focusing not on presence in a purely Heideggerian way, hauntology calls into question the very distinction between being and nonbeing. Like differance, hauntology exceeds (and precedes) the ontological. But it is Heidegger's spirit that allows us to consider the role of techng in our current context.

Sterne writes, "It is true in conversation, in large-scale media systems, in human-animal interaction, and in the most subtle dimensions of encountering others. Communication is, above all else, a techne." Techne in contrast with those things that merely derive from nature (physis) or chance (tyche).

It is a word which has numerous connotations each of a somewhat ambiguous nature. Aristotle's stays the most famous designation, wherein it is both practical art and practical knowledge, meaning both the process by which things in the world are produced and the knowledge that accounts for said production. Referring to this Aristotelian model, Heidegger notes that techne, "reveals whatever does not bring itself forth and does not yet lie before us, whatever can look and turn out one way and now another".

Heidegger's "Question Concerning Technology" is arguably the single most important work in the field of the philosophy of technology. Essentially what is happening here is Heidegger attempting to uncover the essence of technology so that we can have what he calls a "free relationship" with it.

Once we understand the real essence of technology, we will learn how to experience it within its own bounds. Now according to Heidegger, what we have until now failed to understand is that the essence of technology isn't technological. It is not, in other words, something like a neutral tool or gadget. Technology is thus instrumental, a means to an end, a human activity that is geared toward the manipulating and controlling of things.

So, in this view, means produce ends, just like causes produce effects. Heidegger is not denying that this is accurate rather this definition represents only this causal, instrumental meaning of the means to the end. He reminds us of the ancient Greeks and their broader conception of causality; a cause is something that brings something about or that which is responsible for something.

The four causes articulated by Aristotle that Heidegger points to are explanations, explanations of what something is made out of, what it is to be a something, what it produces, and what it is for. Together the four causes are responsible for bringing something into appearance (Heidegger uses the Greek here, poisis).

Poiesis is the Greek term for creation or production aimed to bring about an end, as opposed to doing or action such as praxis. These causes create presencè, bringing it forth, "out of concealment into unconcealment." The essence of technology then for Heidegger is not a means but a way of revealing (or aletheia).

In other words, it's a kind of truth. Yet the way that technology (or techne) reveals is problematic. It places an unnatural and unreasonable demand on nature: It forces the assumption that nature supply us endlessly and efficiently.

Humans then, the supposed masters of technology, are challenged in this way, becoming what Heidegger refers to as "standing reserve." Consider the phrase so ubiquitous today: "human resources." Heidegger calls this way of revealing the world Ge-stell or "enframing," a way of ordering people to see the world and each other—as more or less just a stockpile of reserves to he manipulated.

Enframing happens both in us and in the world; for Heidegger it is the revelation of a certain kind of being (essence) (both in human beings and nature) as a standing reserve. Particular kinds of technology in the ordinary sense of gadgets and tools and machines only respond to this enframing—they are the consequence, not the cause, and, as such, help reveal things as standing reserve (for Heidegger this is true of modern science as well).

The danger of technology here is twofold. First, Heidegger finds that we ourselves are this standing reserve. Second, in our role as human standing reserve, we tend to think that we are masters of everything. The truth of the matter, for Heidegger, is that we cannot see ourselves or understand the world clearly.

Enframing keeps that essence of things concealed; it obscures other ways of seeing things, particularly revealing as poiesis (bringing something into appearance). The danger here is the partial, incomplete enframing that is revealed. Poiesis is ultimately the essence of technology.

What Heidegger is arguing is that we need to realise this essence and stop construing technology as mere instrumentality (as a mere means to an end), and overcome the illusion of our pretension that we have complete mastery and control over things. The "saving power" of technology, for Heidegger, is that the essence of technology is ambiguous. The very instrumentality (techne) that threatens us also saves us (as poiesis).

With the accelerated growth of technology in the modern era (consider Norbert Wiener's famous "change changed"), we find two millennia worth of metaphysics standing in the way of language, prioritizing information transmission and efficacy, threatening the prospects for aletheia, the truth of Being, our shared reservoir of preontological understanding of un-hidden-ness or discovery.

For this reason, Derrida's hauntological turn (and differance) offers a more vigorous means of approaching media and communication through considering than do either conventional metaphysics or traditional ontology.

In this way, if truth exists as a "coming to presence," then the technological manifestations of communicative action, as laid out by the medium theory of Innis and McLuhan, disrupt presence by imposing themselves on the (pre)ontological limits of the very engagement. Therefore to speak of communication after Derrida after Heidegger is to speak of a kind of "artifactuality," whereby artificiality, actuality, artifice, and textuality become intrinsically linked in the materialist explanations of the communication environment.

For Derrida, artifactuality refers to the textual production of communication and information by means of the contemporary structural apparatus—teletechnology, or, simply, "the media". There is, thus, a responsibility in responding to and analyzing the media.

"Hegel was right," Derrida observes, "to remind the philosopher of his time to read the papers daily. Today, the same responsibility obliges him to learn how the dailies, the weeklies, and the television news programs are made, and by whom".

Given an understanding that our mediated world is both "actively produced" and, considering the phenomenological medium theory of Innis and McLuhan, "performatively interpreted," mediation is not merely an abstract philosophical concept, but also a deconstructive artifact. The metaphysical presence of every object of being necessitates the projection of itself toward that end. It is this presence and projection that allows us to identify with forms of communication and to rationalize the mediatization process.

If each form renders a different ontological status, then there exists the possibility to disintegrate and distill these essences down to a primordial core, whereby the deconstruction of mediation is possible, and communication itself may be imagined as a possible impossible. Communication as (im)possible centre is often rendered problematic (and possible) through this sense of iterability.

For example, for Soren Kierkegaard, mediation is explicitly linked to repetition, as he describes in his philosophical narrative on Constantin Constantius: "Mediation" [Mediation] is a foreign word; "repetition" [Gjentagelse] is a good Danish word, and I congratulate the Danish language on a philosophical term. There is no explanation in our age as to how mediation takes place, whether it results from the motion of the two factors and in what sense it is already contained in them, or whether it is something new that is added.

Almost two decades ago, Derrida faced a video camera in Toronto and discussed film and television, in Kierkegaardian form, as "a ghost dance" (la danse des fantomes), contemporary technologies like film, television, telephones live on or off of, ill some way, a ghostly structure. Film is an art of the ghost, which is to say, it is neither image nor perception The voice on the telephone also has a ghostly appearance.

It is something neither real nor unreal, something which returns, is reproduced—finally, it's the question of reproduction. From the moment when the first perception of an image is linked to a structure of reproduction, we are dealing with the ghostly.

Sometime later, again on camera, this time at a conference, he rebuked a group of architects in Japan about the necessity to take what he now called "telefacture," or the facsimile, seriously, the need to attend to the new structure of spatio-temporal differance constructed by new techniques of telecommunication, by new powers of production as well as reproduction—information, images, discourse, and even the event in general.

The event itself, like the concept of experience and of the testimony that claims to refer to it, finds itself affected, in its inside, beyond the public-private opposition, by the possibility of the shot and of reproduction from practically anywhere to anywhere.

Derrida is here now moving slightly beyond Heidegger and exorcising the ghost of Walter Benjamin, who once observed of media's iterability:

You can regard all these things as eternal (e.g. storytelling, narration), but one can also see them as temporal and problematic, even dubious. Eternal things in narration. But most likely entirely new forms, genres. Television, gramophone and so forth bring all this to an ominous bottom line.

And within these early notes for the storyteller essay

Benjamin goes on to articulate a fear that it is all repudiated: narration by television, the hero's words by the gramophone, the moral by the next statistics, the storyteller by what one knows about him Tant mieux. Don't cry. The absurdity of critical prognoses.

FILM INSTEAD OF NARRATION

This is Benjamin's antiessentialist response to the domination of traditional ways of thinking about new communication forms. Essentialism, one of the more enduring philosophical doctrines that responds to metaphysical inquiry into the nature of things, states, essentially, that a thing is a thing and is what it is, and not some other thing, because of inherent, immutable properties.

Essentialist philosophical positions thus espouse truths that transcend specific times. The recent trend from essentialism toward more perspectivist (and multiperspectivist) approaches to deeply philosophical questions has resulted in the reification of structural binarisms within thought itself. For example, if we follow the lineage of contemporary critical theory and & construction, we find Hegel on one side, as a builder if you will, and someone like Heidegger on the other dismantling such buildings (Desilet 152).

Medium theory, in that it tends to neglect the spectral effects at work and forces us to remain prisoners of a metaphysics of presence, is closed by its own essentialist view of communication technology. Post-Heideggerian deconstruction can allow us to break with these limits and open the idea of mediation, for as we are often quick to forget, deconstruction was and is simultaneously structuralist and antistructuralist.

According to Heidegger, "metaphysics is Platonism," for "throughout the whole history of philosophy, Plato's philosophy remains decisive in changing forms." Medium theory, like structuralism then, is an ideal of form, an "ideal of metanarrative social cohesion, the idea; of language transparency".

Although the structural conditions make possible systemic changes (and indeed system formation), they also come to represent all that falls away and out of reach of what makes the very system possible.

Placing communication in conversation with phenomenology, deconstruction, and medium theory, encourages and engages (and hopefully will force) ruptures of thought, (ir)resolutions, promises to remain (re)opened, secrets hidden and exposed, sutures closed but oozing, reason and logic at their limits, aporia as understanding.

(Post)Structural Theories of Mediation (?)In this chapter I have provided a brief overview of some characteristics of medium theory and shown how they relate to the writings of Karl Marx and Heidegger's technological question via a series of "hauntings."

Would Marx buy into medium theory? This is an ill-conceived question, for it carries an incorrect assumption—that Marx is concerned with ontological essences rather than with their historically determined and ever-changing function. For Marx, all issues must be dealt with historically. In this sense, we can see how, for him, the "mediums" might be somewhere in the superstructure, not the base.

Are Innis, McLuhan, and other medium theorists trying to move their object of inquiry from the superstructure (culture) to the base (history/economy)? For Innis, the answer might be a clear yes, but for McLuhan it might get a bit more complex. While Marx embraced new technology, he did so within the context of his time and place (not to be confused with being a technophile of the late twentieth century).

In that way, Marx was actually glorying in the city, with its consolidation of workers and its centralizing of scientific discourse. For Marx, this was the gods getting put in their place, not some kind of manifest technological utopianism in the form of a retribalized global village, replete with media, both hot and cool.

Even though there are a number of similarities, as I have shown, in the spheres of Marxism and medium theory, one is still not the other (all medium theorists aren't Marxists, much like all Marxists obviously aren't medium theorists). McLuhan never critiqued anything from a Marxist/Marxian perspective.

For example, he never seemed concerned that radio and television were set up as purely commercial endeavors and never touched on the emancipatory possibilities or hindrances of any particular medium. For Marx, the goal was bringing about in the proletariat a class-consciousness to change their situation. For him, it was about holding up revolution before the masses.

This is why the phenomenological aspects of orthodox Marxism are theoretical, while still only using empiricism. This is similar to McLuhan's call to pay attention; he was never just some promoter of the latest gadget. McLuhan, like Marx, was trying to raise consciousness in the masses and hold the possibility of a better tomorrow before their eyes.

As with Marx, you must make up your own mind what you want from someone like McLuhan. In that sense, both sadly have become whatever the interpreter says they are. The bottom line is that they raise interesting questions, and that might he the most we can ask of theory at this point in our own (post)historical context.

Derrida's theory of deconstruction, then, anticipates a poststructural turn in the changes in mediation, attempting to destabilize the rally of meaning in univocal logo-centrism by dismantling the logic it hides. It is an interpretive gesture similar to Mark Poster's commentaries on electronic writing, in that both attempt to "understand the volatility of written language, in its instability and uncertain authorship."

Thus, language is a destabilization of subjectivity and Derrida can apply these qualities to all forms of writing (differentiating only partially between media form). Deconstruction, then, might be interpreted as Derrida's interpretation of the metaphysical ramifications of the medium.

Poster's concern, on the other hand, is much more in line with that of Innis and McLuhan (though with a more explicit Marxist-Foucauldian slant), in that he distinguishes the differences of media form to assess the significance of these differences as enacted by the new communication technology.

And, unlike the materialism of Innis's time-space biases, Derrida (deconstruction) and Poster (poststructuralism) offer an interpretive approach that could intermingle with traditional medium theory in a way that would permit the exegesis of communication form in a manner that suits the glissandos of electronic media culture.

Derrida, who, for example, has long been an almost entirely unacknowledged theorist of the media, gives time for a detour in Specters of Marx to highlight the threat telecommunication poses to aletheia, noting that teletechnology obliges us more than ever to think the virtualization of space and time, the possibility of virtual events whose movement and speed prohibit us more than ever (more and otherwise than ever, for this is not absolutely and thoroughly new) from opposing presence to its representation, 'real time' to 'deferred time,' effectivity to its simulacrum, the living to the non-living, in short the living to the living-dead of its ghosts.

But if we begin to consider the problematic at work in a deconstruction of the mode of communication, we would undermine the entire logic of mediation (a la Derrida), whereby no medium is adequate to communicate because of the infinite play of differences.

Since mediation itself, in poststructuralist terms becomes a play of difference, there isn't simply a reversal of hierarchy at work (such as the changing dominance of communicative form found in the epochal historiographies of Innis, McLuhan, and Ong). If there is a breakdown in this centre-margin dichotomy we are putting the active verb function of the mode of communication itself under erasure (sous rature), after Heidegger and Derrida, pointing to the inadequacies in the logic of communication form.

Since the medium is of central import (medium theory), yet it is unnoticed if communication is happening (the logic of successful communication), we find that mediation is then both there and not there, present and absent, alive and dead, material and spectral. Thus, if we are to actively disrupt the logic of the communication form, might it be more appropriate to say: The medium [begin strikethrough]is[end strikethrough] the message?

As communication scholars, we must phrase this intentionally with the impossible possibility intact. To place something under erasure, one must of course, write the differance into existence. To elaborate: Derrida, in taking up the practice of sous rature, shows that neither the word "speech" nor the word "writing" are adequate to describe the more abstract play of differences that exist.

Both speech and writing function for Derrida as a play of difference. And what he's doing here is not simply reversing the hierarchy that makes up Western thinking about communication—making writing central while marginalizing speech (as in the infamous cover to La carte postale), he's putting both terms "under erasure." And he does this by infamously drawing an "X" through them, crossing them out, but leaving them present.

And so, to put a binary opposition found in structuralism and communication under erasure, you could write the words [begin strikethrough]speech[end strikethrough] and [begin strikethrough]writing[end strikethrough] as such. This is a device Derrida borrowed from Heidegger and it simply means that both speech and writing are inadequate to describe the general differences common to both.

But the problem is, in discussing them, Derrida cannot simply do without them; they must be used. A clear, rhetorical criticism of putting something under erasure is that it allows us to essentially have our cake and eat it too, so to speak. By using this deconstructive strategy, we're able to use a word or a concept, while simultaneously indicating its inadequate or undecidable nature.

Here are the origins of "arche-writing." It is an invention and an invitation, an expression that illustrates that binaries like speech and writing are really just the spoken and written forms of this play of difference.

Yet, because of the necessity to write this practice into

existence, and by that I mean that this can't exist without the dichotomy of the speech-writing dialectic, we can see how Derrida is somewhat painted into a corner, relying essentially on what he's seeking to deconstruct.

And here we return to the specter, the hauntological. The work of Harold Innis and Marshall McLuhan does breathe a ghostly life into the subjects of late modernity, technology, postmodernity, power, and possibilities of communication discourse, and each have much to offer cultural studies of communicative form and the material logic of power.

The work of Innis is complicated and laced with a certain darkness. His communication project remained unfinished (a fact that Paul Heyer, for one, thinks would have remained even if he had lived another ten years). The reason for this is because it is open-ended.

Innis provided a wonderful map of what communications historiography could be. And for all its pseudoapocalyptic, speculative, quasitheological, proselytizing excess, McLuhan's probes regarding technology and culture remain some of the most sustained in the cultural theory of the twentieth century, at the crux between the modern and the postmodern, and have the opportunity (and do) to bridge the gap between Nietzsche, Mumford, and Heidegger and Baudrillard, Kittler, and Virilio.

It is up to the rest of us to use these maps to discover and explore the worlds they describe, and, in doing so, resurrect the specters of Innis and McLuhan, allowing them to join Marx and Heidegger. and once we are in the presence of the specter incarnate, once we have accepted the material realities of what they have to offer cultural studies, this will mark the end of the spectral, and we will be haunted no more.

But is this what we want, what we wish, what we desire—what we need? We need these specters, these ghosts. Is it really the goal to be haunted no more? We often consider an exorcism to be a removal, but how will this help us? This chapter has offered an understanding of communication in a manner that is at once historical (in the epochal sense), material, linked to spatial and temporal constraints and limitations, as well as both enabled and constrained by the techne and poiesis of the (post)modern lifeworld.

A phenomenological medium theory, coupled with an historical materialist understanding, offers a clarity with which we can glimpse this world. These ghosts of media and cultural studies don't haunt us, so much as we are simply standing on their shoulders. There can be no communication outside this discourse—one that links meaning with materiality and mediation with technology. Language itself is at the heart of this spectral turn, for, as Derrida reminds, there is no "before the machine" (technology), just as there can be no "before language" (communication) or "before capital" (materiality). "These machines," he writes, "have always been there, they are always there, even when they wrote by hand, even during so-called live conversation". The material nature of communication allows us to peer at the power of techne. And of all these modalities, all these glissandos, it is the spectral voice that will guide us into new worlds and new lives.

Chapter 8

Electronic Media of the 21st Century

Since the beginning of the 20th century, government has enacted various pieces of legislation that regulate the communications industry. Limited space on the electromagnetic spectrum has been the justification, or rationale, for regulating the communications industry. The limited frequency space prevents anyone from actually owning any portion of the spectrum. Proliferation of media other than broadcast, such as cable systems and the Internet, had weakened the limited-space argument. Along with amendments and revisions to regulatory legislation, there have been complete rewrites since the first communication legislation was enacted in 1910. Rapid technological advancements provided the requirement for such modifications and rewrites.

This chapter has two objectives. It first examines the development and enactment of the Telecommunications Act of 1996, which is a complete overhaul of telecommunications regulation. Accordingly, it examines the political and social issues debated between the legislative and executive branches of government before the new legislation was signed into law.

Second, this chapter explores the new issues and implications created by the passage of the legislation and its effects on the telecommunications industry in the 21st century. This exploratory chapter highlights only portions of the telecommunications act that relate to broadcast or cable regulation.

Other than acknowledging that telephone companies now can offer cable service, regulatory issues of the telephone industry in particular are not examined. Primarily, this chapter provides and examines highlights of regulatory changes relating to technology and programming issues in broadcasting and cable.

TELECOMMUNICATIONS ACT OF 1996

Despite the amendments and revisions that have been added throughout the years, Congress saw no choice but to completely replace the obsolete Communications Act of 1934. Because communication technology has grown by leaps and bounds over the last few years, the Communications Act of 1934 was considered an antiquated document.

Edmund L. Andrews states that advances "in technology and rapid change in the marketplace have made [the 1934 act] increasingly outdated and, many experts believe, [the 1934 act] has been harmful to competition and consumers." For that reason, Congress decided to replace the 1934 act with a new, more modern piece of legislation that would adequately regulate the electronic media of the 21st century.

While attempting to change current telecommunications regulatory legislation, both the Senate and the House of Representatives passed bills. Both bills had basically the same objective: "to allow all telecommunications companies to compete head to head in one another's markets, with as little government regulation as possible."

The leading supporters of the Senate bill, S. 652, included former Commerce Committee Chairman Larry Pressler (R-South Dakota) and Ernest Hollings (D-South Carolina). The Senate version of the bill passed 81 to 18 on June 15, 1995. On August 4, 1995, the House of Representatives; passed its version of the telecommunications bill (H.R. 1555) with a vote of 305 to 117.

The leading supporters of that bill were House Commerce Committee Chairman Thomas Bliley Jr. (R-Virginia) and Telecommunications and Finance Subcommittee Chairman Jack Fields (R-Texas).

A primary objective of both the Senate and House bills was to "promote competition in the telephone and cable markets while easing regulations on cable prices and broadcast-station ownership."

The debate for such a bill was "propelled by the widespread sentiment in Congress and the telecommunications industry that legislation is needed to spur competition and investment in advanced telecommunications networks."

A House and Senate conference was established to reconcile the differences between the two bills. The conference consisted of eleven senators and thirty-four representatives. Some of the committee members only addressed certain parts of the legislation. For the bill to replace the 1934 act several issues needed to be resolved.

There were specific issues that President Clinton stated he could not support in the House version of the bill. Furthermore, the Clinton administration stated that it was "committed to enactment of a telecommunications reform bill." Additionally, there was strong debate regarding the issue of what to do with the digital spectrum.

Television stations eventually will change from an analog channel to a digital channel, and former Senate Majority Leader Bob Dole (R-Kansas) wanted the remaining channels to be auctioned. There also is debate regarding the amount of spectrum the government plans to make available to broadcasters. Auctioning of the channels was expected to raise billions for the U.S. government.

After all of the negotiations, Congress passed the Telecommunications Bill on February 1, 1996. In the House the vote was 414 to 16, and in the Senate the vote was 91 to 5. After passage by Congress, the bill was sent to President Clinton, who signed it on February 8, 1996. In regard to the passage of the bill, Carney stated: "In the course of one afternoon.

The House and Senate swept away sixty-two years of telecommunications policy, paved the way for a more dynamic information superhighway, [and] suppressed decades of bickering between industries. This will be the biggest change in the government's role in communications since 1934."

TELECOMMUNICATIONS ACT HIGHLIGHTS

The Telecommunications Act of 1996 still requires broadcasters and cable companies to continue to observe the "public interest, convenience, and necessity" rule. As Krasnow, Longley, and Terry observe, the FCC' s powers to regulate are limited, at times, because of the fact that regulatory decisions must be based on the "public interest" standard.

The public interest standard is mentioned and maintained throughout the Telecommunications Act. As specific regulations are presented, there is some discussion regarding how well it was embraced by all parties involved in the process of creating the legislation.

BROADCAST OWNERSHIP

The primary issues that the House, Senate, and the president had trouble resolving included particulars relating to broadcast ownership. Both the Senate and the House wanted television national audience caps regarding broadcast ownership changed from 25% to 35%. Further, both the House and Senate wanted the ownership caps for radio to be eliminated completely.

After negotiations, it was determined that station ownership could not exceed 35% of the nation's TV homes. For radio, the national ownership limits were eliminated while the local ownership limits were relaxed.

The 1996 Act repealed the duopoly rule for radio station ownership, stipulating that in a market with forty-five or more stations an owner may operate eight stations, in a market with thirty to forty-four stations an owner may operate seven stations, in a market with fifteen to twenty-nine stations an owner may operate six stations, and in a market with fourteen or fewer stations an owner may operate five stations.

The Republicans pushed for even fewer regulations in

this area, but eventually accepted the suggestions of the Democrats. This caused some anger among those in the Republican party because of the perception that the Republicans allowed the Democrats to gain the upper hand with this issue and several others.

OPEN VIDEO SYSTEMS

Before the Telecommunications Act, there existed a "cross-ownership" restriction that prevented telephone companies from offering cable service in the same areas where they were offering telephone service. The cross-ownership restriction provided cable companies protection from the large, established telephone companies. The 1996 Act lifted the cross-ownership restriction in an effort "to stimulate local competition in the multi-channel video market."

The Act allows telephone companies to provide video services in one of four ways: (1) as an over-the-air provider; (2) as a common carrier; (3) as a cable television operator; or (4) as an open video service. The open video service is a newly created hybrid service(30) that allows telephone companies to offer video services and act as both a cable system and common carrier simultaneously.

The 1996 Act requires that if demand is greater than existing available space, the telephone company cannot control more than one third of its system's capacity. These open video systems are not franchised locally. Local authorities, however, are allowed a portion of the open video system's revenues, which is similar to franchise fees that cable operators are required to pay to municipalities.

Also, traditional cable systems may opt to offer video services via an open video system and thereby avoid many regulations that normally apply to cable systems and to avoid all of the regulations that apply to common carriers. Open video systems are required to provide channels to local noncommercial and commercial broadcasters.

Healey states that open video system operators must abide by cable regulations that do the following: (1) require the operator to pay for any commercially broadcast programs that it carried voluntarily; (2) bar the duplication of certain network, sports, and syndicated programs; (3) regulate contracts to transmit programs known as carriage agreements; (4) bar the billing of programming that customers had not requested but had not canceled either; (5) bar programme distribution arrangements that prevent competition; (6) protect customer's privacy; and (7) bar employment discrimination.

Unlike the regulatory issues discussed thus far, other issues required several months of negotiations. Before agreements were reached, the Senate and House of Representatives agreed upon several things rather early in the process:

- Broadcast licensing;
- Advanced television and spectrum flexibility;
- Direct broadcast satellite;
- Must-carry rules;
- V-chip and TV programme ratings;
- Cable deregulation;
- Signal scrambling for indecent programming;
- Cable right of refusal of public and leased-access programming;
- Closed captioning; and
- FCC funding.

BROADCAST LICENSING

The agreement reached regarding broadcast licensing extended the license terms for television and radio to eight years. The previously amended 1934 Act allowed for television licenses to be renewed every five years and radio every seven years.

The 1996 Act streamlines the license renewal process by automatically renewing broadcasters' licenses if: (1) the station has served the public interest standard; (2) if there have been no serious violations by the licensee of the rules and regulations of FCC; and (3) if there have been no other violations by the licensee that might constitute a pattern of abuse.

Competing applications are reviewed only if a license is not renewed. The 1996 Act also requires broadcasters to maintain a "summary" in their public files of all complaints they receive from viewers pertaining to violent programming.

ADVANCED TELEVISION SERVICES AND SPECTRUM FLEXIBILITY

The Telecommunications Act of 1996 allows the FCC to assign licenses for advanced television services, and the licenses are limited to existing television stations. Advanced television service is defined as digital broadcasts. If the broadcaster receives a second channel, then one of the two eventually must be returned to the U.S. government. The public interest requirement continues to apply to the second channel if one is assigned to the broadcaster.

Critics suggest that broadcasters are getting a "sweet" deal by having the new digital frequencies automatically assigned to them rather than having to purchase the rights to use the new frequencies. Former senator Bob Dole believed the provision was a multibillion dollar give-away.

Andrews stated, "Government officials estimate the licenses would be worth anywhere from $11 billion to $70 billion, if the Government auctioned them in the way it is doing for licenses to operate new wireless phone services."

DIRECT BROADCAST SATELLITE (DBS)

Complete control of "direct-to-home satellite services" is granted to the FCC under the Telecommunications Act of 1996. This prevents local communities, including homeowners associations, from prohibiting direct broadcast satellite dishes.

The must-carry rule was established in April 1965 and requires all cable companies to carry the signal of local stations within a sixty-mile radius of the system. The must-carry rule is maintained in the new telecommunications bill. The Telecommunications Act requires the FCC to act upon must-carry complaints within a 120 days of the filing date.

Additionally, the Act stipulates that markets are to be defined by commercial publications that delineate television markets based on viewing patterns (or Nielsen's Designated Market Area map) when considering the must-carry issue.

RESTRICTIONS ON OBSCENITY, INDECENCY, AND VIOLENCE

The 1996 Act established the fines for transmitting obscene, lewd, lascivious, filthy, or indecent material with intent to annoy, abuse, threaten, or harass another person at $250,000 for individuals and $500,000 for corporations. This includes broadcasting media, cable systems, and computer networks. Section 501 of the Telecommunications Act of 1996 is cited as the "Communications Decency Act of 1996."

Immediately after the Communications Decency Act was passed, there was a challenge as to whether it was constitutional. There were several lawsuits filed, and in mid-1996 at least two federal courts prevented its enforcement. In June of 1997, the Supreme Court, in a 7-to-2 decision, ruled that Internet communication indeed was protected by the First Amendment.

In Reno v. American Civil Liberties Union, the court stated that the Internet deserved the same protection as, media such as books, magazines, or newspapers. Thus, the Supreme Court essentially invalidated Title V of the Telecommunications Act.

The Supreme Court dismissed the government's argument that if children were not prevented from accessing indecent material over the Internet then the Internet would not grow to be an important and pervasive media outlet.

The government's rational was that the general public would not access the Internet because of the risk that children might be exposed to indecent material. The Supreme Court rejected this argument stating that it was unpersuasive.

V-CHIP AND TV PROGRAMME RATINGS

The Telecommunications Act requires television sets to be sold with a V-chip, or violence chip, which allows for the "ability to block programming based on an electronically encoded rating." The entertainment industry was required to develop a ratings system for "violence, sex and other indecent materials and to agree voluntarily to broadcast signals containing such ratings."

The bill requires the FCC to develop a ratings system if the industry fails to meet that requirement. The FCC was charged with the duty of overseeing the development of standards for blocking technologies.As a result of such findings, the Act states that there is a "compelling governmental interest" in providing parents the means to block such influences.

CABLE DEREGULATION

The 1996 Act deregulates cable rates for the expanded basic tier which usually includes such networks as MTV, Lifetime, ESPN, and Cable News Network. The cable companies are allowed to increase prices on the expanded basic tier within three years of the telecommunication bill's enactment (or on March 31, 1999).

The bill requires that equipment rates continue to be regulated. Further, the Act allows for the complete deregulation of small cable companies, defined as including 50,000 or fewer subscribers. The Act allows for cable systems to be free from rate regulation if "a telephone company offers cable service by any means that is comparable to the competing cable system."

SET-TOP BOXES

With the 1996 Telecommunications Act, consumers now are able to purchase their own set-top boxes in retail stores. Cable companies are allowed to continue providing set-top boxes, but they no longer may subsidize the boxes by subscription fees. Discussion over this issue caused the "first major impasse" on the telecommunications bill.

Cable companies opposed the sale of set-top boxes in retail stores, asserting that it would "freeze the current technology in place." The new rules regarding set-top boxes were designed to prevent theft of cable services. The rules expire in a market where: (1) there are competing multichannel video providers, (2) there are competing sources of set-top boxes, and (3) where the rules stifle competition and do not promote the public interest standard.

SIGNAL SCRAMBLING FOR INDECENT PROGRAMMING

The bill requires cable operators to scramble any audio or video of programming that subscribers deem "unsuitable" for children. This service must be provided at no extra cost to the subscriber.

CABLE RIGHT OF REFUSAL OF PUBLIC AND LEASED-ACCESS PROGRAMMING

Under the new bill, cable companies can refuse to broadcast programs that contain "obscenity, nudity, or indecency."

CLOSED CAPTIONING

The Federal Communications Commission was required to look into the possibility of making closed captioning a requirement for video programming. The Telecommunications Act of 1996 stipulated that the FCC can waive the requirement for certain classes of programs if closed captioning is economically burdensome.

FCC FUNDING

Finally, the bill authorizes appropriations needed by the FCC to carry out the provisions of the 1996 Act. Quello' s comment could not have been more foreshadowing. Others held similar opinions regarding the future of telecommunications regulation.

Approximately a year after Quello's remark, both the Senate and the House of Representatives introduced different versions of a bill that essentially would do exactly what Quello suggested, that is, modernize the regulatory framework under which the entire telecommunications sector operates.

Simply put, modernization was needed because when the Communications Act of 1934 was enacted, telephone, telegraph, and radio defined the field. Today, "television, cable, cellular, and satellite only scratch the surface of modern digital telecommunications." Hence, a new piece of legislation was needed to accommodate technological advances.

The Telecommunications Act of 1996 serves as that modernized regulatory framework for the telecommunications industry that Quello suggested is needed to help in the proliferation of new media. The 1996 legislation essentially creates "one marketplace for telecommunications services " Technological developments will transform the multimedia world as we know it today.

The Telecommunications Act of 1996 attempts to regulate media as a whole rather than as individual entities. Chong suggested this approach was needed for there to be a healthy and prosperous development of multimedia technology in the United States. To illustrate how just one aspect of the telecommunications bill attempts to converge the electronic media, examine the overlapping markets of the telephone and cable companies.

The cable companies will be allowed to offer telephone services and the telephone companies will be allowed to offer cable services. Fundamentally, the 1996 Act takes a deregulatory approach and relies on the marketplace as a control over electronic media policies and procedures. The telecommunication legislation diminishes barriers that have prevented widespread competition and work toward the convergence of all media.

Because of the belief that competition is good, the Act allows for competition between and among different telecommunication outlets. As one could expect, new competition is not welcomed by the entire electronic media industry.

For example, the industry opposed the cable-telco cross-ownership rules. Only time will allow observers of the telecommunications industry to determine the new legislation's effectiveness. The Telecommunications Act has created an ironic juxtaposition. Technology and programming were specific areas that the new legislation attempts to deregulate, or regulate in certain circumstances (e.g., violent programming).

The foundation of the legislation is built upon deregulatory theory. Head, et al. Suggest that there are many motives fueling efforts to deregulate, such as a need to discard outdated rules, simplify complex rules, ensure that rules actually can achieve their intended objective, and lighten administrative roles.

Additionally, they suggest that deregulation also originates from ideological motives stemming from the belief that the government should play a limited role in the everyday lives of Americans. This approach relies on the marketplace to regulate industries.

Yet the marketplace approach of regulating industries does not always work effectively. On one hand, the Telecommunications Act of 1996 essentially promotes the convergence of technology by disassembling the cross-ownership restriction and by establishing specific regulations regarding the promotion of direct broadcast satellite, set-top boxes, closed captioning, and cable deregulation.

On the other hand, it attempts to regulate programming through must-carry rules, v-chip technology, signal scrambling for indecent programming, and cable right of refusal of public and leased-access programming.

Meyerson suggests that if "these new combinations do not compete with one another, then the Act may have only permitted the creation of large, deregulated monopolists (or oligopolists)." Monopolies were just what the Clinton administration wanted to prevent.

Finally, another juxtaposition includes the requirement that programme ratings be implemented. The industry was required to create a ratings system that would be content-based and would alert parents about programming they might want to prevent their children from viewing by way of the new v-chip.

Initially, the industry created ratings that were age-based. Critics argued that the age-based system would not provide enough information to make a decision.

The industry argued that content-based ratings would be confusing and that advertisers might not want advertise during programming that had a perceived negative rating. Eventually, the industry adopted a content-based ratings system. Overall, it will require time to determine the effectiveness of the Telecommunications Act of 1996.

Chapter 9

Audience Valuation and Minority Media

All advertiser-supported media Organizations operate in what is best described as a dual product marketplace. That is, media organizations produce one product—media content—that is either given away or sold in an effort to attract the second product—audiences. The attention of these audiences is then sold to advertisers seeking consumer exposure to commercial messages. The audience and content markets are tightly inter-related. Success or failure in the "content market" is dependent upon success or failure in the "audience market" and vice versa.

For this reason, policymaking involving the preservation and enhancement of competition and diversity of sources and content within the media industries has been—and continues to be—guided by research on how various market and institutional factors affect what media organizations are able to charge for their audiences.

One recent manifestation of this general concern with source and content diversity involves the viability of minority-owned media outlets. Per the directive of Congress (Telecommunications Act of 1996), the Federal Communications Commission (1996) initiated an investigation into the barriers affecting minority-owned media outlets and the associated availability of minority-targeted programming.

One of the barriers that may face minority-owned and -targeted media outlets is the possibility that minority audiences are valued at a much lower level by advertisers than majority audiences. If this is the case, then minority-targeted media outlets face a substantial hurdle to remaining viable, as their ability to monetize their audience is compromised by lower advertiser valuations of their target audience. Lower audience values lead to lower revenues, lower levels of investment in programming, and an overall diminished ability for such outlets to compete and remain viable.

In this way, the nature of the content market (in terms of the diversity of available sources and content offerings) is affected by the dynamics of the audience market. This study investigates the possibility of lower valuations of minority audiences through a quantitative analysis of the determinants of the value of commercial radio station audiences.

MINORITY MEDIA AND DIVERSITY POLICY

The general policy imperative that drives concerns about the viability of minority-targeted media outlets stems from policymakers' long-standing commitment to diversity in the sources of information and the content that these sources provide.

The diversity principle extends, in part, from the traditional democratic theory notion of a well-functioning "marketplace of ideas," in which citizens' abilities to participate effectively in the democratic process are contingent upon their abilities to consider a wide array of ideas and viewpoints from a wide array of sources.

Diversity concerns have economic motivations, as well, since policymakers have sought to maximize the choices available to media consumers, thereby increasing their overall satisfaction.

The availability of content targeting minority interests has long been perceived as an important means of providing such content diversity. As the FCC (1948) noted as far back as 1948, "It has long been an established policy of the Commission that the American system of broadcasting must serve significant minorities among our population". Research has demonstrated that minority audiences focus much of their media consumption on minority-targeted programming and outlets—and even increase their media consumption—when such services are available.

This suggests that such content is highly valued by its target audience. It is important to emphasize that such diversity is seen as benefiting not only those who are targeted by minority-appeal content, but those whose tastes are "majoritarian" as well.

For the "marketplace of ideas" to enhance citizen knowledge and the consideration of diverse viewpoints, citizens must be exposed to diverse points of view. It has been argued that this exposure diversity is particularly vital within the context of minority media so that greater cultural understanding and social cohesion can be achieved.

In an effort to identify the potential barriers facing minority-targeted media content, the FCC commissioned a study of the value of minority audiences to advertisers. The results of this study raised the possibility that advertisers may place significantly lower values on minority audiences and that these lower valuations may arise, in part, from advertiser misconceptions about minority spending patterns and product purchasing decisions.

A recent NTIA survey raised similar concerns about the challenges associated with selling minority audiences to advertisers (National Telecommunications and Information Administration, 2000).

The NTIA survey found that minority broadcast station owners cited obtaining advertising as their most common difficulty.

Lower advertiser valuations of minority audiences have significant implications for the viability of minority-targeted media outlets since the provision of minority-targeted content potentially involve financial challenges not faced if more mainstream content options are pursued.

In such a situation, the diversity of content long valued by policymakers can be undermined by the valuations placed upon different segments of the media audience by advertisers.

AUDIENCE VALUATION

Those minority audiences may be valued at a lower level than majority audiences may be a reflection of the basic economics of the audience marketplace. Advertisers typically value various audience segments differently, based upon their demographic characteristics. These demographic characteristics are presumed to correlate with purchasing power and purchasing behaviour.

Thus, for instance, younger audience members generally are valued more highly than older audience members (i.e., 50+) due to factors such as their presumed greater inclination to switch brands, their higher levels of disposable income, and their lower levels of availability in the media audience. Income is another important factor that guides advertiser valuations of media audiences.

Some products and services are likely only to be purchased by consumers of certain income levels. For this reason, advertisers frequently will use income as a variable by which to screen out certain media outlets. There are a number of possible reasons why ethnicity may factor into audience valuations as well. To a certain degree, ethnicity correlates with income.

The median family income for Whites is almost $46,000, compared with approximately $30,000 for African Americans and $33,000 for Hispanics. Thus, advertisers seeking higher-income consumers may avoid minority-targeted media outlets. It is also the case that African Americans and Hispanics consume significantly more television and radio on a weekly basis than Whites.

The associated greater ease with which minorities can be reached by advertising messages may reduce their value to advertisers. Finally, some within the minority media community argue that advertisers form their valuations of minority audiences on the basis of severe misconceptions about minority product preferences and purchasing habits, which leads to a devaluing of minority audiences.

Regardless of the reason, there is a growing body of evidence that such "minority discounts" do exist. Ofori's analysis of commercial radio stations found that stations with formats that targeted minority audiences earned less for their audiences than stations with general interest formats.

However, because this analysis focused only on formats, and not on audience composition, no strong conclusions regarding the relationship between audience composition and audience valuation could be drawn. An earlier analysis by Webster and Phalen found that greater proportions of non-Whites in a market had a significant negative relationship with the average cost of reaching 1,000 television viewers within a market.

This analysis controlled for income variations across markets, suggesting that ethnicity was not simply a proxy for income. The Webster and Phalen study focused on advertiser expenditures at the market level, leaving open the question of the existence of such effects at the outlet level.

No research has, at this point, directly examined the relationship between actual demographic composition of media outlets' audiences and advertiser valuations of these audiences to see if there is a significant relationship between audience ethnicity and audience value. The study presented here attempts to fill this gap through an analysis of a sample of commercial radio stations.

It is important to emphasize that lower valuations of minority audiences may make economic sense from an advertiser's perspective. Regardless, such lower valuations may undermine the viability of minority-targeted media content. Such impediments to the economic viability of minority-targeted media could undermine the principles of source and content diversity that long have been objectives of electronic media regulation in the United States.

Given the nature of the policy issue, this analysis utilizes a dependent variable—the power ratio—that provides an indication of the extent to which an individual station is capable of monetizing its audience. Power ratios are computed by dividing a radio station's share of the total radio advertising expenditures in its market by its share of the total radio listening audience in that market. Thus, a power ratio greater than 1 suggests that a station is able to capture a share of advertising dollars that exceeds its share of the total audience.

Such a station is "overselling" its audience. A station with a power ratio of less than 1 is capturing a share of advertising dollars that is lower than its share of the listening audience. Such a station is "underselling" its audience. Because the power ratio controls for audience share, it provides a measure that is uniquely well suited to assessing the impact of audience composition on audience value.

Power ratio data were obtained from the 1999 Media Access Pro commercial database produced by BIA Research. For the regression analysis, the natural log of the power ratio was used as the dependent variable. This transformation was conducted in accordance with the conclusions of Bates' research into the various methods and models employed in the analysis of the value of broadcast audiences, which found models employing such a transformation to be both theoretically appropriate and to provide a better fit to the data than models without such a transformation.

An emphasis on audience composition has been maintained for the independent variables, as well. Station power ratios for 1999 are regressed against Fall 1999 Arbitron data on the demographic composition of individual stations' audiences. Thus, instead of incorporating each station's ratings or share points, or raw number of listeners for the different demographic groups listening to each station, this analysis employs percent composition data.

Arbitron provides data on the percentage of each station's audience that is comprised of various demographic groups (according to age, gender, and ethnicity). Thus, for example, Station A's audience may be 40% African American, while Station B's audience may be 80% African American. Clearly, such figures provide no indication of which station has the larger number of African-American listeners. Station A may reach more African Americans than Station B if Station A's total audience is much larger.

The use of pure composition figures was deemed most

appropriate given the nature of the dependent variable. Using raw numbers or rating/share points would not as effectively address the issue of the viability of minority-targeted media outlets, given that minority-targeted media outlets are not defined in terms of audience size, but in terms of the extent to which the composition of the outlets' audiences consists of minorities.

Arbitron breaks down each station's audience into men and women for seven age Categories. Arbitron provides data on the average quarter-hour percentage of each station's 6:00 a.m.-to-midnight audience that is comprised of each of these demographic categories.

For the purposes of this analysis, these demographic categories were collapsed to produce two independent variables: (a) the percentage of a station's audience comprised of men within the ages of 18 to 54, and (b) the percentage of a station's audience comprised of women within the ages of 18 to 54. These two demographic categories roughly represent the audience groups with the highest demonstrated value to advertisers.

Thus, it is presumed that there will be a positive relationship between MEN1854 and WOM1854 and station power ratios. Broadcast band was included as a dummy variable (AMFM; 0 = AM; 1 = FM) to account for the likelihood that FM stations are able to charge more for their audiences than AM stations because of the better sound quality of FM signals.

The station's average quarter-hour share (6:00 a.m. to midnight) of the listening audience (SHARE) also was included as an independent variable to account for the possibility of advertisers paying a premium for larger audiences, independent of the composition of those audiences. Although this analysis focuses on the issue of audience composition, research has suggested that advertisers will pay more on a per audience member basis for larger audiences.

Such patterns may be due to the efficiencies derived from engaging in fewer transactions in order to reach the desired number of consumers. Or, this premium may be derived from the value advertisers associate with the likely greater reach of a single ad placement relative to two ad placements that achieve the same level of audience exposure.

In the latter case, there is the possibility that some consumers appeared in both audiences (unless the advertisements are run simultaneously on different channels), thus the overall reach in the latter case is lower. To capture the ethnic composition of each station's audience, the two composition-based ethnicity variables provided by Arbitron were employed.

The first of these is the percentage of a station's average quarter-hour audience that is African American (AQBLACK). The second is the percentage of a station's average quarter-hour audience that is Hispanic (AQHISP). It is important to note that Arbitron does not report ethnic composition for stations in all of the markets that it measures, but only in those markets where there is a significant minority population; nor does the company provide data on ethnic groups other than African Americans and Hispanics in any of its markets.

A number of market-level variables were included as control variables to account for the possibility that station power ratios vary in accordance with market size and demographic fluctuations. Two ethnicity variables (percent Hispanic in the station's market [HISPANIC]; percent African American in the station's market [BLACK]) were included, as was per capita income in the station's market (PERCAP).

Market size was controlled using total radio advertising revenues in the market (MARKETREV). This variable was very highly correlated with other potential measures of market size, such as total population and number of radio stations in the market. The use of a market-size variable that most directly reflected market value was deemed most appropriate, given the nature of the issues being addressed.

The inclusion of these market-level independent variables addresses the possibility that variations in market size and demographics affect audience share and revenue share (the two components of the power ratio) disproportionately, independent of a station's audience composition. Perhaps a more likely relationship involves possible interaction effects between audience ethnicity and market conditions.

Thus, for instance, the extent to which African-American/ Hispanic audience composition affects audience value may be different in markets with higher African-American/ Hispanic compositions than in markets with lower African-American/Hispanic compositions, given the different supply and demand dynamics for African-American/ Hispanic audiences in markets that are heavily African American/ Hispanic versus those that are not.

Similarly, in larger or wealthier markets, advertiser demand for African-American/Hispanic audiences may be different than in smaller or less wealthy markets. For these reasons, six interaction terms were created.

Two inter action terms were created for interactions between audience ethnic composition and market ethnic composition to address the possibility that the effect of audience ethnicity on audience value varies in accordance with market ethnic composition, Two interaction terms also were created for interactions between audience ethnic composition and market size to account for the possibility that the effect of audience ethnic composition on audience value varies in accordance with market size.

Finally, two interaction terms were created for interactions between audience ethnic composition and market per capita income to account for the possibility that the effect of audience ethnic composition on audience value varies in accordance with per capita income in a station's market.

Utilizing interaction terms typically raises problems of multicollinearity between the main effect independent variables and their associated interaction terms. The recommended procedure for reducing such multicollinearity problems is to "centre" each main effect independent variable used in the computation of the interaction terms.

Centreing involves subtracting the independent variable mean from the independent variable value for each case. These centreed independent variables were then used as the main effect variables in the multivariate analysis and to compute the interaction term used in the multivariate analysis.

Although it would have been desirable to also incorporate data on the average income levels of the audience members for each station studied, such data were not available via the data sources obtained for this analysis. As was noted above, station-level audience income delta are not part of Arbitron's syndicated reports (the reports obtained for this study) and are only available to Arbitron clients for an additional fee.

This limited availability of audience income data even to advertisers likely limits the extent to which such data are employed in radio buying decisions. Regardless, such data would have made it possible to separate the effects of income from the effects of ethnicity.

Given, as was noted above, that ethnicity is correlated with income, it is possible that advertisers are using ethnicity solely as a proxy for income. Although previous research has provided evidence that contradicts this assumption, the analysis presented here cannot address this issue directly.

However, as was noted above, even if lower valuations of minority audiences are largely a function of lower income levels, such lower valuations still could undermine the source and content diversity that policymakers traditionally have sought as well as the provision of content serving minority interests and concerns.

Finally, it is important to address a number of limitations in the scope of the database. First, Arbitron does not measure all radio stations in the United States. Of the roughly 13,000 radio stations in the United States, only about 6,000 are in Arbitron-defined and measured radio markets.

Moreover, as was noted above, Arbitron does not provide data on the ethnic composition of station audiences for all of the radio markets it measures. Generally, Arbitron only provides such data in markets where there is a significant minority population. These factors limit the number of stations eligible for analysis and weight the stations included in this analysis toward those in markets with large African-American and Hispanic populations.

The number of eligible stations was limited further by the fact that not all commercial radio stations report their revenues to BIA Research (BIA's reported response rate is roughly 80%). In cases where station revenues are not reported, it is impossible to compute the power ratio that serves as the dependent variable for this analysis.

Due to these limitations, within this data set there is a total of 810 stations with Hispanic audience composition (and revenue) data, 1430 with African-American composition (and revenue) data, and a total of 461 commercial radio stations with reported revenues and with both African-American and Hispanic audience composition data available.

It is this latter set of stations that is the focus of this analysis as these stations represent the only context in which it is possible to investigate simultaneously the effects of both of the minority-audience characteristics at issue on audience value.

In sum, while previous research has explored the relationship between audience ethnicity and audience value via market-level demographic data, market-level CPMs, and differences in power ratios across programme formats, the approach outlined here moves beyond these approaches by directly examining the relationship between the audience composition of individual media outlets and their ability to successfully compete for available advertising dollars.

The mean power ratio of stations that target minority audiences was first compared to the mean power ratio of stations that do not target minority audiences. For the purposes of this analysis, minority-targeted stations were defined as those stations for which the majority of the station's average quarter-hour audience (i.e., greater than 50%) is comprised of African-American and/or Hispanic listeners. In this means comparison, stations with a minority audience of greater than 50% (n = 121) have an average power ratio of.82, compared with an average power ratio of 1.06 for other stations (n = 340).

This difference is statistically significant at the.01 level. As these results suggest, minority-targeted stations tend to undersell their audiences, meaning that their share of the total radio audience is greater than their share of the total radio advertising revenues in their markets.

Of particular importance is the fact that correlations between the main effect variables and their associated interaction terms generally are modest. Before these variables were centreed, some of the correlations between main effect and interaction terms were as high as.90, a level indicative of a potentially serious multicollinearity problem.

There remain, however, a few strong correlations between some of the interaction terms. There is a similarly strong correlation between the Hispanic versions of these interaction terms. However, tolerance statistics for all four of these independent variables are reasonably high (ranging from.39 to.52), alleviating concerns about multicollinearity in the multivariate analysis.

Hierarchical regression was employed due to the inclusion of interaction terms. When working with interaction terms, hierarchical regression is necessary in order to determine whether the interaction terms provide significant explanatory power beyond that provided by the main effect variables.

Using hierarchical regression in this context also makes it possible to better examine the relative contribution of market-level versus station-level independent variables. (Given the nature of the dependent variable, it was presumed that station-level independent variables would provide greater explanatory power than market-level independent variables).

The first set of independent variables entered into the model was the market-level control variables. These variables alone explain none of the variance in station power ratios. There is a negative relationship between modulation type and power ratios, with AM status having a negative effect on power ratios.

Both the MEN1854 and WOM1854 demographic

composition variables are positively related to power ratios, indicating that the greater the extent to which a station's audience is composed of men and women 18 to 54, the greater the station's power ratio. A station's overall audience share (SHARE) also is positively related to a station's power ratio, providing evidence that sellers of audiences are able to charge a premium on a per audience member basis for larger audiences.

Finally, in terms of ethnicity, both the AQHISP and AQBLACK variables are negatively related to power ratios, suggesting that ethnic composition exerts a downward pressure on a radio station's ability to monetize its audience. The magnitude of the beta coefficients indicates that the age/gender independent variables are the most important in terms of explanatory power, followed by the ethnicity variables. The AQBLACK and AQHISP coefficients are similar in size, though African-American audience composition seems to exert a slightly stronger downward pressure on audience value than Hispanic audience composition.

The six interaction terms were added to the equation. The addition of interaction terms explains only an additional 5% of the variance in the dependent variable (the adjusted R2 increases from.32 to.37); however, this improvement in explanatory power is significant at the.01 level.

Only one of the six interaction terms is statistically significant. The significant negative coefficient for the AQHISP*MARKREV interaction term indicates that the magnitude of the negative relationship between Hispanic audience composition and station power ratios decreases slightly as market size increases.

The analyses presented here represent the next step forward in determining the extent to which advertiser valuations of minority audiences affect the viability of minority-owned and minority-targeted media outlets. The results conform to those of previous studies, which found that minority audiences are more difficult to monetize than non-minority audiences.

This study also has extended previous research by

examining the value of minority audiences at the level of individual media outlets and by employing detailed data on the demographic composition of the audiences for those outlets. Future research should seek to better separate possible income effects from ethnicity effects.

From a media policy standpoint, however, whether lower valuations of minority audiences are purely a function of income or also are a function of other factors such as advertiser perceptions of minority spending and product usage patterns, the implications for diversity in the electronic media are the same—the viability of minority-targeted media content suffers.

It is important that these findings be placed within the broader context of the economics of minority media. Minority-targeted media content suffers from not only the potentially lower valuations of minority audiences but also the fact that, by definition, it appeals to a small audience. Smaller audiences mean smaller revenues, particularly when the audience is not highly valued by advertisers (if the small audience segment being targeted is highly valued by advertisers, then, of course, revenue potential increases).

Recall that this analysis also found that stations with larger audiences are able to charge more on a Per audience member basis than stations with smaller audiences, a finding that further illustrates the compounding negative consequences of being a niche programmer. These economic handicaps result in lower incentives to produce such programming and, consequently, lower levels of availability of such programming.

Moreover, lower levels of audience size and value both exert downward pressures on the production budgets of minority content, which further undermine the ability of such content to compete and remain viable. The smaller and less valuable the potential audience for a media product is, the smaller the likely investment in programming. At the same time, research shows that audiences are drawn to content with higher production budgets over content with smaller production budgets.

Together, these processes create a situation in which minority content loses some of its appeal—even to minority audiences—relative to majority content. The differential in production budgets may be enough for some minority audience members to find the majority content more appealing than the content targeted at their particular interests and concerns.

Such defections further undermine the viability of minority-targeted content and contribute to the availability of minority audiences in non-minority content that further discourages advertisers from advertising on minority-targeted media outlets. In the end, the lower valuations that advertisers place on minority audiences feed into an economic process that works against minority-targeted content being able to compete and remain viable in both the audience and content markets.

The end result is lower levels of availability of minority-targeted content. This Perspective suggests that policymakers seeking—at the general level—to preserve and promote diversity of sources and content in the electronic media, and seeking—at the specific level—to promote minority ownership of media outlets and the production of minority-targeted content, need to investigate new strategies and tactics.

Previous policy initiatives, such as minority preferences in the license allocation process and minority tax certificates, have focused on increasing the likelihood of minorities becoming owners of media outlets.

The results presented here suggest that if policymakers want to preserve and promote minority-targeted media outlets, their efforts may need to address the barriers not only to establishing such media outlets but also to maintaining the financial viability of such outlets once they are established.

Possible mechanisms might include subsidies for minority-targeted media outlets or education campaigns designed to counter any advertiser misconceptions about minority media audiences that may be driving down their value.

Of course, such recommendations are premised upon the

notion that existing levels of minority-targeted media content are not sufficient.

Whether—and to what extent—this is the case is a question that is beyond the scope of this analysis. The analyses presented here suggest that the economic handicaps associated with targeting minority audiences may lead to a disconnect between the availability of minority audiences and the availability of minority-targeted media content. Future research should explore this issue in greater detail.

However, in order to effectively address this issue, and the necessity of a policy response, policymakers need to work toward establishing more concrete objectives in terms of the desired levels of both ownership and content diversity in the electronic media marketplace.

Chapter 10

Preparing the Next Generation of Journalists

The news industry has been undergoing a fundamental paradigm shift since the end of last century. An increasing number of media companies around the United States, such as the Washington Post in Washington, DC, Media General in Virginia, the Tribune Company in Chicago, and New England Cable News, have taken solid steps to merge different media such as newspapers, television stations, radio stations, and online journalism companies to disseminate news content on multiple media platforms.

As a result, in a metropolitan area, one company would own print, TV, and online venues. Media call this industrial trend "media convergence," though the concept means much more than media mergers. Media convergence muddies the lines among broadcast journalism, print journalism, and online journalism, leaving college journalism educators to wonder whether traditional journalism programs have become dinosaurs.

After surveying 200 newspaper publishers worldwide, the World Association of Newspapers (WAN) found, "Despite a somewhat gloomy outlook for wholesale convergence in media companies worldwide in the near term, convergence is already being implemented with varying degrees of enthusiasm and speed among the world's media companies".

The Innovation International Media Consulting Group estimates that at least 100 of the world's multiple media companies are planning and implementing integration strategies. South and Nicholson drew a sketch of a converged media company:

Daily journalists need to embrace the 24-hour news cycle, with continuous deadlines. And the story needs to be reported and produced for a multi-platform audience. That may mean delivering content first to the Web and cell phones, a streaming video broadcast later in the day, a TV talk-back interview still later, and a "second day" interpretive story for the next morning's newspaper.

Dominic Gates (2002) pointed out, "Convergence with broadcast and online media is the shape of things to come for newspapers." The trend remains controversial. Critics complain that such cross-ownership of both a television station and a newspaper in the same market is a threat to democracy because it limits the number of voices1.

Delegates of the Communication Workers of America, a 60,000-member guild, passed a resolution in June of 2002 at the group's annual convention in Las Vegas, pledging to increase public awareness about the risks of ongoing media convergence. The delegates complained that shrinking media markets are a threat to editorial diversity and job security.

In 1975, the Federal Communications Commission (FCC) ruled that no new broadcast licenses would be granted to companies that own a major daily newspaper and a local television station in the same city. Fairness & Accuracy In Reporting (FAIR) calls on the FCC to roll back limits on media consolidation. The Newspaper Association of America (NAA), on the other hand, has asked the FCC to appeal the rule. On June 2, 2003, the FCC voted 3 to 2 to relax or eliminate some ownership restrictions, such as a rule barring media companies from owning television stations in markets where they publish daily newspapers.

Although some lawmakers and advocacy groups are still fighting in the courts and on Capitol Hill to overturn the FCC's new media ownership rules, these rules will be likely to encourage cross-media ownership in the years to come.

The mergers have raised questions about whether they are good for the craft of journalism itself. Critics complain that by requiring journalists to be jacks of both trades, print and broadcast, the journalists will be masters of none.

Robert J. Haiman, president emeritus of The Poynter Institute, compared the media convergence trend to an Amphicar, a cross between a boat and a car. The Amphicar, hawked in Florida during the 1950s, flopped. "It flopped because people quickly discovered that while it really was an ingenious combination of a car and a boat, it was a lousy car (because it also had to be a boat), and it was a lousy boat (because it also had to be a car)".

Willingly or unwillingly, many news practitioners' functions are gradually changing or are expected to change as media convergence rolls on. For a reporter in a converged media environment, knowing how to write is probably no longer enough. S/he could be expected to write the same story for different media in a timely manner.

Ideally, s/he can readily talk in front of a video camera. As a photographer, knowing how to tell a story both in video and in still images is more and more in demand. A designer should know how to prepare still graphics for print, moving graphics for television and dynamic graphics for the Web. At the online version of the Chicago Tribune, for instance, staffers are supposed to cover stories, take pictures, operate video cameras, and create digital pages.

The editors, too, need a wider variety of skills than the traditional paper editors. Along with infrastructure changes and the attempt to create synergy among the various media outlets, a new breed of journalists-digital or multimedia journalists-is expected.

As media jobs become more demanding, some news practitioners are beginning to team up to complete projects. At the same time, fear, confusion, and frustration from news practitioners are creeping into newsrooms. Carr wrote: "Convergence frightens many people who wonder whether their current skill sets have prepared them for-or will even be needed in-that great undiscovered country, the future.

This is probably the primary reason why I still find such great hostility to convergence among certain journalists."

Killebrew (2001), a mass communications professor from the University of South Florida, suggested that "journalists must be prepared to either crosstrain themselves or seek training from other sources while management must be prepared to give them the opportunities and time to do so."

The 1999-2000 president of the Association for Schools of Journalism and Mass Communication (ASJMC), Shirley Staples Carter, questioned whether, in the midst of the "Internet revolution," programs are prepared to educate journalists of the future. When specifically talking about writing, Keith Hartenberger, manager of news and programming for Tribune Regional Programming, said that journalism schools should make their students aware of the many ways to present the news.

"It's a multimedia world out there," he said. "If you're just being prepared to write newspaper stories, you won't be prepared". "At some point, this [cross-media training] is something we're going to expect from everyone".

Media convergence, as a trend that is gradually shaping the landscape of the media industry in the new century, has called into question the conventional journalism school practice of having separate tracks-print, broadcast, etc. Journalism educators around the country also are trying to figure out what they should do, if anything, to better prepare students for the converged media.

For instance, should journalism educators consider merging different sequences such as magazine, newspaper, broadcast, and photojournalism, or still teach all such courses as if they were unrelated media? "Traditionally defined segments of the communications industry are less and less distinguishable for technological and market convergence," observed Moon.

Are college journalism educators themselves both theoretically equipped and technologically prepared to teach their students for converged media? What do media companies expect from future news practitioners? What do current news practitioners in converged media feel is lacking? For both news practitioners and professors, the two most urgent questions cry for answers: Should journalism schools train specialists or fit for-all generalists? And how should college journalism education balance the teaching of critical thinking and technical skills?

Apart from all these education-related questions, we are also interested in finding out what are the driving forces behind the media mergers, who are regarded as the beneficiaries of this trend, and how people's political beliefs are related to their attitude toward teaching media convergence in colleges? These questions pertain closely to college journalism education, which has been the subject of debate and criticism for two decades.

A national survey was conducted among colleges, daily newspapers, and commercial television stations to explore the issue of how journalism schools should prepare students for the trend of media convergence from the perspectives of news editors, news professionals, and journalism professors. The study measured the level of general support for convergence education and determined if a new model of journalism education was called for.

If so, it examined whether consensus existed among the three groups on the direction educators should take when revisiting programme designs. Where consensus was not apparent, divisions among the sample of educators, editors, and reporters were defined. The goal of the study is to provide evidence that will help journalism educators make informed decisions about how to respond to media convergence in their curricula and courses and lay an empirical foundation for further discussions and conversations about media convergence.

The search results show that media convergence is a comparatively new topic in media research, though articles about it have inundated the Internet, magazines, and newspapers. Most research writings appeared no earlier than 1998. Many writings have addressed one of the toughest questions: What is media convergence? How to define "media convergence" had a direct bearing on how we conducted this study. Out of these writings, we identified four categories of media convergence that directly affect how journalism will be taught in colleges.

CONTENT CONVERGENCE

As Tremayne noted, decades ago, the term media convergence referred to the content convergence between competing newspapers and even among newspapers, magazines, and television. Today, pure content convergence continues on the Internet. For instance, the St. Petersburg Times has incorporated local Channel 10's TV news into its online newspaper though they are independent business entities. In other words, media convergence may not necessarily be tied to media merger.

Form convergence (or technological convergence). Around the mid-1990s, as Tremayne and Wurtz noted, computer technology and Internet technology made possible the convergence of all forms of mediated communications including video, audio, data, text, still photo, and graphic art for "on-demand" audiences.

Using these different forms to tell news stories on the World Wide Web has been widely regarded as the future of mass communication regardless of the fact that most online news sites have had a hard time making ends meet, let alone making a profit. Form convergence, often called technological convergence, has been a fundamental force to guide and lead convergence in the market, industry, and regulation.

CORPORATE CONVERGENCE

Since the late 1990s, media convergence has been escalated to the level of media mergers. The News Centre located in Tampa, Florida, owned by Media General, and the Tribune Interactive, owned by the Tribune Company, for instance, are the products of media mergers.

In The News Centre, WFLA-TV, The Tampa Tribune, and Tampa Bay Online operate out of the same building. They share daily tips and information, spot news, photography, enterprise reporting, franchises, events, and public service. Each of the three entities in The News Centre has its own independent newsroom, but they issued a joint statement of coverage principles, titled "News Centre Pledge".

The Tribune Interactive has brought together the interactive functions of the company's four newspapers and more than a score of television stations including WGN-TV and CLTV. The individual media outlets have their own newsgathering staff, but their coverage is enhanced by their multimedia desks in the Chicago Tribune newsroom and the Tribune Media Centre in Washington.

"A synergy-team of print editors and TV news veterans at the Chicago Tribune work together to manage resource sharing and the relationship". Media merger has made both content convergence and form convergence handy. Corporate convergence via vertical and horizontal integration, mergers, alliances, and acquisitions will make traditionally defined segments of the communications industry less and less distinguishable.

Role convergence. Russial identified several examples of role convergence in newsrooms. For instance, the roles of reporter and librarian, the roles of copyeditor and compositor, the roles of graphic artist and Web designer, and the roles of photo editor, darkroom technician, and photographer are all converging in different media.

In more recent years, content convergence, form convergence, and especially corporate convergence have sparked more in-depth role convergence among news practitioners.

For instance, Victoria Lim from The News Centre in Tampa revealed at a February 2002 conference on media convergence at the University of Florida that she primarily works as a television reporter for WFLA-TV, but she also has to write for the company's newspaper, The Tampa Tribune, as a senior consumer investigative reporter and for the Web company TBO.com on a daily basis; at the time of the conference, she was working on 31 stories.

A newspaper reporter may also produce a newspaper in QuarkXPress or serve as a TV news anchor, while a newspaper photographer may shoot video stories or produce interactive online stories in Flash. Role convergence requires that both reporters and editors re-equip themselves both journalistically and technologically.

Of the four types of convergence, role convergence has the most direct effect on future journalism education. Within the media industry, there are serious doubts about whether training cross-media journalists is possible or desirable. When asked whether reporters of the future must be equally skilled in print, TV, and online, Forrest Carr, news director of WFLA-TV at The News Centre in Tampa, said no.

He said he believed that there would always be areas of specialization and students may still choose specialties, but said that it no longer makes any sense to pretend print journalists and electronic journalists are in different professions. On the other hand, he said that journalists who have skills in TV, print, and online media certainly will be more valuable to their employers; and he emphasized that prospective employees must be willing to work in an environment where reporters cooperate across platforms.

In most cases currently, he said, cooperating across platforms simply comes down to the sharing of tips and information. Charles Kravetz, the vice president for news and station manager of New England Cable News (NECN), the largest regional news network in America, concurs with Forrest Carr.

When asked "Do you see a time when all journalists will have to be able to file stories on all platforms (print, TV, radio, online)?" Kravetz said: "I am not sure that is the way it is going to work out. This notion we had that one-journalist-fits-all-media is perhaps not that realistic. There are very few people we will talk about in the future that are TV/newspaper/internet reporters".

Gates agreed, "The 'backpack journalist'-a superhack master of multimedia who can do it all and who routinely packs a laptop and a video camera along with the tape recorder and steno notebook-may be the subject of avant-garde j-school courses, but it's not likely to become the norm."

Some other media executives have tried to define the

extent to which role convergence is expected. Gil Thelen, executive editor and senior vice president of The Tampa Tribune, for instance, gave suggestions to journalism educators based on his two years of experience in The News Centre.

"The fully formed, all-purpose, multiplatform, gadget-laden journalism grad is NOT what we're looking to hire. Journalism schools must continue to produce graduates who are competent in one craft area: reporting, design, producing, directing, editing." However, Thelen encouraged journalism schools to train writers to write for print, online, and broadcast and train print photographers to learn how to shoot and produce TV packages.

Thelen said that cultural resistance is the biggest hurdle for converging newsrooms, and that employees or current journalism students need to learn to cooperate and collaborate across newsrooms.

What is unclear is whether these media administrators' predictions are limited by the status quo of the current generation of news practitioners who might not be very well prepared for convergence or who might even resist the notion of media convergence.

At Brigham Young University, students with multiple skills are more valued and feel more comfortable in the converged media environment. In addition, sharing tips and information does not entail convergence. Reporters have been doing this for decades. It seems that keeping convergence only on the level of sharing tips and information can hardly justify the high cost of rebuilding infrastructures like The News Centre.

We are interested in finding out what expectations media companies have for future journalists. From news professionals' self-evaluations of their preparedness for media convergence, we should also be able to infer what is most desirable in the media industry nowadays.

In the face of increasing demand for technically skilled journalists-conversant with QuarkXPress, Photoshop, Avid, and Dreamweaver and able to crunch statistics using spreadsheets and other statistical methods in order to uncover the hidden story-should longstanding staples such as ethics, law, and theory remain at the heart of journalism curricula?

Or should such materials, commonly grouped together as "critical thinking", share equal hilling with technology or "skills" training? In other words, how should journalism schools balance the teaching of professional skills and that of critical thinking in an era when technology penetrates every facet of news gathering, preparation, editing, production, and delivery?

Convergence further complicates this age-old battle in journalism education. Abraham noticed that the goal of most restructuring in journalism institutions is to provide an integrated skills environment where students would get the chance to practice the skills of multimedia production. Abraham argued: "The role of journalism academy should be very different from that of the industry.

Its role should not simply be to inculcate skills that will help students to flag down jobs. They should aim to provide a scholarly background for a deeper intellectual understanding of our lives, media forms and of communication in general".

The dean of the University of Nevada at Reno thinks the ability to use multiple media skills is essential. Brigham Young University, which has built a working converged newsroom into its curriculum, expects students to graduate with multiple skills. University News Director, Dean Paynter, said, "We expect our students to more than anchor, more than report, and more than produce.

The best ones can do it all, including write for the newspaper". Mitchell Stephens (2000), professor of journalism and mass communications at New York University, holds up the other end. "In a world where corporate pressures on 'content providers' seem to be increasing and civic affairs decreasing, the argument for emphasizing the basics does have much to recommend it."

Thomas Kunkel (2002), dean of the Philip Merrill College of Journalism at the University of Maryland, sums it up:

"Today's journalists, first and foremost, must be strong critical thinkers who know enough about geography, history and the human condition to understand why events play out as they do. They must be intellectually curious. They should speak a second language. They should read something other than Jim Romenesko's MediaNews site. They ought to have a world view."

A controversy in late 2002 at Columbia University demonstrates how volatile the argument is currently. The debate arose when the graduate school of journalism at Columbia University halted its search for a dean. The new university president, Lee Bollinger, wanted to re-evaluate the school's mix of craft versus theory (Babcock), and the move created a flurry of opinion about the journalism school's existing curriculum.

This critical curriculum question is often reflected in the questions of whether and how new technology classes should be included in the existing curriculum and how they should be taught. Some journalism schools are preparing to embrace the wave of media convergence in their new curricula by converging print and electronic media sequences to adapt to the industrial trends and the new technological environment.

Blanchard and Christ warn that universities with limited resources will no longer tolerate duplicating specializations with separate courses such as writing for television, writing for newspapers, writing for public relations, and writing for advertising. Blanchard and Christ add that the communications revolution (the media's convergence and related trends) is making journalism and mass communication's traditional sequences obsolete.

Actually, Blanchard and Christ's opinion is not something new. Early in 1972, the University of Iowa School of Journalism already eliminated its sequences but at the expense of being denied reaccreditation by ACEJMC. About thirty years later, their decision seemed to be finding more sympathy.

Many schools are still exploring where to go. In October 2001, seventeen professors and leaders of new media from thirteen journalism programs across the country gathered in Berkeley, California, and had a discussion about new media in journalism education.

The University of Nevada, Reno, offered several different elective courses in new media, but it did not have a special sequence. It was struggling with how to incorporate them in other classes. The University of Florida had a concentration in online media, which was equivalent to other concentrations such as reporting and editing and photojournalism.

Students who were not in that concentration couldn't always squeeze in the online media courses because they did not have any leftover électives they could take in the school. American University had three divisions, journalism, public communication, and visual media, but they did not work together very well most of the time.

The University of South Carolina was restructuring its graduate masters programme in newspaper leadership and was focusing it on convergence. The University of Maryland had an online curriculum, but it was not formally structured as such. Northwestern University had an introductory New Media course at the undergraduate and graduate level, which was offered as an elective.

It was packed with everything from new skills training to wrestling with the business issues of new media to actual production. After three admission cycles, enrollment declined. The University of Minnesota established the Institute for New Media Studies, which merged broadcast journalism and print journalism programs to make them a concentration with the idea that future journalists would work in a multi-channel environment and should know how to operate within all those channels.

Although editors and academics sometimes agree on the qualifications a journalism student needs, an ideal curriculum doesn't always include convergence preparedness courses. In a 2000 poll, editors and educators agreed "on the same five of 14 types of knowledge considered most necessary for journalism graduates and listed them in the same order of importance".

Technical skills were not mentioned in the top five, surpassed instead by "understanding of a journalist's responsibility to the public, understanding of the ethics of journalism, knowledge of current events, broad general knowledge, and knowledge of government".

With so much variance across universities, we are interested in finding out how many journalism schools have revamped their curricula to prepare students for the trend of media convergence, what professors' attitudes are toward teaching critical thinking vs. teaching technical skills and training generalists vs. training specialists, and what editors' and news professionals' attitudes are toward the same issues. In this regard, several scholars and news practitioners have tried to give advice to journalism professors and students in the context of media convergence.

In 2002, David Bulla from the University of Florida presented his "Media convergence: Industry practices and implications for education" to the AEJMC annual conference in Miami. This is the first research writing of its kind. The theme of the paper is the closest to that of this study. Bulla's study looked at the changing nature of contemporary mass communications practices, focusing on multimedia or converged journalism.

It described what scholastic journalism scholars are doing to prepare their students for these changes and provided recommendations to educators about how to update curricula to account for convergence.

The research questions for that study were: (1) what are journalism educators currently doing to incorporate convergence into their curricula; and (2) what abilities, skills, and attitudes do professional journalists expect from their newest employees? Media convergence in Bulla's study was defined as multimedia journalism, which means reporting, writing, and disseminating content in two or more media platforms.

Because of the controversy about media mergers, Bulla tried to find answers to some hot issues concerning democracy including: Does corporate media merging reduce public discourse and hinder democracy? Will it ultimately mean the need for fewer and fewer reporters, as the development of other technology has meant a decline in the number of employees in other areas of the production process? All these questions pertain to our study.

Bulla obtained a sample of 114 news practitioners working at newspapers, television stations, wire services, magazines, radio stations, and online publications in the United States. The sample was randomly selected from Editor & Publisher and Yahoo lists of media companies in the U.S. Media Web sites. With a response rate of 36 percent, Bulla interviewed 41 news practitioners. Bulla also interviewed college educators, but he did not state how he sampled them.

What is unclear is the extent to which the Yahoo list and Editor & Publisher list overlap each other and if a sample from two potentially overlapping lists is any longer a random sample. In addition, since Bulla's questions were almost all unstructured, that is, he conducted interviews,10 he did not really need a random sample.

Researchers strive for depth rather than breadth and don't mean to claim external validity in the statistical sense by conducting interviews. Finally, if he did need a random sample, a sample of 114 people with a 36 percent response rate could be statistically defective because of big statistical errors. Bulla needed a better research design to make his study valid and reliable.

Some scholars doubt whether journalism school professors are theoretically and especially technologically prepared to teach media convergence. In an article written for Journalism Education magazine, John Irby, a professor from Washington State University and a veteran newspaper editor and publisher, for instance, was concerned about the disconnection between the newsroom and the classroom.

Irby (2000) asked: Are universities and educators effectively preparing students for the work force? Do educators understand what newspapers are looking for in future reporters and editors? Does the newspaper industry have a responsibility in the division between educators and professionals? Are journalism educators "discounted" by professionals who believe those who teach couldn't succeed in newspapers?

Irby said older generations of newspaper reporters also appeared on radio and television periodically though they had no training; they never even felt like it was part of their job and thus did not take it very seriously. But now, he continued, print journalists do need to take it seriously; journalism educators need to re-evaluate, and probably modify, the separatetrack approach in training print and broadcast journalists.

Irby believed that there is still a need for specialization, but he told students to take both broadcast and print courses and told them that computer literacy is as crucial as the old-fashioned kind. A study about the impact of media convergence on journalism education without consulting Robert J. Haiman's article "Can convergence float?" (2001) should be considered incomplete.

Haiman's fervent talk against media convergence raised some challenging questions that educators must face. Haiman, president emeritus of The Poynter Institute, argued that the converged media world is one from which good journalism, and good journalists, are going to be in great need of defence.

He stuck to his notion of the mission of good journalism he stated 40 years ago: "To inform the public about the public's business, creating a society that is equipped with the knowledge it needs to make the right civic decisions more often than it makes the wrong civic decisions, and thus helping to perpetuate self-government and democracy."

Expressing his deep concern for journalism, Haiman said: "I think that convergence may end up being good, maybe even very good, for media companies. I fear, however, that it is going to be bad, and maybe even very bad, for journalism." He continued to explain:

I think it is going to be bad for journalism because, even if it goes as well as it possibly can, I believe that it is going to distract journalists, journalism teachers, and journalism students away from that single most important imperative of the craft - to create an informed society capable of intelligently governing itself. And if it does not go well, I fear it is going to subject journalists to time, resource, craft, and ethical pressures, all of which will be bad for journalists, bad for journalism, and bad for the country.

In his talk, Haiman mentioned a top education reporter who had done a "superb job" for more than 18 years. Now, he had to do short reports for the TV station with which that newspaper was converged.

However, "he's not exactly ready for prime time." After this reporter retires, Haiman is afraid that that he will be replaced by "someone who may not report like a buzz saw and write like a dream, but who probably will report and write education okay and who will also look good and sound good on television."

"When that happens," he continued, "the journalism quality of all of the education reporting coming out of that converged news operation is going to go down." We believe that few people would disagree with Haiman's point that quality content is the king, to use his own words, but Haiman's above comment could be limited, again, by the performance of the current generation of reporters who are not prepared for media convergence.

Haiman was suggesting that a future reporter who has been trained to work for different media platforms and who has learned more about reporting would produce reporting of less quality. In our study, we would like to find out to what extent Haiman's concern is shared by editors, news professionals, and professors.

While convergence is still in its infancy, Haiman suggested that journalists, journalism students, and journalism teachers do three "terribly important things":

- For journalists who want to keep good journalism alive in the converged world to take a blood oath to fight, scrap, kick and scream whenever any attempt is made to dilute good journalism values.
- For journalism schools and journalism teachers to offer students the right curriculum to function best

in that converged world, and this does not mean offering new courses in convergence.

- For journalism students to emphasize the right areas of study and take the right courses so they will be able to defend themselves against the evils of convergence, prosper in that new world, and contribute to the effort to sustain informed self-government.

Haiman said, "If we decide to teach anything about convergence at Poynter, that is the lesson I hope we'll teach."

To students, Haiman said that the journalists who will be the most successful in the converged world are the same ones who are the most successful today, and they are the ones who are best trained in six areas: reporting, writing, editing, ethics, and media law, research techniques and specialized knowledge such as business, finance, law, science, health, aging, and the environment.

Since the top reporter in education Haiman mentioned can hardly survive the converged media world, our question is whether gaining knowledge in these six areas is sufficient and what else, if any, students need to learn. Do students need to learn any new skills? What new skills do news practitioners need?

Also, we would like to see how the attitudes of the respondents from these three groups toward media merger affect their views of how to train future journalists. As South and Nicholson (2002) commented, "If the industry doesn't agree on what new skills journalists need, it will be hard for journalism schools to know what to teach."

LARGER CONTEXT OF THE STUDY

The questions concerning teaching skills vs. critical thinking and training specialists vs. generalists are not new. They have been contextualized in ongoing conversations across disciplines over decades on many campuses in the United States.

But such conversations take on new meanings in journalism schools when many reporting jobs today are becoming high-tech-oriented and many news companies are demanding high-tech skills from new hires upon their graduation. The impact of such industrial demands on universities brings us back to the core issue-the role of the university in the shaping of the young souls in its charge.

In other words, how should a university achieve the desired product-a truly educated human being for newsrooms. The question of teaching skills vs. critical thinking winds down to a perennial competition between acquiescing pervasive vocationalism with its emphasis on skills training in an attempt to enable college students to survive outside academic institutions and establishing the relevance of the broad spectrum of knowledge to the career goals and lives of individuals.

E. D. Hirsch argues: "Narrow vocational education, adjusted to the needs of the moment, is made ever more obsolete by changing technology What is required is education for change, not for static job competencies". Probably no one has better expressed than Joanne G. Kurfiss the importance of imparting critical thinking as skills of analyzing and constructing arguments, as construction of meaning, and as the manifestation of a contextual theory of knowledge.

"Critical thinking can result in a new way of approaching significant issues in one's life or a deeper understanding of the basis for one's actions. Or it might result in political activity".

Along the similar line as Kurfiss's critical thinking theory and unlike Allan Bloom, who condemns the introduction of non-Western materials into the university curricula so as to protect the curriculum from the contamination of ideological conflict, Jerry Herron also highly promotes the teaching of critical thinking by calling on faculty to bring their conflicting ideologies into open engagement so that students can discover what is at stake in different ideas and can see their representational meaning.

The questions are whether universities should totally give up the teaching of skills today and how the needs of the job market and the goal of college education can be in harmony. In other words, can the teaching of common traditional content and the teaching of higher order skills join forces? Patracia Graham, ex-dean of the Harvard Graduate School of Education, argues that we need both commonality and flexibility in American education and there is no reason we cannot have both at once.

The question of training specialists vs. generalists is an extension of a larger conversation about reforming the fragmented curricula in higher education. Often classified as "cultural right," Ernest Boyer, Allan Bloom, and E. D. Hirsch share similar views about the problems in higher education. They point out that the university now is anarchistic.

There is no vision of what an educated human being is. The curriculum is disjointed and disciplines are fragmented into smaller pieces. Undergraduates find it hard to see patterns in their courses and relate what they learn to life. Careerism conflicts with the liberal arts.

And finally, schools have failed to thoroughly carry out the educational goal of promoting mature literacy for all our citizens. They all agree that an educational reform is needed to teach more common traditional content apart from the higher-order skills that are commonly emphasized.

Boyer calls for a balance between individual interests and shared concerns while the actual priority is given to the latter. To promote a liberal education, Boyer advocates the "integrated core" or "enriched major"-a programme of general education that introduces students not only to essential knowledge, but also to connections across the disciplines, and, in the end, to the application of knowledge to life beyond the campus.

Boyer points out, knowledge becomes important only when we use it and apply it to humane ends; therefore, the undergraduate experience should not only generate new knowledge, but channel that knowledge to the service of the society.

It is a matter of invigorating "the claims of community while protecting with full vigour the dignity and origins of each individual," to use Boyer and Kaplan's words. In a similar vein, Bloom calls on teachers to look toward the goal of human completeness and to provide students a liberal education, in which learning is both synoptic and precise.

To Bloom, liberal education feeds the student's love of truth and passion to live a good life. It also requires that a student's whole life be radically changed by it. Bloom offers an ivory tower vision of the university-"the good old Great Book approach"-undergraduate students spend four years reading certain generally recognized classic texts for answers to philosophical questions of personal and human identity and aspirations.

Bloom thinks that man may live more truly and fully in reading Plato and Shakespeare than at any other time because then they are participating in essential being and are forgetting their accidental lives.

In accordance with Boyer's and Bloom's points of view, Hirsch argues that "the greatest human individuality is developed in response to a tradition, not in response to disorderly, uncertain, and fragmented education" and "only by accumulating shared symbols, and the shared information the symbols represent can we learn to communicate effectively with one another in our national community".

However, Hirsch places emphasis more on the content of education, ensuring that students acquire all the "right" elements of knowledge that will enable them to get along in the Real World. He believes that neither the content-neutral curriculum of Rousseau and Dewey nor the narrowly specified curriculum of Plato is adequate to the needs of a modern nation.

Hirsch calls for a curriculum, including extensive curriculum and intensive curriculum with an emphasis on the former, which is traditional in content and provides students with a common core of cultural information. "The conception of a two-part curriculum avoids the idea that all children should study identical materials" Hirsch says.

Based on our literature review, media convergence in our study is defined as the assimilation of media content for multiple media platforms. Media convergence may involve any combination of the convergences of media contents, media forms, media companies, and roles of news practitioners.

Our general research question is how college professors should prepare students to cope with media convergence. To be specific, should college professors prepare generalists who can competently work in multiple media platforms or prepare specialists who know inside out how to work for one particular medium platform?

And how should journalism schools balance the teaching of critical thinking and technical skills? Corresponding to these two questions, we also would like to find out if college journalism educators themselves are both theoretically equipped and technologically prepared to teach their students about media convergence. The study serves both as an attitude finder and a fact finder.

We believe that professors, editors, and news professionals are the best candidates to answer these questions. Editors represent the media companies to hire news staffers with news reporting abilities desired by the company. News professionals work in the forefront of news reporting and know best about what news reporting abilities they need.

The attitudes of the editors and the current generation of news professionals toward media convergence will have a great implication on future journalism education. Professors run journalism schools, and they have the final say about where their schools are going. Their attitudes toward journalism education in terms of media convergence will have the most direct influence on the kind of education journalism students will receive and how the students will perform in tomorrow's media.

Editors include daily newspaper editors in charge of newsroom operations or online news operations and news directors in charge of newsroom operations in a commercial TV station with news content, both in the United States. News professionals refer to non-management news staff, such as reporters, anchors, photographers, designers, producers, Web staff, etc., working in American media companies. Journalism professors are defined as full-time instructors with any academic rankings who teach journalism courses in a U.S. journalism school, department, programme, or division, which could be administratively affiliated with an institution with a name like College of Communications or Department of Communications Studies.

To obtain opinions about media convergence, we could have targeted our survey only at those editors and news professionals in a converged media environment. The opinions obtained from those editors and news professionals, however, could be biased. Those media companies that have not gone through convergence must have a reason for not doing so. We also wanted to find out what they are doing about convergence. Balanced views both from the converged and un-converged media companies will better assist colleges in their strategic planning.

We conducted a national survey among editors, news professionals, and journalism professors with three different versions of online survey questionnaires posted on a school Web site. Respondents were asked to fill out the questionnaire online and submit answers online as well. The answers went through a commercial form handler and reached the primary investigator's email address.

By doing so, the primary investigator had no way to detect who answered the questionnaire unless the respondent voluntarily revealed his/her email address to request the findings from the study.

There were twenty-two questions in each of these three questionnaires. Almost all questions were close-ended. About half of the questions used a 5-point Likert Scale from "Strongly Agree" to "Strongly Disagree." Some questions across the three questionnaires shared similarity, so that comparisons could be made when analyzing data.

A text field was created for respondents to provide feedback to the survey freely. The textual answers in the text field will be reported along with the statistics to illustrate and explain the quantitative findings. All questionnaires went through pilot tests. The unit of analysis was each participant. In order to conduct a systematic random sampling of editors and news professionals, we needed a list of newspaper editors and TV news directors in the United States and a list of newspaper and TV news staffers. We found that such lists did not exist, though lists of newspapers and lists of TV stations did exist in multiple places online like Editor & Publisher Yearbook and Broadcasting Sr Cable Yearbook. Therefore, we decided to construct our own.

To do so, we went through two steps. First, we constructed a combined list of daily newspapers and TV stations so that we could sample these news institutions. Second, we visited the Web sites of all sampled news institutions to find the email of the editor/news director and the email of one news professional randomly chosen.

Then, we visited each of those Web sites to find the email address of the managing editor, chief editor, online editor, or equivalent in each of those dailies and sent out a survey invitation email to him/her.

In total, we extracted 674 TV stations with a valid URL. Since this population is smaller than that of the newspapers, we over-sampled it. Instead of sampling every other four, we sampled every other station. Then, we visited each of those Web sites to find the email address of the news director or equivalent in each of those TV stations and sent out a survey invitation email to him/her.

We also sampled one news professional out of each of the sampled U.S. dailies and TV stations for the survey. Since there was always more than one professional in a company, we simply randomly clicked on one name and picked him/her and made sure that s/he was on the news staff.

Then, we sent him/her a survey invitation email. If an individual email address was not available, we replaced it with a generic email address and specified whom the email was for. S/he was asked to fill out a questionnaire that was worded in a slightly different manner. In total, we successfully sent out invitation emails to 398 news professionals.

We also needed to conduct a systematic random

sampling of college journalism professors, but we were disappointed that all lists we found had many J-schools, even major ones, missing.

In total, the new list contains 205 alphabetically ordered U.S. J-schools that contain 2,194 journalism professors. We sampled one out of every four professors from the virtually running list of all journalism professors across the schools. For instance, if a school had six journalism professors, we picked the fourth one; then, the second journalism professor from next school was picked.

We sent an invitation email to every professor in the sample. In total, we successfully sent out 500 emails. The three samples of editors, news professionals, and professors included 1,421 cases. We understood that nonresponse had been a serious problem with online surveys in recent years.

In order to counter possible low response rates in our survey, we created three samples for editors, news professionals, and professors containing roughly 500 people for each group, which were much larger than the sample sizes for populations recommended by Mildred Patten (2000) in her book Understanding Research Methods: An Overview of the Essentials so that, if low response rates occurred, we could base our confidence limits on the actual number of responses themselves. We also sent out one reminder email to the samples, which drastically boosted the response rates, especially for professors and news professionals.

FINDINGS AND DISCUSSION

After two weeks of online data collecting in November 2002, we received 223 responses from professors (a 44% response rate), 151 responses from editors (a 29% response rate), and 142 responses from news professionals (a 35% response rate). The overall response rate is 36%. As Singletary (1994) notes, returns of 30% to 40% are common in mail surveys.

The response rates of this online survey seem typical. However, the response rates are still comparatively low. A response bias is potentially present. Many respondents (41%)

left textual answers to explain and illustrate their answers to the close-ended questions and/or made comments on the topic.

By the end of 2002, 19% of the newspapers and commercial television stations with news content in the United States had gone through media mergers. Being merged or not has to do with the size of a company. Larger companies tend to have been merged while smaller ones have not. Roughly half of the news professionals surveyed (48%) reported that they produced news content for multiple media platforms on a routine basis; that was true both in merged media (50%) and non-merged media (48%).

In other words, media merger is not the precondition for practicing news for multiple media platforms. The pressure on news professionals to learn to produce multimedia content is also felt in many non-merged media companies. This finding confirms that media convergence is not necessarily related to media merger.

A typical editor or news director was a man (71%) between 36-45 years old (42%) with a bachelor's degree (76%) who had worked for at least two media (57%) for more than 20 years (53%). A typical news professional was either a man (52%) or woman (48%) between 26-35 years old (43%) with a bachelor's degree (84%) who had worked for at least two media (60%) less than ten years (62%).

Editors had generally worked for more years than news professionals, but they did not have more multiplatform experience than news professionals. As more news companies are practicing cross-media reporting with or without their companies being merged, it is important that editors with multiplatforrn experiences are chosen to direct newsroom businesses. Many editors need cross-media training more urgently than news professionals do if the news company they work for produces news contents for multiple media platforms on a daily basis.

Should J-schools Train Specialists or Generalists?

Gil Thelen (2002) said that writers should learn how to

write for multimedia and still photographers should learn how to shoot videos, but he was not interested in hiring people with multiple sets of skills. We designed four questions to test how popular Thelen's opinion was.

The majority of the respondents (84%) agreed or strongly agreed with Thelen that journalism students should learn how to write for multiple media platforms. One-way ANOVA shows significant difference among the means for professors (4.35), professionals (4.05), and editors (3.99). Tukey HSD post hoc tests show that professors were more positive on this statement than editors and professionals, while no significant difference existed between editors and professionals.

A similar number of respondents (85%) agreed or strongly agreed with Thelen that journalism students with a visual emphasis should learn how to produce and edit photos, videos, and online interactive images. One-way ANOVA shows significant difference among the means for professors (4.55), professionals (4.22), and editors (3.91).

Tukey HSD post hoc tests show that professors were more positive on this statement than professionals, while professionals were more positive than editors. Most respondents (78%) agreed or strongly agreed that all journalism majors should learn multiple sets of skills, such as writing, editing, TV production, digital photography, newspaper design, and Web publishing.

Oneway ANOVA shows significant differences among the means for professionals (4.28), editors (3.99), and professors (3.86). Tukey HSD post hoc tests show that news professionals who worked in the forefront of news production felt this need more deeply than other respondents. Editors also had such an expectation for them.

There is no significant difference between editors and professors. These findings support the growing evidence that news professionals are being asked to wear multiple hats. The findings also indicate that Thelen's view has its market at this moment when news professionals with multiple sets of skills are highly desirable but not easy to find.

Such a view may change as more journalism graduates

equipped with multiple sets of skills enter the job market. The professors' textual answers show that some of the difficulties J-schools have come across include the lack of a friendly curriculum, lack of credit hours to include the components of convergence content, lack of willing cooperation among faculty from different sequences, and lack of expertise, interest, or even time for some professors to develop new courses on convergence.

When asked whether journalism students should still have a specialization, such as writing, photojournalism, broadcasting, and new media, over half (63%) of the respondents agreed or strongly agreed. Over a quarter of the respondents (28%) were negative and 9% were not sure. One-way ANOVA mean comparisons show no significant difference of attitude among professionals (3.42), editors (3.51), and professors (3.72).

Comparing the support rate for this question to those for the first three questions, it is fair to argue that editors, news professionals, and professors emphasized the importance of cross-media training more than that of specialization, though they believed that specialization should not be neglected either.

Currently, students in many J-schools specialize in one area by subscribing to a sequence such as news-editorial, magazine, photojournalism, and broadcast. When asked whether sequences should be reorganized considering the trend of media-platforms merging in the industry, 56% of the professors agreed or strongly agreed, 22% were not sure, and another 22% disagreed or strongly disagreed.

The concept of sequences is being shaken among professors though it is still being accepted as a legitimate means of training students in various specialization areas in some J-schools. Speaking on behalf of herself and her colleagues, Professor offered some special insight on this issue:

We can't teach for the "now." We have to prepare students for when they graduatewhich in most instances is now five years out. And, we feel a commitment to expose them to all types of writing in all platforms so they can be flexible about their career choice at the front end of their academics. Then, they can apply the skills to a specialty area where they are totally proficient.

"Flexible" is a key term repeatedly seen in editors' and news professionals' textual answers as a suggestion for future journalists. Editor 's statement is typical: Our job descriptions are open ended and new hires understand that they are being hired for their skills. They may be hired today to cover the city beat. In six months or in two weeks, if necessary, a person with Quark skills may be asked to fill in or shift duties to include pagination of a particular section. It is important that hires stay flexible.

The new hires, wrote Editor, "need to understand that the information they gather and process can have many different uses, audiences and shelf lives. They need to understand the complexities of the audience mix and be able to respond." "Those unwilling to be flexible may find themselves in a difficult scenario later in their careers".

From a different perspective, Professional concurred: "Students must be flexible, have a vigorous skill set and be prepared to get laid off and move around in the changing media arena." In short, "young journalists must be prepared to fill a variety of roles if they hope to succeed". "The most successful journalists are those that take on assignments willingly, can learn and want to learn".

Specialization in journalistic jobs is still honored, but is losing its favour to cross-media capability in converged media. Today, professionals with different specializations team together to work on multiple media projects. Tomorrow, it is likely that one-man bands will be more and more desired in newsrooms.

Most respondents (93%), especially professors, agreed or strongly agreed that journalism students should both learn technical skills, such as online information search and Web design, while learning critical thinking skills in media law, ethics, etc. One-way ANOVA shows significant difference among the means for professionals, editors, and professors. Tukey HSD post hoc tests show that professors were more positive on this point than editors and professionals, while no significant difference existed between editors and professionals.

But, should journalism students spend more time on learning critical thinking skills than on technical skills? Opinions were divided. More than half of the respondents (62%) believed that should be the case, but 19% of the respondents were not sure and another 19% of them did not agree. Oneway ANOVA shows significant difference among the means for professors (3.21), professionals, and editors. Tukey HSD post hoc tests show that editors were more positive on this point than professionals, and professionals were more positive than professors.

Throughout all the answers from the three groups of respondents, critical thinking was highly regarded as being more important than technical skills. Editors, news professionals, and professors all liked to see good stories, and good stories come from good thinking ability. An editor said: "Journalism graduates need to have a broad, well-rounded education; be critical thinkers; have the ability to write clearly; have a serious work ethic; and know computer basics - in that order".

"You can teach a monkey to type," echoes a writer. Therefore, he strongly suggested that J-schools "get more critical thinking skills pounded into the skulls of the students". While highly emphasizing the importance of critical thinking ability, editors did not mean to neglect the importance of teaching technical skills in schools. We will develop this point when we discuss the next question.

Comparing the professors' highest mean for the first question and their lowest mean for the second question, it is clear that professors saw critical thinking as highly important, but preferred a comparatively balanced approach for the teaching of the two sets of knowledge. One professor's comment illustrated this observation:

Knowing technical skill alone will not make you a "good" journalist. Critical thinking is vital not just to a career but to life itself. Without developing your ability to discern and evaluate, you will become "the prey" of society. Next, a technical skill is critical to a career in journalism today.

Even print Journalism is very high tech these days and all electronic media require extensive computer knowledge as well as other technical skills. I would place critical thinking skills first on your list of things to do because a developed mind will make it that much easier to develop a creative and technically sound understanding of the technical side of the business.

From a holistic view, there was no substantial disagreement between classrooms and newsrooms when we examine the issue of teaching critical thinking vs. teaching technical skills. Compared to Terry's 2000 poll, this study shows that professors gave a higher status to technical skills in journalism curricula in 2002 than they did in 2000. This is a period during which media convergence garnered its momentum. In short, all respondents generally agreed that J-schools should place emphasis on teaching critical thinking, but at the same time, should not neglect teaching technical skills.

News professionals were asked, "If you wish to possess the technical skills you don't have now, do you prefer to learn them at work or wish you had learned in school?" Editors were given the same question with a slightly different wording. Chi-Square test shows that the difference between editors and news professionals is significant. This finding well supplements the findings from the preceding questions. It suggests that editors not only looked at future journalists' critical thinking ability, but also hoped that future journalists would already possess the skills needed in a converged newsroom when they are hired.

On the other hand, most professionals preferred that they spend most of their school time on gaining critical thinking ability and learn skills largely at work. The professionals' general preference, to some extent, also reflected their need for technological update at their current positions, so that they can better qualify for multimedia productions.

Many editors and reporters said that school is the best

place for journalism students to explore every facet of the media and acquire basic technical skills, though some advanced skills can only be learned on the job. Learning skills while in school, they said, can build confidence and an expansive and broad understanding of the entire field and help with damage control and communication in newsrooms.

"If editing and the technical skills were more prevalent in college courses," wrote a multi-tasking editor, "I think I could stave off a lot of headaches when the students become professionals." An internship was the news professionals' and editors' most recommended venue for enhancing and learning more technical skills and gaining other practical experience. Reporter said: "While I value my college education, my internship and first job provided me with the most valuable skills today."

Another reporter said: "While education is great, students who work in media while in school fare much better in the real world." Some editors had complaints about graduates with a 3.5 GPA but no practical experience and no published news work. An anchor/reporter said that it is important even "for a freshman or sophomore in college to visit a newsroom and shadow someone.

So many students wait until they are juniors and seniors to do this and then they realise they made a mistake in selecting their major. You will learn more by watching and doing". One reporter said, "To remain competitive, education must continue throughout a career".

The implication of the discrepancy from this finding suggests that Jschools should place emphasis on teaching critical thinking, expose students to new technology, and design a comprehensive internship programme for students to gain real-world knowledge and further develop their crossmedia technical skills.

Both editors and news professionals were given this unstructured question with slightly different wordings. We read through all the answers, and categorized them into the following nine facets in random order: Multimedia production: producing and editing news stories on video, for the Web, and for print; re-purposing the same story for different media.

New technology: knowledge of software for producing video, Web sites, graphics, newspapers, and magazines; knowledge of how to operate a computer and use the Internet. Good writing: knowing how to write to make people remember and/or take action, write about the beats with an expert's view. Good editing is also expected. Critical thinking: having good news judgment, understanding what is legal and ethical, knowing how to report with insight, knowing how to crunch statistics.

Computer-assisted reporting: expert's knowledge of conducting online information search, database knowledge. On-camera exposure: how to report like a TV news anchor before a camera for a newspaper reporter. Visual production: A newspaper writer must know how to take photos, or a TV reporter must know how to shoot video.

SECOND LANGUAGE: KNOWING HOW TO FLUENTLY SPEAK AND READ A FOREIGN LANGUAGE

Time management: well organizing time to work for multiple media platforms; the ability and willingness to work as a team to produce multimedia news stories. Then we ranked these facets according to the percentage scores each facet got separately from the editors and the news professionals:

This ranking shows more agreement than disagreement between editors and news professionals. No matter how technology changes and whether media are converged, editors and news professionals believed that learning how to write good stories is still the top priority and writing is the very basic skill all news professionals should learn.

One editor pushed the importance of good writing to the extreme: "I've worked in markets 170 to 20, and having training in multiple media will not help you get a job, but being a good writer will". Most editors and news professionals, however, did believe that learning multimedia production, new technology, and computer-assisted reporting are also among the top priorities.

"I would strongly urge students to prepare themselves to the best of their ability to be able to report/edit the news in a variety of platforms and to learn how to truly engage readers/listeners/viewers in what they are writing about," said Editor.

Editors and news professionals both believed that it is not very important for a newspaper reporter to learn how to talk like an anchor in front of a video camera. This skill was even regarded as being less important than knowing how to speak a second language. Some editors and news professionals also mentioned learning how to manage time for producing multimedia news stories.

Editor hoped that journalists in a converged environment would learn to avoid "extra" work by working "smarter" and with greater awareness of the requirements of the different publishing media.

This finding, again, shows that editors valued critical thinking ability more than news professionals did. Editors wanted news professionals to be good thinkers first, and the latter wanted most to learn how to express their thinking in different media.

Since some authors such as Haiman expressed the concern about the possible decline of work quality if news professionals have to "re-purpose" stories for multiple media platforms, we tried to find out to what extent this concern was shared by editors and news professionals. Opinions split. Thirty-eight percent of the editors and professionals agreed or strongly agreed that the quality would deteriorate, 40% disagreed or strongly disagreed, and the other 22% were not sure.

Editors and professionals showed no significant difference on this attitude T-test. Such a concern was not prevalent in the news industry.

In response to such concerns, the news director from a converged media company wrote: "When reporters do cross platforms we give them the time to finish the project for all three platforms. Quality does not suffer. If we were to try to force reporters to cross platforms while operating under daily deadlines then quality could suffer depending on the nature of the story and the extra time consumed".

Another editor summed up this issue: "Some employees can capably handle multiple media and tell stories effectively. Others cannot. Certainly strong technical skills and training can help, but it's not just dependent on that; it depends more on the attitude and aptitude of the journalist".

Quality multimedia work also involves a solid understanding of different cultures in different media. Editors both for and against media convergence noted the difficulty of merging different media with different cultures, and editors in those merged media called for flexibility in aptitude and willingness to cooperate across platforms. For instance, Editor wrote:

Clarity of what convergence means to the news organization is vital and often lacking. This causes unneeded anxiety.

Managers have to realise that each medium has its own culture, language, skill set and timetable and is naturally skeptical of anything unfamiliar. It is also true that these same journalists' stock in trade is learning a new culture, language, skill set and timetable-on a daily basis.

Therein lies the hope for an efficient news operation running on all cylinders and an effective -maybe even happy-staff. If most editors and news professionals are not concerned about the quality of the work prepared for multiple media platforms and if news professionals are given enough time to complete their cross-media work, there is little reason to worry that future journalists, if well trained both theoretically and technologically for multiple media platforms, will produce work of poorer quality.

Training students to practice news in multiple media platforms will help bridge newsroom cultures from different media and eventually erase such differences. We have noticed that no significant statistical differences existed between the editors and news professionals from the converged media companies and their counterparts from the not-yet-converged media companies when they answered the questions reported above.

How are J-schools Coping with Media Convergence?

From 1998 to 2002, about 60% of the J-schools in the United States redesigned their curricula or developed new courses to prepare students for practicing news in multiple media platforms. A typical journalism professor was a man (71%) between 46-55 years old (42%) with a doctoral degree (63%) who worked in news media for one to ten years (48%), may still be practicing news (45%) in one way or another, and conducted academic research (66%).

More professors claimed that they were theoretically equipped (81%) than technologically prepared (53%) to teach students how to report news in multiple media platforms. More than half of the professors (57%) had not taught any journalism courses in the last five years where skill sets were beyond their own expertise; 25% of the professors taught one such course and 11% taught two.

Nevertheless, the majority of the professors (84%) added content about media convergence either to their existing courses or to new courses or participated in cross-media team-teaching in the last five years.

Worries, concerns, and, sometimes, misconceptions about media convergence appeared in professors' textual answers. For instance, a professor from Montana said: "convergence is not happening".

A professor who no longer practiced news said, "In my judgment, the writing portion of preparing news for print and for the Web is exactly the same". Another professor maintained that it was not necessary to teach cross-media news practicing because "few 'want ads' for newspaper reporter and editor positions specifically listed multimedia platform skills as required or preferred experience for new hires".

Many professors worried that media mergers would restrict the number of voices in a community. They regarded media mergers as a grand experiment in the profession and waited for the FCC's ruling on the cross-ownership of different media in the same market.

Wait-and-see-that was the strategy some universities took for teaching media convergence. One professor said that he needed to see the substantive contribution media convergence could make before he would be more serious about this phenomenon.

He said that J-schools should be cautious about embracing convergence. Some other universities didn't have the time and resources to teach convergence courses or make major curriculum changes.

Most professors, however, did believe that media convergence was a reality; and "anybody serious about practicing media needs at minimal an acquaintance with various media and at best multiple competencies," as Professor said.

Many professors (and editors and news professionals as well) had a clear opinion as to which comes first, teaching critical thinking or teaching technical skills. While acknowledging the need for incorporating media convergence content in curricula, especially the technological components, professors cautioned against sacrificing conceptual and theoretical courses such as law, ethics, history, cultural studies, critical perspectives, etc.

Professor analogized critical thinking as meat and potatoes and technical skills as dessert and side dishes and argued that "the meat and potatoes need to come before one begins to worry about the dessert and side dishes (or side shows)." This viewpoint was popular. Professor wrote:

It's the message, not the medium, that is of paramount importance. If students cannot understand and appreciate the underlying concepts, principles and ethics of journalism, then they cannot produce the type of content that will be of value to a free society. A thorough grounding in journalism must come before any training in tools. The tools are means to an end, not the end in and of themselves.

Incidentally, a reporter had similar thoughts: The

medium isn't the message, the message is the message. In short, the fundamental analytic and synthetic skills of the news writer are paramount to the message. The medium does not alter the reporter's craft of interpreting news events in the context of the society in a way that will make sense for the receiver of the information.

Additional skills may be desirable, but for the most part they can be learned on the job. Obviously, the more skills one can offer, the better the employment opportunity. Those ancillary skills should not come at the expense of thorough proficiency as a news writer.

We fully understand why these respondents emphasize the teaching of critical thinking and the fundamentals of good reporting over the teaching of technical skills, and we strongly agree with their opinions.

But, we also see the danger of over-stretching the point by treating the two sets of knowledge as two opposing poles. Those arguments are based on the presumptions that message and medium can be easily separated, content and form can be detached, and readers for different media are from the same population.

But, is that right? It is true that content is the king. It is true that "the medium does not alter the reporter's craft of interpreting news events." News practice, however, is not only about news-gathering and writing. It also includes production, editing, and delivery. Without a solid grasp of grammar and style, how can a writer effectively express his/her good analytical thinking?

Without knowing the available features and limitations of online news delivery, how can messages be constructed to their fullest potential? Without understanding the technical difference between video news and print news, how can messages be constructed appropriately? In the digital era when almost all steps of news transmission involves technology, if professors don't teach students technical skills, will the computer majors, who know little about news practices, be expected to produce newspapers, TV news, and online news?

Writers, for instance, do not necessarily have to be conversant in constructing news reporting with Flash for online presentation or know how to operate a video camera to shoot video stories. But knowing the principles and rules of news video-taping and what Flash or other software can offer will surely help writers more effectively convey their messages and better cooperate with visual reporters. Creativity distinguishes artists and artisans.

Critical thinking ability distinguishes master journalists and technical writers. But artists must first know what artisans know and a master journalist must possess all that a technical writer knows for a living. Skills are intrinsic instead of extrinsic to ideas.

Teaching critical thinking and teaching technical skills are not mutually exclusive. Teaching journalism students how to express their critical thinking with conversant technical skills in different media seems to be a big challenge for J-school professors in the years to come. From the professors' textual answers, we have observed different philosophical approaches to teaching convergence.

Unlike some professors who took the wait-and-see approach, a professor from the University of Texas at Austin claimed that "convergence is already happening, and journalism schools should be leading the parade and not following it". A popular viewpoint was that "skills across platforms must be taught, but more importantly storytelling, ethics, and critical thinking skills should be even more important in the journalism school curriculum". One professor from Texas Christian University said that it maintained the existing sequences but required broadcast students to take print courses and vice versa.

Team-teaching was an often-used approach in some J-schools such as Indiana University for courses involving multiple sets of skills while professors learned from each other. Another professor, from the University of Colorado at Boulder, said convergence meant that "students work together to produce multimedia content for the Web-not that each individual should attempt to become proficient in all media".

To overcome the hurdle of the ratio limited by the ACEJMC accreditation standards between journalism courses and liberal arts courses, a professor from Bowling Green State University suggested that journalism undergraduate students stay for five years and devote the fifth year entirely to practice.

Some professors said that journalism students only need to know a little about the practices in media other than their own while some other professors firmly maintained that students should "be the master of many arts and the explorer of all".

All respondents were asked, "Do you think that merging media companies such as television station, newspaper, radio station, and online news from a local area will benefit any of the parties listed on the left?

Check all entries that apply." The entries included "The general public," "News professionals," "Media companies," "Nobody," and "Not sure." We designed this question about the legitimacy of media merger as a barometer for testing the respondents' political view on media convergence.

We presumed that a respondent's answer to this question could be related to his/her way of answering other questions regarding teaching media convergence or requirement for new hires.

Most respondents (66%) from all three groups pointed to media companies as the beneficiary of media mergers. In comparison, only 37% of the respondents said that media mergers also benefit the general public, and even fewer (27%) said that media mergers benefit the news professionals.

By reading the percentage numbers horizontally, we can find that consistently fewer respondents believed that media mergers benefit the general public or news professionals; also consistently more respondents believed that media mergers benefit media companies.

It is also noticeable that 47% of editors believed that media mergers benefit the general public while the other 53% didn't. Editors' opinions on this point were roughly equally split. This finding indicates that media merger is a grand experiment in the media industry. Its benefits to the general public, which can better legitimize media mergers, are to be explored in the years to come.

By reading the percentage numbers both vertically and horizontally, we also find that editors were the most positive about the benefits media mergers could bring to all three parties while professors were least sure of such benefits. It is logical to reason that management personnel, such as editors and news directors and the companies they represent, are the primary forces behind today's media merger movement.

The question is that, since most professors, editors, and even news professionals believed that media mergers do not benefit news professionals and hardly benefit the general public, why do most news professionals still want to be trained to be cross-media practitioners and why are so many Jschool professors enthusiastic about training such graduates?

Considering the editors' most positive attitude toward media convergence, we wonder if news professionals are under the pressure to do so, and J-school professors are under the pressure to follow the industrial trend. Our surmise is partially corroborated by some textual answers.

A news anchor from a merged media company agreed that new hires should have received cross-media training in writing and visuals and should possess multiple sets of skills. She showed her understanding for media mergers:

The merging of media companies is almost a daily occurrence. The pool of entities providing news services is shrinking. I think there is a danger that the public will lose in this race for media giants to accumulate wealth. At the same time, with the amount of competition in the industry from cable networks, the Internet, DVD's etc., I see the financial need for companies to merge to survive.

A newspaper reporter also from a merged media company expressed a similar feeling: "I am not all for the media convergence At the same time I find it quite beneficial to be savvy in all branches of the industry. It helps the journalist become more knowledgeable about her or his job". News professionals were not alone in having such feelings. Here are two excerpts from two professors who have expressed similar feelings: It's a harsh reality that I checked the box saying that news companies are the ones that are sure to benefit from media convergence. It may not be great for the public or even for news professionals who are going to be asked to bring more and more skills to the table and to have more and more responsibility on the job. Even so, convergence in one way or another is gonna happen and we need to prepare our students.

Finally, my answer on merging media companies reflects my disdain for the corporatization and concentration of control in the media. I think we ought to train mass communicators for a converged world, but as professors we ought to fight like hell against media mergers.

Very few respondents (19%) believed that media mergers benefit all three parties, the general public, news professionals, and media companies, but about one third of the respondents (35%) believed that media companies are the only beneficiaries to such a practice.

These 35% respondents, who were almost equally proportionally found in editors, news professionals, and professors groups, could be regarded as the most critical toward media mergers. We compared these 35% respondents with the rest of the sample and found no significant difference in their answers concerning the necessity of teaching journalism students cross-media writing and visuals and teaching multiple sets of skills.

Always, more respondents believed that professors should teach all those things. In short, the respondents' political view was not directly tied to their views of teaching students cross-media practices.

As an experimental industrial trend, media convergence in the sense of media mergers is still in its formative stage. Whether it will sustain its momentum to reach popularity in the nation and how its advantages balance against disadvantages are yet to be seen.

While there seems to be a good deal of support for cross-media education, on some questions, professors are more gung-ho than editors and news professionals about the trend.

The legitimacy of media mergers needs repeated tests before such mergers can be truly accepted as a healthy development and a full-force education of media convergence can be seen in many in J-schools.

Media convergence, however, is not tied to media mergers. Media convergence, initiated and made possible by digital technology, is more than media mergers propelled largely by financial considerations. More pervasive is the media convergence in the senses of content convergence, technological convergence, and especially role convergence, which have occurred not only in merged media companies but also more in non-merged ones.

No matter whether media mergers will continue, the other three forms of media convergence, which are not subject to the FCC regulations, are likely to continue to develop. Most editors and news professionals in this survey are not from merged media companies.

Many editors, news professionals, and professors do not yet see media mergers as beneficial to the general public and news professionals. But, their backgrounds and political views do not prevent them from sharing with other respondents with different backgrounds and political views many opinions regarding where future college journalism should go.

Such common understanding is shaping a force to push forward the education of media convergence in campuses nationwide.

To better direct newsroom businesses in a converged media environment, many editors need cross-media training. Many opportunities are out there for news companies and universities to work together to explore the issue of media convergence and provide mid-career professionals and editors cross-media technological training.

It seems sensible that opportunities for learning multimedia skills should be made available both on campus and through off-site continuing education programs that are geared for midcareer news professionals as technological developments continue to evolve.

Multi-dimensional news reporting in multiple media

platforms will be tomorrow's way news is presented. Therefore, dealing with media convergence in college journalism education is an urgent necessity. The wait-and-see strategy will place a Jschool in a disadvantaged position over the long run.

These findings tell us that J-schools do need to provide cross-media knowledge and experience to their students, so that the latter can better qualify for cross-media jobs in the future. Media convergence poses both challenge and opportunity to J-schools for them to reconsider their current curriculum design, sequence setting, faculty composition, teaching methods, and internship approaches.

Many professors, editors, and news professionals have expressed concern that media mergers will eliminate voices in a community, thus potentially eroding democracy. However, media mergers did not start only these days. As a TV reporter wrote in the textual answer, when she first went to Philadelphia years ago, there were five daily papers.

Now, there are two; and they are both published by the same company. Philadelphia is not alone in such media reduction. The question is whether the general public feels that it is less well-informed than it was thirty or forty years ago and that democracy has been eroded by such media reduction prior to media convergence.

This is a topic for another study. Nevertheless, students should be exposed to such a legitimate concern and learn to take a critical look at the phenomenon of media mergers.

J-schools should continue to teach critical thinking courses and meld critical thinking components into the teaching of all courses. Critical thinking is the cornerstone of journalism education. However, technology courses or course components should also be given the status they deserve.

In other words, there should be a balanced curriculum to include both kinds of courses, and many cross-media related courses should contain both components. An ideal curriculum should balance the load of technical skill-based courses and critical thinking courses, weighting toward the latter. Critical thinking and technical skills can go hand in hand rather than being competitors for class time. A balanced curriculum can help students better gather, produce, edit, and deliver quality news; more creatively and professionally materialize their ideas; and make them better fit into the market, especially in an economic downturn.

University of Florida professor Melinda McAdams, one of the Washington Post's first online editors, told colleagues that if colleges don't teach journalists the technical skills they will need, no one else is likely to take on the responsibility." The reality they'll face in the world is they'll have to teach themselves".

The classroom should be the first stop for students to at least get exposed to and get familiar with the technology for cross-media practices, though they can become more proficient with such technology through internship and their future jobs.

With all that said, technology courses should not dominate journalism students' education, and technology should not be taught for the sake of technology. Technology must serve the purposes of doing good journalism.

Apart from teaching students multimedia productions, new technology, and computer-assisted reporting, J-schools still need to place good writing-the very basics of being a journalist-as the top priority for all journalism students regardless of sequences or specializations.

Many respondents point out that the teaching of technology should not be at the expense of the teaching of critical thinking. Many J-schools have no more elective hours for students to learn cross-media technology within the existing parameter of curriculum. For such schools, curriculum redesign is a necessity.

Though some J-schools such as Indiana University School of Journalism have eliminated sequences to provide a comprehensive education to all journalism students, we expect that sequences will continue to exist for some time in some other J-schools. However, it has become increasingly important to encourage students from all sequences to learn technology and reporting skills from other platforms.

Sequences in many J-schools are regarded as dinosaurs because it no longer makes sense to teach broadcast and newspaper, for instance, as two unrelated bodies of knowledge in the era of media convergence and students can opt for a specialization without sequences but with professors' advice.

Most respondents expect that future journalists will be competent in producing news in multiple media platforms while being particularly strong in one area. It appears that students will be prudent to opt to specialize in either print or television and take several electives in a secondary platform, either radio or online journalism. Versatility and specialization should be equally important.

The majority of the editors do expect that future writers will be able to and willing to write for multiple media platforms, and photographers and designers will create multimedia visuals, though such expectations will not be converted into requirements in job ads for a while because "too many newsroom dinosaurs have to die off first," as Editor put it.

But chances are they will, as Nelson (2002) predicted. Most editors even expect that new hires will possess multiple sets of skills to become "superhack masters of multimedia," to use Gates's term. The needs are out there, but whether the training of such superhack masters will become the norm, as Gates questioned, largely depends on whether J-schools are willing and able to develop those "avant-garde" courses. Apart from the technological aspect, students also need to learn to cooperate and collaborate across newsrooms so as to bridge different newsroom-cultures.

Students need to be both theoretically and technically prepared for media convergence. The findings from this study show that more than half of the J-schools in the United States have redesigned their curricula or developed new courses to cope with media convergence, but professors need to be better prepared technologically.

Team-teaching is one approach to solve the problem, but will the teaching of media convergence be more effective if a

activists to feminist activists, have harshly criticized the video game industry's "violent" and "sexual" content, I believe a communication (rhetorical/feminist) perspective, particularly a Burkean perspective, is uniquely well-suited to shedding light on the presently shadowy discourses of video gaming.

In order to uncover the system of meaning of video gaming, in this analysis, I examine the discussions and "reviews" of games in prominent publications and Websites dedicated to video gaming (particularly, Game Informer Magazine, TwinGalaxies.com, Internet Gaming Entertainment, and G4). In many respects, as discourses for and by video gamers, these texts reveal the "meaning" of video gaming for these gamers by explicating the unique perceived pleasures of playing interactive computer games.

Nonetheless, initially, I should note that the world of video gaming is remarkably diverse with many niche markets such as educational games, card games like video poker and solitaire, and aerobic exercise games. This analysis does not cover the vast diversity of interactive digital media but rather emphasizes one segment of the video gaming population, what is sometimes referred to as "heavy gamers" or "hardcore gamers" or increasingly just as "gamers."

These so-called garners are largely responsible for purchasing the most popular video games and constructing the discourses of garner magazines and Web-based discussion forums. As I highlight in the manuscript, gamers are the driving force of the video game industry and strongly influence the conventions of the most popular video games. On the other hand, as the analysis demonstrates, alternative voices are emergent in the gaming community and may offer alternative video gaming experiences.

Drawing upon Burke's conceptualization of perfection, I argue that most popular video games contain a remarkable uniformity, particularly by consistently utilizing an entelechial motivational system. Further, as an entelechial system of meaning, "gamer" discourses promote a dangerous mix of competition, conquest, hierarchy, and aggressive domination.

Based upon Martin Heidegger's conception of mastery, I

conclude that these discourses encourage a patriarchal form of mathematical mastery and perfection for video gaming that ultimately promotes subjugation via dehumanization. Further, because video games are imbedded in the broader discourses of digital/information technologies, this analysis offers insights into the relationship between feminist rhetorical theory and emergent communication technologies.

KENNETH BURKE AND THE ENTELECHIAL PRINCIPLE

"[Humanity] is goaded by the spirit of hierarchy (or moved by the sense of order) and rotten with perfection". As his definition of humanity clearly reflects, hierarchy and perfection are central to Kenneth Burke's understanding of motivation. Burke refers to the principle of perfection as the "entelechial principle".

Expanding on the concept originally created by Aristotle to describe the telos of natural processes (e.g., a seed becoming a plant), Burke describes entelechy as: "intrinsic to symbol-using as such there is the 'principle of perfection,' the delight in carrying out terministic possibilities 'to their logical conclusion,' in so far as such possibilities are perceived".

In this respect, entelechy is the desire of someone or something to move toward its perceived (symbolic) state of perfection or completion—"the striving of each thing to be perfectly the kind of thing it was" or "the perfection (that is finishedness) of which that kind is capable".

As a symbolic process, for Burke, entelechy is most dangerous when imbedded in systems of meaning such as "scientific nomenclatures". For instance, "Entelechy is illustrated, for Burke, in the scientific 'perfection' of the vocabularies of genetic manipulation, and in the creative clutter of technology that now threatens our existence". In other words, systems of language serve as a motive force toward a desired entelechial state of perfection.

As Lindsay states, with entelechy, "Burke is concerned with tracking down the logic of perfection implicit in symbols, terminologies, nomenclatures". In this project, I am engaging in a similar undertaking, uncovering the logic of perfection in the vocabularies and discourses of gamers. I argue that the discourses of gamers function as an entelechial system of meaning based upon mathematical mastery. The implications of this entelechial system emerge largely from issues of gender implicit within these video gaming discourses.

GENDER AND VIDEO GAMING

Built upon the language and discourses of science, pervasive communication technologies play a unique role in contemporary cultural processes, particularly conceptualizations of gender. Previously, feminist scholars have identified mastery and control as primary values of both masculinity/patriarchy and science/technology. For instance, feminist critics interested in the role of technology and popular culture in contemporary gendered identity formation has examined the "integration of biotechnology and technology within our gendered bodies".

In general, feminist scholars often argue that technology is not a neutral "tool" but is "filled" with discourses that promote particular gendered power configurations, gendered notions of self/identity (the body), and implicit values for masculinity and femininity.

More specifically, the video gaming industry has often been described as a male-dominated domain. Most popular video games feature male protagonists (or highly sexualized female protagonists) and are primarily marketed to young men. Independent marketing research indicates that "heavy gamers," males between the ages of 14 and 17, are driving the video game industry (i.e., video game makers are creating games that primarily appeal to this demographic).

Further, research has concluded that arcade and computer games are often filled with stereotypical and even degrading images of women accompanied by graphically violent narratives. Nonetheless, video gaming extends well beyond this adolescent male market with growing evidence that girls and adult men and women are increasingly playing video games—as many as 56 million people between 35 and

50 are playing video games and around one-third of console-game players and 40 percent of computer-game players are female.

The diversity of video game players does not appear to be changing the types of games produced by the video game industry. In fact, "the bikini babes" and "damsels in distress" that pervade video gaming alienate many women who enjoy playing computer games.

For instance, many video games' narratives and imagery fit well with adolescent male fantasies—e.g., the packaging and images of popular games like Blood Rayne and Xtreme Beach Volleyball depict young women in revealing clothing in poses conventionalized in "soft core" pornographic magazines such as Maxim and Playboy with the clear intent of attracting the gaze of the adolescent, heterosexual male consumer.

This "male-dominance" of the video gaming context also emerges from the social norms surrounding video game players. As Lucas and Sherry (2004) concluded, "Based on established social norms, video games are perceived to belong in the male domain, and female players and male players alike experience greater social acceptance by staying within sex-role expectations".

The adolescent (heterosexual) male emphasis of the video game industry is perhaps best exemplified in the cable network G4's television series "Video Game Vixens," an awards show for female video game characters which aired in the summer of 2005. The programme was promoted by the network as "The hottest, sexiest and most lethal videogame babes will get your heart racing and your palms sweating in G4's irreverent new awards show". The "awards show" included categories such as "dirtiest dancer," "best booty," and "most dangerous curves."

Some video game advocates defend these sexualized and violent female video game characters (or "avatars") as empowering to women—while virtually always scantily clad and with the impossible proportions of a Barbie doll (or perhaps, more appropriately, a Playboy playmate), these women are "fighters" and therefore "empowered". The notion that this quasi-"girl power" is positive for women is highly problematic, bell hooks clearly identified the inconsistencies of the messages in these video games—rather than challenge patriarchy:Now women can be killing machines, but adolescent about everything else That is what one sees in 'Charlie's Angels,' the women kill as ruthlessly and as brutally as any men, but when it comes to sex that drops out and they are little girls.

It is a tremendous burden. (online document)Frankly, to view these depictions of women in popular video games as "empowering" is a rationalization based upon a distorted "it could be worse" logic. While women can offer resistive, alternate readings of these characters, the dominant reading (particularly by most gamers) is clearly promoting patriarchy by reproducing images of highly sexualized and childlike women performing for a heterosexual male gaze.

On the other hand, not all representations of women in video games rely on sexist stereotypes. In popular games such as Half-Life, Radiata Stories, and Elder Scrolls, women are not sexualized and often are represented as competent, intelligent, and assertive. Unfortunately, in an industry courting the young male consumer (gamers), these representations remain a minority. As Jansz and Martis concluded:

Gender stereotypes are particularly robust with respect to physical features. Men are still represented as hyper muscular characters, and women hyper sexualized characters. In other words, quite a few women became leaders in games, but they continue to function as 'eye candy' for their consumers, the gamers.

Further, popular video games usually involve narratives of violent conquest. For instance, of the 83 games with nine or higher ratings (with ten the highest rating) by the most popular gaming publication, Game Informer: 18 were sports simulation games (games such as NCAA Football 2005 and Gran Turismo 4, which reproduce sporting events), 7 were "puzzle" oriented games (e.g., games such as Super Mario

Bros and Lumines in which the player moves through layers of a puzzle), and 58 were "violent conquest" games (games such as Halo 2 and Doom 3 in which the primary objective is to violently defeat and/or kill enemies to advance through missions or stages).

Like other forms of entertainment media such as television and film, video games typically involve characters who perform actions within stories. In fact, often the narratives of video games are taken directly from feature films, books, and television programs (e.g., Spiderman, The X-Files, The Lord of the Rings)—and, increasingly, the inverse is also true (e.g., Resident Evil, Final Fantasy, Tomb Raider). In some respects, the narrative form of video games follows the conventions of other entertainment media such as films and comic books.

These consistent patterns within video gaming narratives have fostered generic conventions and expectations that consistently emphasize violent conquest. A journalist describing a video game convention in 2003 observed, "A few genres dominate: first person shooting games, fantasy multiplayer games, sports re-creations, movie fie-ins".

Based upon the reviews of the most highly rated games by Game Informer, the narratives of these "violent conquest" games are remarkably consistent. While there is variability in the "specific objective" such as tracking down a terrorist as a spy (Splinter Cell: Pandora Tomorrow) or defeating a criminal as a super hero (City of Heroes) or killing monsters in a fantasy world (Fable), the template of the story is essentially the same: Violently defeat the "enemy" and progress to the next "stage."

The reviewers consistently described the process of reaching these violent objectives as the primary source of pleasure derived from playing the game. For instance, the review for Devil May Cry 3 stated: "The sense of accomplishment you get when you master your skills and beat one of the insane bosses into submission makes all the toil worthwhile".

As this example demonstrates, the general emphasis of

many of the reviews was the "technique" for killing the enemy. The review for Resident Evil 4 described the game's most appealing characteristics as:

This time around, everything that so much as raises a finger at you must die—preferably by a nicely placed headshot. A remarkable new targeting system allows this feat to be handled with the utmost precision. On this note, I've never seen so many heads explode in my life.

The new over-the-shoulder perspective coupled with abeautifully crafted laser sight makes for a lethal and satisfying combat experience.

Further, even in the sports-related games, the "techniques" for dominating the "enemy" (the other team, the other drivers, etc.) were still the primary focus of the reviews. The reviewers referred to the application of these techniques as "control."

Previously, scholars have argued that the "interactivity" of video games provides the player pleasure because the game makes "it possible for players to gain control over the elicited arousal". This control is a source of pleasure for the gamer. As the review for NCAA Football 2005 stated:

I loved scoring first as an away team and causing the crowd to eat a big plate of shut the hell up. You can also get things under control by calling a timeout, during which your coach boosts the morale of a particular segment of your team, such as the WRs. This is what a big-time NCAA game feels like, and I love it. The game also contains some nice brutal hits, including user-controlled ones by pressing the L2 button.

In general, the themes of the vast majority of the most popular and "well-respected" games are remarkably consistent: dominate the "enemy" via skillful (usually violent) techniques. At this point in the discussion, I should note that not all popular video games follow these conventions. More specifically, not all popular games have a win-state or the goal of ultimate victory.

Frasca (2003) distinguished between "the most widely popular" ludus video games which provide "us with two possible endings: winning and losing" and much less pervasive paidia video games which leave "its main goal up to the player".

Games such as The Sims, SimCity, Nintendogs, and Animal Crossing do not involve violent conquest or competitive conflict. As I examine in the conclusion of this analysis, these non-violent, non-competitive, more "open-ended" gaming conventions may offer viable alternatives for the gaming community.

While both conservative and liberal critics have been quick to point out the violence and sexism that is ubiquitous in video gaming, social critics and scholars have rarely offered an explanation concerning the underlying motivation to play these sexist and violent video games.

In the following analysis, I argue that the discourses of these games create an entelechial motivational system drawing players toward a perceived state of perfection. Further, video games' patriarchal and sexist discourses emerge from the pursuit of an entelechial state of perfection that ultimately encourages subjugation via dehumanization.

VIDEO GAMING AS AN ENTELECHIAL MOTIVATIONAL SYSTEM

In the reviews of the 83 top rated video games (9.0 or higher) from Game Informer between December 2003 and August 2005, two words were recurring: "addictive" and "master." First, variations of "addiction metaphors" were sprinkled throughout the reviews of all types of games with statements like, "absolutely addictive gameplay" and "one of the most addictive and rewarding time sucks in recent memory".

As these statements suggest, these addictive qualities were not characterized as negative but as the highest compliment the reviewer could offer a game. As the review for the game Max Payne 2 stated, "At its heart, this is a shooting gallery—the world's coolest, most stylish, and addictive shooting gallery".

In fact, both inside and outside the gaming world, video gaming is often descibed as a compulsive or "addictive" activity. For instance, on Thanksgiving 2002, Shawn Wooley committed suicide while sitting in front of his computer playing the multi-player fantasy video game, EverQuest. Publicly, his mother blamed his suicide on an "addiction" to EverQuest.

This incident drew tremendous media attention and fed an already growing perception that video games were addictive. Popular periodicals ranging from Newsweek to The Washington Post to National Public Radio reported stories concerning the "addictive" quality of EverQuest or "EverCrack"—a term popularized by the game's players. Recently, an online support group for "EverQuest Widows" (i.e., significant others of EverQuest "addicts") has attracted over 6,000 members.

This perceived video game addiction is closely tied to the gamer's pursuit of "higher scores" and "new levels." For gamers, status is measured precisely and numerically. Once the gamer has "completed" all levels or reached the "high score," he/she has "mastered" or "beaten" the game. Again, this status relies upon the mastery of the "skills" of the video gamer's avatar.

For instance, the review for Jade Empire stated, "By game's end I had dabbled in or mastered over a dozen different fighting styles". Similarly, the review for Doom 3: Resurrection of Evil stated, "once you become proficient in the use of your environment and the new toys, RoE will suck you in and keep you enthralled until the last demon lies gibbed at your feet".

Game reviewers characterized the video gaming experience as mastering skills to ultimately "beat" the game: "While I beat the game in about 12 hours, much of my time was spent repeating a handful of tough stages scattered throughout the game".

The more "skills" (e.g., accurately shooting a gun, timing a punch) the video gamer masters, the greater status the video gamer achieves.

This is referred to as "deep play" or the "near-obsessiveness" with "gaining points, devising a winning (or at least a spectacular) strategy, and showing off their prowess to other players during the game and afterward, during replay".

The review for Onimusha 3: Demon Siege described this process: "Each character will upgrade their weapons and skills through the course of the game Without a combo-laden combat system, Demon Siege relies heavily on timing and strategy to master each of the three warriors". Ultimately, these techniques or skills allow the player to advance to new, increasingly challenging game stages.

In many respects, the perceived addiction derives, in part, from the desire to "see the end" and "beat" the game. This is a distinctly entelechial process based upon a desire for completeness, finishedness, and perfection. As the review for Halo 2 stated:

- You begin this roller-coaster ride, and you just want to keep playing till you reach the end (and even then I instantly restarted the game on its Heroic and Legendary levels—which offer a whole new level of death and destruction).

In the gamer vocabulary, advancing to new stages in the game is considered "leveling." Leveling is often based on what Gee (2006) calls challenges that "feel hard, but doable" or each task becomes slightly more difficult but always within the reach of the player. Players continue developing more and more complex skills until they achieve, in Gee's words, "mastery".

In violent conquest games, leveling generally occurs by reaching a particular "objective" (which typically requires the skillful execution of enemies). In sports-oriented games, leveling occurs when players "master" the skills associated with driving the car, throwing the football, shooting the ball, etc. The pleasurable experience of developing skills to reach a new level was clearly described in the review for Ninja Gaiden:

- Each weapon (and its upgrades) brings with it a different set of moves and strategies. When you begin the game, you have a standard set of attacks at your disposal. A few stages later, you'll find yourself with more moves than you know what to do with.

You'll be bouncing off of enemies' heads, tossing them into walls, launching into the sky and spearing them, and even summoning the power of the gods to create a whirlwind of ice With 16 lengthy stages, Normal and Hard difficulties, and secrets buried around every comer, Ninja Gaiden is capable of keeping you hooked for the better part of the year.

From start to finish, this game captivated me to no end and wowed me like few others have. The more skillful and knowledgeable the player becomes, the more the player can control aspects of the game with advanced combat skills, magic, weaponry, etc.

The convention of leveling originally emerged from the video game producers' desire to have players plug "more and more quarters in the arcade machine" with "the revelation of the new level the reward for having survived and mastered the previous environment".

Even though 21st century gamers usually play video games from their homes on console machines and PCs, these "quarter plugging" conventions remain. Today, in most games featuring avatars, gamers seek to develop the "best" or "strongest" characters possible—this is the central purpose of the game.

In fact, the intense desire for the strongest character has fostered online auctions for already created, highly advanced characters. By purchasing powerful characters, gamers can more quickly advance to new levels in the game and achieve greater status in the video gaming community.

An organization entitled "Twin Galaxies" compiles the "high scores" for hundreds of video games. On its website, the organization describes its mission as "to verify 'official' world record high-scores and crown new world champions." For instance, according to Twin Galaxies, only four video gamers have played a "perfect" game of Pac-Man reaching the score of 3,333,360, the maximum number of points allowed in the game.

As the highest plateau on the hierarchy, these "word

champions" represent the absolute, "perfect" completion of the game. This hierarchy resides in the inherent "gameness" of video games: "quantifiable outcome means that the outcome of a game is designed to be beyond discussion".

The gamer's primary objective is to reach the highest level of the hierarchy (moving up each "level") in order to reach a teleological endpoint. In fact, Burke's articulation of the entelechial principle in Language as Symbolic Action almost seems to be specifically describing the gamers' discursive system:

The principle of perfection (the "entelechial" principle) figures in other notable ways as regards the genius of symbolism. A given terminology contains various implications, and there is a corresponding "perfectionist" tendency for men (humans) to attempt carrying out those implications.

Thus, each of our scientific nomenclatures suggests its own special range of possible developments, with specialists vowed to carry out these terministic possibilities to the extent of their personal ability and technical resources.

For Burke, the ultimate objective when analyzing an entelechial system is "the tracking down of implications within a particular vocabulary". In the case of gamers' discourses or vocabularies, the implications stem from the technical pursuit of a "perfect" state of mathematical mastery.

TECHNOLOGY AND MATHEMATICAL MASTERY

Historically, philosophers and scholars have recognized an inherent link between science/technology and mastery. For instance, Martin Heidegger argued that technology is fundamentally about control and mastery because modern technology is based upon the "the exact science" of physics.

Heidegger describes, "[humanity's] ordering attitude and behaviour display themselves first in the rise of modern physics as an exact science. Modern science's way of representing pursues and entraps nature as a calculable coherence of forces".

The will to master and order our environment derives

from the centrality of technology in the modem world. As Heidegger's use of the term "mastery" suggests, humans seek to "enslave" the natural world, to conquer and exert superiority. Similarly, Kenneth Burke argues that humanity's "rotten" perfection is represented in the "rational" vocabularies of science and technology.

Not only do humans seek to be "better" or "higher" within a hierarchy, humans seek to be perfect or the "highest" element in the hierarchy—in many respects, to achieve mastery. The pursuit of masterful control is central to humans' "analytical" experience in the natural/biological world.

As Burke articulates in Permanence and Change, scientists utilize a language and, like any language—i.e., "the symbolic fog arising from the social order"— scientific discourse promotes a particular orientation to the world that is situated within its unique cultural milieu.

The language of science presupposes that the biological world is rational and organized in mechanistic causal relationships.

Further, according to both Burke and Heidegger, the mathematical discourses of science and technology lack any ambiguity or interpretation because mathematics or "calculation" is exact, absolute, and uniform.

Stated simply, the mathematical discourse of science makes the natural world falsely appear highly systematic, predictable, and fundamentally controllable by humans. Although Burke and Heidegger were concerned with "science" in its broadest sense, both recognized a fundamental connection between the discourse of science and the cultural implications of technology.

As Burke stated, "peculiarly human kinds of nomenclature made possible the kinds of attention and communication that culminate today in the social developments produced by Technology".

Science and technology share a common mathematical language and both construct the natural world as ordered and predictable. Therefore, the discourses associated with both science and technology (including the digital technologies of video gaming) will both typically encourage the desire for a perfect state of mastery.

SEEKING PERFECTION VIA DIGITAL CODE

Underlying Burke's conclusion that humans are "rotten with perfection" is the implicit assumption that perfection (or mastery) is a linguistic abstraction that can never be achieved. Thus, humans are desperately pursuing the unattainable. "Offline" or "face-to-face" communication is far from controlled, ordered, predictable, and symmetrical. In non-mediated contexts, "perfection" is impossible because perfection is immeasurable.

Humans cannot mathematically "calculate" who is the best but rather, through discourse, construct a perceived (albeit imprecise) hierarchy. Further, perfection is a potentially dangerous construct as powerful rhetors can provide simplistic and easily identifiable "measurements" of perfection, such as the Nazis' use of eugenics or advertisers' use of idealized body weight and shape.

As these examples highlight, perfection has been intimately tied to the ideologies and political struggles associated with race, gender, and class (among others). Historically, the central discursive process associated with perfection involved the constant critique, re-definition, and revision of the ambiguous standards by which perfection is judged (e.g., the characteristics that constitute the "perfect" enemy).

Though hierarchies "offline" involve dynamic processes, obscure standards, and constant revision, hierarchies within video game systems are often far more precise, exact, and uniform.

Digital media, in general, refer to technologies that use digitization or data converted into a numerical representation for the purpose of communication. As Evens argues, "The digital is a logic, an abstract code It is this condition—this general principle of operation according to an abstraction whose rules are immanent to its code—that defines a technology as digital".

In video game environments, due to this mathematical code, there exists an inherent order and symmetry. The standards of perfection can remain constant and uniform because the standards are based on mathematical principles within a controlled environment.

With digital technology, software designers can create a controlled, mathematical environment in which perfection (within the limited boundaries of the system) is measurable and, thus, achievable with a sophisticated technical understanding of the mathematical system.

In this respect, entelechy appears especially powerful when coupled with the exact mathematics of scientific and technological discourses. Through the mathematics of digital code, perfection and mastery appear not as an abstraction of language but rather a quantifiable state, a precise score, or a measurable outcome.

Because mastery is defined via hierarchy or power "over" persons or tasks (e.g., mastering a slave or mastering a musical instrument), within these mathematical video gaming environments, who or what is the player the master over? In the vocabulary of gamers, players seek to post the "high score" or to reach the "final level."

Thus, players seek to master other players—players with less power and skill. Further, the player is also competing with the game's programmer, seeking to master the mathematical "puzzle" created by the game designers. In video gaming, this mastery "over" others is often (and, as I explore further below, not coincidentally) coupled with the pleasures of aggressive domination and the dehumanization of "others."

Thus, from a feminist perspective, these hierarchies of mastery and domination must be challenged.Within the entelechial discursive logic of many video game systems, the perfect "end-point" is a "complete" aggressive domination of all others. Like other entelechial systems of meaning, participants never question why they are pursuing a perfect state of mastery and domination-it becomes normalized.

Like scientists pursuing a more powerful atomic bomb

or geneticists seeking "perfect" DNA, once imbedded in the system of discourse, the participants feel compelled to see it to its "logical completion" regardless of the moral consequences. As Burke states:there is a kind of "terministic compulsion" to carry out the implications of one's terminology, quite as, if an astronomer discovered by his observations and computations that a certain wandering body was likely to hit the earth and destroy us, he [she] would nonetheless feel compelled to argue for the correctness of his computations, despite the ominousness of the outcome.

In this sense, the vocabulary "normalizes" the desire for the finished state, even when the state of finishedness is morally problematic. In the case of video gaming, from a feminist perspective, the entelechial endpoint of complete domination of all others has significant ethical implications. Like films (such as Natural Born Killers) that "help to perpetuate the normality of male violence and make challenging and ending it that much more difficult", gamers' discourses normalize the patriarchal values of competition, mastery, and domination.

Specifically, this discourse reflects what Foss and Griffin call "a rhetoric of patriarchy" that is characterized by "a desire for control and domination". For instance, consider the Game Informer review for PsiOps: Mindgate Conspiracy:

Words cannot accurately describe the level of excitement that is delivered when you use telekinesis to levitate an enemy's body and fling them like a rag doll into a blazing incinerator, or tap into mind control to assume the identities of your attackers and obliterate their entire squad.

In many respects, the violent, competitive, and aggressive "play" of "boy culture" pervades many video games—even as video games are played by hundreds of millions of males and females of diverse ages. To put it simply, these video games are not "gendered" as merely masculine; these video games normalize a patriarchal (heterosexual) masculinity defined by the exertion of physical domination and mastery via violence and aggressive competition.

Further, in video game systems, gamers rarely embrace

alternative values such as equality, empathy, or compassion. In fact, these gamer discourses are the virtual antithesis of a feminist-oriented "invitational rhetoric" that is "rooted in equality, immanent value, and self-determination" and resulting in "a relationship of equality, respect, and appreciation".

Of particular concern is the tendency of video gaming environments to position other players as "objects" to be "conquered." This is strikingly represented by the advice for new players ("newbies") provided by a Website for the popular multi-player, online game EverQuest: "There are certain truths about the world of Everquest.

One of those is that killing is the path to power So what does a newbie kill? The easy answer is: everything". In video gamer discourses, the other players are not "real," they are merely "avatars" and the purpose of the game is to conquer the other participants. Although only anecdotal, this observation was painfully evident when I was playing the NFL simulation game "Madden 2005" with my twelve-year-old nephew.

My nephew is remarkably mature for his age and is generally quite empathetic and considerate of others when playing board games or sports in the backyard. But, when playing video games, he mercilessly dominates my "avatar" by scoring as many points as possible in order to try to best his top statistical performances.

Upon humiliating me, he casually replies, "that's the point of the game." It is as though when staring at the screen at my avatar, I am no longer in the room, I am merely a dehumanized object to be conquered. I have observed similar dehumanization processes many times at arcades and playing computer games. I strongly suspect these experiences are not unusual.

When gamers encounter "others" in video game environments, within the mathematical (entelechial) logic of the system, the gamer typically seeks to conquer all "others" and continue to dominate these "others" until mastering the game. In this regard, video gaming discourses of dehumanization and subordination of others should be of great concern to feminist scholars.

Further, as a popular form of interactive digital media, video gaming may reflect broader "mathematical" and "entelechial" discourses of other forms of digital media such as the World Wide Web. Scholars should be mindful of the dramatic potential implications of the emergent discourses of digital technologies: How might the entelechial motivational systems of digital media promote and strengthen existing political and social power hierarchies and even exacerbate the violent suppression or dehumanization of subordinate classes as "others"?

As noted previously in the analysis, although most popular video games embrace the conventions of mastery and domination, a few non-violent, non-competitive video games have found a market in the gaming industry. The non-teleological openness of "paidia" games such as The Sims, SimCity, Nintendogs, and Animal Crossing suggests that video games can emphasize alternative values such as nurturing, social integration, and cooperation.

In fact, in some video gaming subgroups, players creatively alter games in order to offer new discursive orientations to the gaming experience, such as Civilian III players who explored new ways "to win through nonviolent means".

Further, via interactivity and simulation, video games and digital media have the potential to become an exciting form of artistic expression. In addition, Consalvo has demonstrated how heterosexist norms in video games can be "subverted" by players via queer readings and identity experimentation.

These alternative gaming experiences suggest that the relentless pursuit of perfection, mastery, and conquest can be replaced by discourses promoting greater social justice and equality.Feminists should continue to critique and undermine video game discourses of domination, dehumanization, and control. As hooks articulates,

Sexist discrimination, exploitation, and oppression have

created the war between the sexes Feminist movement can end the war between the sexes. It can transform relationships so that the alienation, competition, and dehumanization that characterize human interaction can be replaced with feelings of intimacy, mutuality, and camaraderie. This analysis suggests new applications of Burke's term entelechy for the feminist critique of popular media, particularly interactive, digital media.

Further, in recent years, a number of groups have actively resisted, critiqued, and parodied the hyper-masculine discourses of the video game industry. For instance, "the Game Grrls" actively seek to escape the "fixed identities" perpetuated by images like "video game vixens" common in video games.

In addition to critiquing the apparent "gender stereotypes" pervasive in video gaming, we must also work to more actively criticize and satirize the discourses of mathematical mastery, hierarchy, and technical domination pervasive in the discourses of digital technologies. Too often, video games are simply discarded as "toys" that have little cultural significance.

In a similar respect, only after years of vigilant critique and consciousness-raising, do people today finally recognize the political and social significance of other popular cultural forms (e.g., television, film, and magazines) in shaping our gendered lives. Video games and other forms of digital technology require a similar undertaking. Via continued analysis, critique, and consciousness-raising, communication and feminist scholars can encourage alternative readings, alternative texts, and more complex understandings of the increasingly dangerous discourses of video gaming.

Prominent in the rhetoric of journalism is the phrase "what the public needs to know." But do the traditional criteria of newsworthiness—everyone can recite the list—really specify the kinds of information that individuals need to know to function as citizens?

How much of the daily news produced by your favourite newspaper or television news programme has any practical value for the ordinary citizen in the street? Or is the phrase "what the public needs to know" only a rationalization, a reflexive defence of the routines and traditions that govern how journalism does its day-to-day business? Or worse, is this an arrogant attempt by journalists to define for citizens what should be, from the journalists' insider perspective, necessary knowledge and interest?

Far more topics compete for attention than any news organization possibly can cover, and most public affairs topics are too complex and slow-moving for a simple stenographic approach to reporting. Hard decisions have to be made about which stories to cover and how to write them. Are journalists truly guided by a critically honed sense of what the public needs to know?

Look at the stories on the front page of this morning's newspaper and scan the lead items on the television newscast. Are these the things ordinary citizens need to know? Would they likely attract the attention of Schudson's monitorial citizens who are scanning the information environment for useful information that can affect their lives? How can an ordinary citizen use this information? Are the news media effective public communicators?

George Bernard Shaw once remarked that every profession is a conspiracy against the public. By a conspiracy he meant that every profession, such as the law, accounting and journalism, creates grounds rules and traditions to govern its behaviour with little explicit regard to the needs or convenience of the public whom the profession ostensibly serves.

On rare occasion, prominent journalists do reflect on their professional decisions about which topics to include in the daily news and how to frame those topics, that set of decisions that define the daily agenda of news offered to the public. James Fallows wrote a book, *"Breaking the News: How the Media Undermine Democracy,"* which dealt harshly with the traditional media's choices. And an executive producer of *"Nightline"* once asked in a moment of doubt, "Who are we to think we should set an agenda for the nation? What made us any smarter than the next guy?" Before pursuing the details of these questions about the quality of the media agenda, we consider in some detail that powerful phrase about the role of the media, "set an agenda for the nation."

AGENDA-SETTING ROLE OF THE NEWS MEDIA

The power of the news media to set the nation's agenda, to focus public attention on a few key public issues, is an immense and well-documented influence. Not only do people acquire factual information about public affairs from the news media, readers and viewers also learn how much importance to attach to a topic on the basis of the emphasis placed on it in the news.

Newspapers provide a host of cues about the salience of the topics in the daily news—lead story on Page 1, other front page display, large headlines, and length, for example. Television news also offers numerous cues about salience including placement as the opening story on the newscast, length of time devoted to the story, and promotional emphasis put on it. These cues repeated day after day communicate the importance that journalists attach to each topic. In other words, the news media set the agenda for the public's attention to a small group of issues.

Because of this unavoidable influence on the public mind, the values journalists apply in their decision-making process become crucial. When the traditional news values are applied, one sort of influence occurs. When, however, other values intervene in the process, such as anxiety over ratings or confusing entertainment with substance, quite another sort of influence happens.

The principal outlines of the media's agenda influence were sketched by Walter Lippmann in his 1922 classic, *"Public Opinion"* which began with a chapter titled "The World Outside and the Pictures in Our Heads."

As Lippmann noted, the news media are a primary source of those pictures in our heads about the larger world of public affairs, a world that for most citizens is "out of reach, out of sight, out of mind." What we know about the larger world is largely based on what the media decide to tell us. More specifically, the result of this mediated view of the world is that elements prominent on the media agenda become prominent in the public mind.

Social scientists examining this agenda-setting influence of the news media on the public usually have focused on public issues. The agenda of a news organization is its pattern of coverage on public issues over some period of time—a week, a month, an entire year. Over this period of time, whatever it might be, a few issues are emphasized, some receive light coverage, and many are seldom or never mentioned. It should be noted that the use of term *agenda* here is purely descriptive.

There is no pejorative implication that a news organization "has an agenda" in the sense of specific policy outcomes. The media agenda presented to the public results from countless day-to-day decisions by many different journalists and their supervisors about the relative importance of the news of the moment, or, in some unfortunate cases, their focus on values other than importance.

Some partisan or interest groups attempt to tease out a journalistic political agenda. Most fail to make a persuasive case because of two factors: Their own starting assumptions bias their analyses, and for most general-interest media, there simply is no specific political or ideological agenda.

The public agenda—the focus of public attention—can be assessed by public opinion polls asking the widely used Gallup Poll question, "What is the most important problem facing this country today?" The American public's responses to this question over the past half century provide a fascinating portrait of our political and civic history and yield significant evidence of the agenda-setting role of the news media.

For example, when Chapel Hill, N. C. voters were asked to name the most important issues of the day —in the very first empirical study of this agenda-setting influence—their responses closely reflected the pattern of news coverage during the previous month in the mix of newspapers, network television news and news magazines available to them. Since that initial study during the 1968 presidential election, hundreds of published studies worldwide have documented this influence of the news media on what people think is important.

To summarize the extent of this influence—and to facilitate comparisons from one setting to another—social scientists frequently calculate the correlation between the ranking of issues on the media agenda and the ranking accorded those same issues on the subsequent public agenda. This quantitative measure provides a substantial degree of precision for those comparisons much as a thermometer's precise numbers are better than simply saying it seems cooler today than it was yesterday.

The possible range of scores for this correlation statistic is from a high of +1, perfect agreement between the media and the public on the ranking of the issues; down to 0, no agreement whatsoever about the rank ordering of the issues; and on to a low of-1, a perfectly inverse relationship between the ranks of the issues on the two agendas. The vast majority of comparisons between how issues are ranked on the media agenda—a measure of the relative emphasis by the media on these issues—and how the public ranks the importance of these issues yield correlations of +.50 or better. That is a substantial degree of influence.

The initial study of the agenda-setting influence of the news media in Chapel Hill examined a month during the 1968 presidential election. Others have examined much longer periods of time and found similar evidence of strong agenda-setting effects among the public. A look at the entire decade of the 1960s found a substantial correlation (+.78) between the patterns of coverage in news magazines and the trends in public opinion reflected by responses to the Gallup Poll's question about the most important problem facing the country.

A look at a single issue, civil rights, over a crucial 23-year period, 1954 to 1976, found a similar match (+.71) between public concern about this issue and the pattern of rising and falling front page news in the *New York Times* during each preceding month. A similar analysis of 11 different individual issues during the 1980s found a median correlation of+.45 in the comparison of Gallup Polls and a broad sample of newspapers, television news and news magazines. All of the comparisons were positive except for morality—a topic seldom discussed in the news.

Nor are agenda-setting effects limited to the agenda of national issues. In Louisville, a comparison of public concern about eight local issues with coverage in the *Louisville Times* across 8 years also yielded a substantial match (+.65). The news media have a substantial influence on the content of the public agenda, and the phrase "setting the agenda" has become commonplace in discussions of journalism and public opinion.

Bibliography

Chimutengwende Chen C. "The Role of Communications Training and Technology in African Development." In World Communications: A Handbook, edited by George Gerbner and Marsha Siefert. New York: Longman, 2001.

Head Sidney W. World Broadcasting Systems: A Comparative Analysis. Belmont, CA: Wadsworth, 2004.

Hellack George. Newspapers, Radio and Television in the Federal Republic of Germany. Bonn: Inter Nationes, 2002.

Journalistic Training Centers. Prague: International Organization of Journalists, 2000.

Kang Joon-Mann. "Reporters and Their Professional and Occupational Commitment in a Developing Country." Gazette 40, no. 1 (2003): 3-20.

Lowenstein, Ralph, and John C. Merrill. Media, Messages and Men, 2d ed. New York: Longman, 2002.

Malcolm Bruce. To License a Journalist: A Landmark Decision in the Schmidt Case. New York: Freedom House, 2000.

Martin L. John. "Africa." In Global Journalism: Survey of International Communication, 2d ed., edited by John C. Merrill. New York: Longman, 2001.

Nordenstreng Kaarle, and Hifzi Topuz, eds. Journalist: Status, Rights and Responsibilities. Prague: International Organization of Journalists, 2003.

Ogan Christine. "Middle East and North Africa." In Global Journalism: Survey of International Communication, 2d ed., edited by John C. Merrill. New York: Longman, 2004.

Paraschos Manny. "Europe." In Global Journalism: Survey of International Communication, 2d ed., edited by John C. Merrill. New York: Longman, 2000.

Index

F

G

H

I

J

L

M

N

O

P

Q

R

S

T

U

V

W